Progressive Racism

The Collected Conservative Writings
of David Horowitz

Second Thoughts Books
Los Angeles

ENCOUNTER BOOKS
New York · London

First American edition published in 2016 by Encounter Books, an activity of Encounter for Culture and Education, Inc., a nonprofit, tax exempt corporation. Encounter Books website address: www.encounterbooks.com

Manufactured in the United States and printed on acid-free paper. The paper used in this publication meets the minimum requirements of ANSI/NISO Z39.48 1992 (R 1997) (*Permanence of Paper*).

Book design and production by Catherine Campaigne; copy-edited by David Landau; research provided by Mike Bauer.

FIRST AMERICAN EDITION

LIBRARY OF CONGRESS CATALOGING-IN-PUBLICATION DATA

Names: Horowitz, David, 1939– author. Title: Progressive racism : / by David Horowitz.
Description: New York : Encounter Books, 2016. | Includes bibliographical references and index.
Identifiers: LCCN 2015038178 | ISBN 9781594038594 (hardcover : alk. paper) |
    ISBN 9781594038600 (ebook)
Subjects: LCSH: Racism—United States. | United States— Race relations. | African Americans—Civil rights. | Civil rights movements—United States—History—20th century.
Classification: LCC E185.615 .H674 2016 | DDC 305.800973—dc23
LC record available at http://lccn.loc.gov/2015038178

10   9   8   7   6   5   4   3   2   1

Contents

Preface

In August 2014 the shooting of a black criminal in Ferguson Missouri by a white police officer led to a series of riots lasting several months, and eventually inspired national protests making it the civil rights cause of the Obama era. The protesters' indictment was summarized in a chant "Hands Up, Don't Shoot," which symbolized their claim that the nation's police had declared open season on unarmed black citizens and were killing them for the crime of being black. During the public disturbances surrounding the Ferguson events the president and his chief law enforcement officer, Attorney General Eric Holder, exhibited active sympathy and support for the movement's complaints.

When the facts were finally established by forensic evidence and grand jury testimony, and eventually by a separate Department of Justice investigation conducted by Holder himself, they refuted the movement's central claim.[1] Forensics, video records and the testimony of five black eyewitnesses established that the alleged victim Michael Brown, was targeted for arrest not because he was black but because he had just committed a strong-armed robbery. He did not have his hands in the air and was not shot while surrendering but while attacking the arresting officer whose gun he attempted to wrestle from its holster.

In short, the actions of the crowds that burned the city of Ferguson and looted its community businesses even before the facts

---

[1] http://www.washingtonpost.com/blogs/fact-checker/wp/2015/03/19/ hands-up-dont-shoot-did-not-happen-in-ferguson/.

were in, and which continued their rampages even after the facts were established, were not those of a civil rights protest but of a lynch mob, unconcerned with the evidence, impatient with due process, and intent on ensuring that a severely injured officer who had been the victim of a criminal attack be indicted, tried, convicted and punished. *Or else.* How did the mob "know" that the officer was guilty? Because he was *white.* Mob leaders even demanded that the prosecutor—a white liberal Democrat—be removed from the case because his own father was the victim of a black criminal 50 years previously, and therefore he could not discharge his duties fairly.[2]

This racist thuggery would have been readily recognized as such if the lynch mob had been white. But it was composed mainly of African Americans and "civil rights" progressives, who were supported in their aggression by a media eager to embrace the baseless idea that unarmed black teens were regularly shot in the streets by white police officers who were protected by a "white supremacist" power structure. This, too, was contradicted by the facts. Shootings of black criminals by police have steadily been declining, while the number of whites shot by police officers nearly doubles that of blacks even though black males—six percent of the population—account for nearly forty percent of all violent crimes.[3] Although they constitute only 13% of the population more African Americans are murdered every year than whites.[4] a staggering majority—more than 90%—are murdered by

---

[2] http://thinkprogress.org/justice/2014/08/26/3474838/why-civil-rights-groups-are-calling-for-the-ferguson-prosecutor-to-step-down/   ; http://www.cbsnews.com/news/background-of-prosecutor-in-ferguson-case-has-some-suspicious-of-bias/.

[3] http://www.bjs.gov/content/pub/pdf/ph98.pdf; http://www.bjs.gov/content/pub/pdf/ardo309st.pdf; http://www.fbi.gov/about-us/cjis/ucr/crime-in-the-u.s/2013/crime-in-the-u.s.-2013/tables/table-43.

[4] In 2013 there were 5,537 whites who were victims of homicide, compared to 6,261 blacks. http://www.fbi.gov/about-us/cjis/ucr/crime-in-the-u.s/2013/crime-in-the-u.s.-2013/offenses-known-to-law-enforcement/expanded-homicide/expanded_homicide_data_table_1_murder_victims_by_race_and_sex_2013.xls.

other African Americans meaning that the police, rather than enemies as progressives have made them, are African Americans' best friends and last line of defense against criminal violence.[5]

A second contested incident occurred soon after in New York when a black street criminal named Eric Garner died while resisting arrest after police were forced to apply a choke hold because of his large size. Garner's words—"I can't breathe"—joined "Hands Up, Don't Shoot" as a slogan of those pushing the narrative that America—and especially its police—were irredeemably racist. "I can't breathe" was meant to highlight the progressive mob's view that the choke hold employed to cuff the 300 pound Garner had actually strangled him. So pervasive was the assumption of police guilt in the case that the slogan was featured on the warm-up jerseys of star athletes and became a national *cause celebre.* According to the activists, another unarmed black suspect had been murdered because he was black.

This time the charge of racism was particularly ludicrous since it was leveled against a police force half of whose officers were minorities.[6] The sergeant on the scene in charge of the fatal arrest was an African American woman, a fact studiously ignored by the media intent on pushing the narrative of police racism. Eventually the autopsy report showed that unknown to the police who arrested him Garner was suffering from multiple maladies including heart problems, asthma and morbid obesity. It was these conditions that caused the normal trauma of a resisted arrest to result in the collapse of Garner's pulmonary capacity and his subsequent death in the ambulance later.

---

[5] In 2013, 90% of black homicide victims were killed by other blacks. http://www.fbi.gov/about-us/cjis/ucr/crime-in-the-u.s/2013/crime-in-the-u.s.-2013/offenses-known-to-law-enforcement/expanded-homicide/expanded_homicide_data_table_6_murder_race_and_sex_of_vicitm_by_race_and_sex_of_offender_2013.xls.

[6] http://nypost.com/2014/09/08/nypd-is-as-diverse-as-new-york-city-itself/.

In other words, both accusations—of racism and strangulation—were false. But because of the pervasive influence of progressive prejudice in the culture at large, the lynch mobs were ultimately successful. To forestall the threat of future violence stemming from future "protests," the careers of the white officers involved in the fatal arrests were terminated. Ferguson officer Darren Wilson was forced to go into hiding to keep from being killed himself.

The furor of these events spurred much commentary as racial arsonists like Al Sharpton tried to make local tragedies into a national "crisis." A fact lost in this shuffle was that progressive lynch mobs had been doing this work for decades. Three other recent cases show the desperate effort of progressive vigilantes to keep alive the notion of America as a racist nation. One is the destruction of the career and fortune of TV cooking personality Paula Deen, a supporter of President Obama who had given more than a million dollars in charity to help inner city African Americans. In addition to being white, Deen's offenses were a groundless discrimination lawsuit against her brother that was later dismissed, and her use of the forbidden word "nigger" in a remark made to her husband in private after being mugged by a black criminal during a bank robbery twenty-five years earlier. (She volunteered the remark in a deposition connected to the lawsuit.[7])

An even more celebrated case was the public lynching of three innocent Duke University LaCrosse players, the result of a nationwide hysteria whipped up over the rape claims of a drug-addicted black prostitute by Al Sharpton, Jesse Jackson and other progressives, including 88 Duke professors who signed an ad condemning the students. Before the evidence exonerated them, they had to endure termination of their school careers, a year of public condemnation by national news networks, and onerous fees for their

---

[7] http://www.tmz.com/2013/06/19/paula-deen-n-word-racist-deposition-sexual-harassment-oyster-house/3/#comments-anchor.

legal defense.[8] Finally, there was the rush to judgment and demand for punishment of George Zimmerman, falsely portrayed as a "white Hispanic" to make him racially culpable in the shooting death of Trayvon Martin.[9] As in the Ferguson case, the president and his attorney general led from behind as Sharpton and Jackson poured gasoline on the racial fire they had ignited.

What these events show is the way America's political culture has been tragically warped by progressives through their rejection of the color blind standard established by the Constitution and once championed by the civil rights movement and its leader Martin Luther King. Progressives have been able to persuade an influential section of the country to believe that whites are guilty before the fact and blacks are innocent even when the facts show they are guilty. The racial morality play of "white supremacy" and black "oppression" provides an indispensable myth for advancing their political agendas, which is why it has proved so durable.

The fact that racial injustice is the most problematic aspect of the nation's heritage is also the reason that it is the focus of the progressive assault on America and its social contract. For obvious reasons, progressives largely concentrate on one race—American blacks, or "African-Americans" as they have come to be known through at least five permutations of linguistic political correctness since World War II: "coloreds," "Negroes," "blacks," "persons of color" and—only then— "African-Americans." The injustices of slavery and segregation and the historic sufferings of this community form an arguable basis for the progressive indictment, but only by systematically ignoring the historic gains—unprecedented and unparalleled—of this same community, which are the

---

[8]Stuart Taylor and K. C. Johnson, *Until Proven Innocent: Political Correctness and the Shameful Injustices of the Duke Lacrosse Rape Case*, 2008.

[9]http://articles.latimes.com/2012/mar/27/opinion/la-oe-goldberg-trayvon-martin-race-20120327. It is my own opinion that Zimmerman was indeed culpable, but that doesn't make the actions of the lynch mob any less deplorable. See Part IV, chapter 12 in this volume, "Second Thoughts About Trayvon."

direct result of America's tolerant and individual-centered social contract.

Progressive attacks on a chimerical "white supremacy" have been destructive for all citizens. The principal target of this racism, as already noted, is the idea of equal treatment for all individuals under the law, an idea that progressives seek to replace with group identities and group privileges based on race and gender. The idea of an equality of individuals without regard to race, ethnicity or gender, on the other hand, is the very idea that informs the *American* identity, and unites its diverse communities into a single nation.

There will always be racists and bigots. Only utopians will fail to understand this and seek to deploy the coercive powers of the state to make everyone believe as they do. By contrast, people connected to the realities of this world recognize that America is the most tolerant of societies. Americans' cultural acceptance of racial, ethnic and gender minorities is virtually without parallel in human history. Interracial marriage, once the strongest racist taboo is now hardly noticed, whether among ordinary Americans or cultural celebrities; large American cities—Detroit, Philadelphia and Atlanta—are run by African American administrations and an African American has been twice elected to the White House. In their battles with "white supremacy," progressives cling to a past that is already remote. They have become the true reactionaries of our time, and it is hardly surprising that they are its new racists as well.

Introduction

This is the sixth volume of my writings called The Black Book of the American Left. It is also one of the most important, as its subject—race—goes to the heart of the most problematic aspect of America's history and heritage, and is thus the focus of the progressive assault on America and the American social contract.

The first essay in this volume, "The Reds and the Blacks," explains how this assault is shaped by the left's melodrama of "oppression" and "social justice," and is merely an extension of Marx's discredited formulas of "class oppression." Parts I & II of the text that follows address the falling-away of the civil rights movement from the mission and values championed by Martin Luther King. An introduction, "Memories in Memphis," is the account of my visit to the "National Civil Rights Museum" housed in the motel where King was murdered. This visit provided a summary moment in my efforts to understand these historic events. "Memories in Memphis" first appeared as the opening chapter in *Hating Whitey and Other Progressive Causes.* The original title of that book published in 1999 was "Hating White People Is a Politically Correct Idea." This was an accurate description of the culture promoted by the new leaders of the civil rights movement, and—equally important—was the undeniable thrust of what was being taught in university curricula devoted to the malevolent race, gender and class "hierarchies," which tenured leftists falsely claimed as structures of American society. The book was rejected by my publisher, Basic Books, whose editor told me, "We will never publish a book with that title." His response indicated how completely the literary culture had succumbed to the new dispensation. I had to find an obscure publisher in Texas to get the book in print, and thus the upshot of trying to right an injustice was a dramatic diminishment of my career as an author.

Both essays, "The Red and the Black" and "Memories in Memphis," were written in 1999, and the opening chapter of Part II, "The Race Card," two years earlier. All the other chapters in this volume are organized in chronological order to form a running journal of the conflicts that accompanied the transformation of the civil rights cause. Until this transformation it had been a movement to integrate African-Americans into America's multiethnic democracy. In less than a decade it had become a movement led by demagogues to refashion racial grievances into a general assault on white people and on the country they were said to "dominate." In its core agendas, the new civil rights movement was an assault on the basic American social contract, and in particular the 14th Amendment's commitment to equal rights under the law and thus to race-neutral standards and race-neutral governmental practices. Post-King civil rights became a movement to institutionalize racial preferences—the same kind of discriminatory practices that characterized segregation—and to recreate a race-conscious political culture in which blacks and a handful of designated minorities were singled out as the groups to be racially privileged. On other the side of the coin, whites were made targets of exclusion, suspicion and disapprobation.

Part III recounts an effort I undertook in the spring of 2001 to oppose a campaign by the left to gain reparations for slavery. This was a cause that had been first proposed in 1969, during the civil rights era, and rejected by every major civil rights organization. At the time of the proposal there were no slaves alive to receive reparations, while the vast majority of Americans who would be forced to pay reparations were descended from immigrants who had arrived in America well after slavery had been abolished. The clear goal of the radicals who launched the reparations campaign was to indict America as a racist society, and to sow the seeds of racial conflict. It was also an obvious shakedown effort of the kind that had come to characterize the civil rights leadership of Jesse Jackson and Al Sharpton. In the winter of 2001, I published an account of these battles titled *Uncivil Wars: The Controversy Over Reparations for Slavery*, which explained why the issue of race was at the heart of the left's assault.

Democratic congressman John Conyers was the author of the legislative bill supported by the reparations movement. During the controversy, a Republican majority in the House of Representatives prevented Conyers's legislation from being passed out of the Judiciary Committee and sent to the House floor, a fact that the left seized on to insinuate that Republicans were racists. Yet when Democrats won control of the House in 2008 and Conyers became chair of the Judiciary Committee under a newly elected African-American president, he did not bring the reparations bill to the floor. The reparations issue, which had been infused with such moral urgency until then, was apparently no longer a priority and disappeared from public view. Few episodes seem better designed to illustrate how race had become a political weapon for a movement driven more by its anti-American and anti-white animus than a desire to correct actual injustices.

Part IV of this volume examines the way attacks on a chimerical "white supremacy" have fostered a new progressive racism whose consequences have been destructive for all citizens. The principal target of this racism is the idea of equal treatment under the law—the idea that informs the American identity and unites its diverse communities into a single nation.

As in previous volumes, I have edited the individual pieces to eliminate repetitions where possible and enhance the overall readability of the text.

PART I

The Reds and the Blacks

The Reds and the Blacks

The Communist Manifesto is probably the only Marxist text that most of his millions of followers have actually read. During the last century, his disciples went about killing a hundred million people in attempts to create the utopia he promised, but these disasters have had no effect on the fantasy that inspired them. It is almost a decade since the collapse of the empires that Marxists built, but it is already evident that its lessons have not been learned. Today, few people outside the halls of academia may think of themselves as Marxists, or publicly admit to pursuing socialist illusions.[1] But behind protective labels like "populist," "progressive" and even "liberal," the old socialist left is alive and powerful, and in steady pursuit of its destructive agendas.

Three ideas advanced in Marx's famous tract make up the core of this contemporary leftist faith. The first and most important is the belief that modern, secular, democratic societies are ruled by oppressive "alien powers" (as Marx referred to them). In Marx's vision, even though industrial nations had dethroned their hereditary rulers

---

May 20, 1999, http://archive.frontpagemag.com/Printable.aspx?ArtId=24277.

[1] Since this was written, the situation has changed fairly dramatically. A Pew poll taken in 2011 reported that 49 percent of 18–29 year olds had a positive opinion of socialism. This change had already taken place a few years earlier. See "Little Change in Public's Response to 'Capitalism,' 'Socialism,'" Pew Research Center, December 28, 2011. http://www.people-press.org/2011/12/28/little-change-in-publics-response-to-capitalism-socialism/.

and vested sovereignty in the people, this did not mean they were actually free. Though liberated from serfdom, workers were now "wage-slaves," chained to capital as effectively as they had been chained to the land under feudalism. According to Marx and his disciples, capital is the alien power that rules the modern world in the same way landed aristocracies presided over it in the past. Electoral democracies are fictions within the framework of capitalist societies. Behind the democratic facade, the capitalist "ruling classes" control political outcomes and keep their citizens effectively in chains.

The second idea of the Manifesto flows naturally from the first: politics is war conducted by other means, and specifically class war. The third idea is that victory in this class war leads to a world without chains—a rupture with the entire history of humanity's enthrallment to alien powers.[2]

In response to the collapse of communism, and to distance itself from that failure, the modern left has revised its vocabulary and expanded the notion of alien powers to include race and gender. The target is rarely described anymore as a "ruling class," but as a trinity of oppressors: a class-race-and-gender caste. In the war against these hierarchies, race carries the greatest moral weight and political impact. Consequently, racial grievance is the spearhead of the modern radical cause, although gender and class grievances are not far behind. Oppressed blacks and their grievances are deployed to undermine the bulwarks of the social order. And they are effective. In the past several decades, racial preferences to redress past injustices have been the most successful elements of the assaults on the standards and practices of the old order based on individual rights and equality before the law.

The left's stated goal in subverting these classical liberal norms is to "level the playing field," which is a precise translation of Marx's classless society into politically palatable terms. According to those who hold this view, the Civil Rights Acts failed to achieve

---

[2] Kenneth Minogue, Alien Powers: The Pure Theory of Ideology, 2008.

"real" equality, meaning an equality of results—which is the communist ideal. Previous civil rights reforms had focused on making institutional processes fair, and eliminating legal barriers to political power, education and jobs—in other words, to providing individual opportunity. For Martin Luther King and the civil rights movement he led, leveling the playing field meant extending to blacks the constitutional protections accorded to all Americans; making all citizens, regardless of color, equal before the law. It meant creating neutral rules that rendered color or ethnicity irrelevant to the competitions of civic and economic life. This was King's idea of a "color-blind" society. Color would no longer affect individual outcomes, certainly not through the agency of the state. In King's vision, the playing field would be level once government ceased to play racial favorites, as was the practice in the segregated South.

But the elimination of racial barriers through the passage of the Civil Rights Acts did not lead to equal results. To the left, whose collectivist vision discounted individual achievement and individual failure, this could only be explained by the persistence of covert prejudice—"institutional racism," which is the contemporary left's version of Marx's alien power. According to the left, procedural fairness, the original goal of civil rights reforms, was actually a mask for an "institutional bias" that preserved an unequal status quo. Just as Marx had derided "bourgeois democracy" as a political smokescreen to preserve the power of a ruling class, so the post-King civil rights left dismissed equality of opportunity as a smokescreen to preserve the superior position of a dominant race. The term "white supremacy," favored by racist demagogues like Louis Farrakhan, now became a term loosely applied by broad sectors of the left.

According to the new ideologues, educational admissions tests, for example, are culturally rigged to appear neutral while in practice they favor applicants of the dominant color. If facts alone were the issue, this claim would be easily refuted. Asian immigrants, who struggle with both a foreign language and an alien culture, consistently score in the highest ranges on standardized tests, surpassing whites and gaining admission to the best schools available. In fact, affirmative action measures in education are designed by the left to limit opportunities for Asian minorities, while favoring low-scoring Hispanics and blacks.[3] But where ideology is concerned, facts do not matter. Within the ideology, only one explanation is possible for persistent inequalities: the hierarchies of race, class and gender, and their system of oppression.

When the left demands a level playing field, it is not interested in neutral rules and equitable standards. It is interested in combating the alien powers of the race-class-gender hierarchy and their alleged oppression of blacks and other designated minorities—the new stand-ins for Marx's proletarians. The left is oblivious to the experience of persecuted minorities who have been successful, such as Asians, Armenians, and Jews. It is not interested in the cultural factors that shape individual choices. It is not interested in individuals and their freedom, and therefore in securing an equitable process. It is only rhetorically interested even in equal results. What drives the left is its quest for the power to fundamentally reshape the social order by state fiat, to enforce its own prejudices and preferences, which it calls "social justice."

If the left actually set out to achieve an equality of results, it would have to invade and then control every inch of the private sphere. Consider what it would mean to implement this demand. It is true that 40 percent of America's African-American children are poor, a condition that handicaps them in any educational competition. The left accounts for the resultant disparities by its mythical construct, "institutional racism," which allegedly blocks their way. Since the fault is "institutional" rather than individual, the remedy is institutional reform: rigging educational and performance standards to force an equality that doesn't currently exist.

---

[3] "Pacific Islanders" are the one Asian group defined as an "underrepresented minority," not coincidently because they are the one Asian group that was the subject of American colonialism.

But the primary reason that African-American children are poor is cultural, not institutional or racial. If it were racial, there would be no (or only a small) black middle class, whereas the black middle class is now the majority of the black population. Statistically speaking, a child born into a single-parent family is five times more likely to be poor than a child born into a family with two parents, regardless of race.[4] Eighty-five percent of African-American children in living in poverty grow up in single-parent households.[5] It is that circumstance—and not "institutional racism"—which actually handicaps a portion of the African-American population and denies them opportunity. By the time such children are ready to compete, they may suffer from dysfunctional behaviors, or have developed disabling habits, or have internalized attitudes hostile to academic achievement, or simply lack the supportive environment that a middle-class, two-parent home provides. The excessive dropout rates among students who take advantage of racial preferences to overcome these inequalities are the statistical indicators that these parenting handicaps are real, and that no rigging of institutional standards can make up for them.[6]

In the face of such realities, what can "leveling the playing field" mean? How can the state make up for the irresponsible behaviors and mistakes of the biological parents? By forcing them to get married? By compelling them to look after their children? By requiring them to teach their offspring to study hard and not be self-abusive? Is this even practical? Is it wise? Should the state

---

[4] "Marriage: America's Greatest Weapon Against Child Poverty," Robert Rector, Heritage Foundation, September 5, 2012, http://www.heritage.org/research/reports/2012/09/marriage-americas-greatest-weapon-against-child-poverty.

[5] Stephan Thernstrom and Abigail Thernstrom, America in Black and White: One Nation, Indivisible (New York: Simon & Schuster, 1997), p. 237.

[6] Richard Sander and Stuart Taylor, Jr., Mismatch: How Affirmative Action Hurts Students It's Intended to Help, and Why Universities Won't Admit It, Basic Books, 2012.

become a Big Brother for those who fall behind, taking over their lives and curtailing their individual freedom? Yet that is the logical inference of the proposals of the left.

To achieve the benevolent outcomes that progressives promise would require a government both omniscient and wise, a utopia that has never existed. Such a state would have to mandate comprehensive transfers of opportunity and wealth, and would conduct a relentless battle against human nature to overcome the resistance to its impositions by those unwilling to give up their liberty or the fruits of their labor. The call to level the playing field, pushed to its unavoidable conclusion, is a call for the systematic subversion of American individualism and democracy, the destruction of individual freedom and the creation of a totalitarian state. The level playing field requires a totalitarian state to eliminate the disparities resulting from human nature and private circumstance. Yet the totalitarian state is itself a hierarchy of forbidding dimensions.

In the aftermath of communism's collapse, such a prospect may seem remote, which is why the dangers inherent in these progressive reforms are often discounted. But the efforts to undermine the system of individual rights are already well advanced. Moreover, it is the nihilistic ambition behind the radical assault that presents the most immediate threat. For it is possible to destroy the foundations of social trust without establishing a socially viable alternative. Underlying the idea of racial preferences is a corrosive premise that the white majority is fundamentally racist and cannot be fair. For those who embrace the idea, the institutions, traditions, rules and standards that white majorities have arrived at over the course of centuries merit no respect. Affirmative action race preferences are an assault on the very system of economic and legal neutrality that underpins a pluralistic democracy. By denigrating the rule of law as a mask for injustice and oppression, the left undermines the very system that makes democracy—and racial equality—possible.

To support race preferences, the left demands that government abandon the principle of "color-blindness" and equal protection under the laws. It does so in the name of opening doors that allegedly remain closed, since it claims that minorities are still "excluded" or "locked out." But its only evidence for this is statistics that show disparities between minority representation in certain jobs or educational institutions and their representation in the population at large. The villain, according to the left, is the invisible power called "institutional racism." (It has to be invisible because actual discrimination against minorities is already outlawed.)

No one seriously contends that admissions officers at America's elite colleges are racists. In fact, college admissions offices are normally desperate to recruit as many eligible minority applicants as they can, offering them large financial rewards for being "underrepresented." As a result of California ballot Proposition 209, the University of California system is one of the few institutions legally required to eliminate the racial preferences it put in place for minorities. Yet the UC system is still spending $160 million annually on outreach programs designed to increase minority enrollments.[7] Since this is the case, it is hard not to conclude that any deficiencies in minority admissions are the result of individual failures to meet academic standards.

The idea that America is a country ruled by racist precepts and powers, as leftists claim, is absurd. If African-Americans are oppressed, what would explain the desire of so many blacks to come to America's shores and—in the case of Haitians—to risk their lives in doing so? Are they longing to subject themselves to a master race? In fact, the reason they want so desperately to immigrate is that in America they have more rights, more opportunities, more cultural privileges, and more social power than they do in countries like Haiti, which has been independent and run by black governments for more than two hundred years. This difference is attributable to America's pluralistic democracy. Because

---

[7] "Increasing Minority Enrollment at the University of California Post Proposition 209: UCLA's Center for Community College Partnerships," Ramona Barrio-Sotillo, 2007, p. 57, http://udini.proquest.com/view/increasing-minority-enrollment-at-goid:304826328/.

culture and not race is the determinant factor, Haitian-Americans are freer and more privileged in America than they would be in any black-run country in the world.

The civil rights movement was supported by the vast majority of the American people, including federal law enforcement and the military, and by ninety-percent pluralities in both congressional parties. Since those victories were achieved, public-opinion surveys have shown a dramatic increase in the goodwill of whites generally towards the African-American minority, and an equally precipitous decline in attitudes that could reasonably be called bigoted. Large increases in the number of black officials elected by majority white constituencies, and huge income transfers authorized by a predominantly white electorate to black communities, provide solid empirical evidence of these attitudinal changes. There would be no affirmative action preferences at all if not for the support of white officials elected by white voters seeking racial fairness.

The justification advanced for racial preferences is illogical on its face. The white majority that allegedly cannot be fair in the society at large is also a white majority in government. If government programs are required to compel whites to be fair, how can whites have designed and instituted those same programs? If the white majority is racist, how can the government it dominates be relied on to redress racial grievances? The question is absurd because the premise is absurd. In fact, it is America's white racial majority that ended slavery, outlawed discrimination, funded massive welfare programs that benefited inner-city blacks, and created the very affirmative action policies that are allegedly necessary to force them to be fair.

The end result of racial-preference policies masquerading as affirmative action is also perverse. In the long run, subverting the state's neutrality by eliminating the principle of color-blindness will work against minorities like African-Americans. Groups that are numerically larger are bound to benefit more from political redistribution schemes than smaller ones. Over time, as the displacement of blacks by Latinos in urban centers like Los Angeles already makes clear, the racial spoils system will transform itself into a system that locks blacks out.

Civil rights is just one battlefield in the left's war against America. The big guns of this war are directed from the centers of intellect in the university, where tenured radicals have created an anti-American culture and used the academic curriculum to indoctrinate broad sections of the nation's youth. The thrust of this curriculum was summarized in a text by a constitutional law professor at Georgetown, one of America's elite universities: "The political history of the United States ... is in large measure a history of almost unthinkable brutality toward slaves, genocidal hatred of Native Americans, racist devaluation of nonwhites and nonwhite cultures, sexist devaluation of women, and a less than admirable attitude of submissiveness to the authority of unworthy leaders in all spheres of government and public life."[8]

Of course, the political history of the United States is exactly the reverse. It is in large measure the history of a nation that led the world in eliminating slavery, in accommodating peoples it had previously defeated, in elevating nonwhites to a position of dignity and respect, in promoting opportunities and rights for women, and in fostering a healthy skepticism towards unworthy leaders and towards the dangers inherent in government itself. This view of American history is now called "conservative," but only because leftists currently shape the political language of liberalism and have been able to redefine the terms of the political debate. There is nothing "liberal" about people who deny the American narrative as a narrative of freedom, or who promote class, race, and gender war in the name of social progress. But leftists have successfully created a political vocabulary in which "racist" describes those who defend the constitutional framework of individual rights, and attempt to guard it against the nihilistic advocates of a political bad faith.

---

[8] Robin West, Progressive Constitutionalism: Reconstructing the Fourteenth Amendment, Duke University Press, 1994.

PART II

Decline and Fall
of the Civil Rights Movement

Memories in Memphis

On a recent trip to the South, I found myself in Memphis, the city where Martin Luther King, Jr. was struck down by an assassin's bullet just over thirty years ago. Memphis, I discovered, is home to a "National Civil Rights Museum," created by a local trust of African-Americans active in civil rights causes. Tucked out of the way on a city side-street, the museum is housed in the building that was once the Lorraine Motel, the very site where Dr. King was murdered.

Except for two white 1960s Cadillac convertibles, the parking lot outside the motel is empty, part of the museum's plan to preserve the memories of that somber day in April three decades ago. The cars belonged to King and his entourage, and have been left as they were the morning he was killed. Above them, a wreath hangs from a balcony railing to mark the spot where he fell. Beyond is the room where he had slept the night before. It, too, is preserved exactly as it was, the covers pulled back, the bed unmade, the breakfast tray laid out, as though someone would be coming to pick it up.

Inside the building, the first floor of the motel has vanished completely. It has been hollowed out for the museum exhibits, and the cavernous room has become a silent stage for the dramas of the movement King once led. These narratives are recounted in docu-

---

September 30, 1999, http://archive.frontpagemag.com/Printable.aspx? ArtId=24316. This was also the introductory chapter to David Horowitz, *Hating Whitey and Other Progressive Causes*, Spence, 1999.

ments and photographs, some the length of wall frescoes, bearing images as inspirational today as then. In the center of the hall, the burned shell of a school bus recalls the freedom rides and the perils their passengers once endured. Scattered about are small television screens whose tapes recapture the moments and acts that once moved a nation. On one screen, a crowd of well-dressed young men and women perpetually braves police dogs and water-hoses, vainly attempting to turn them back. It is a powerful tribute to a movement and leader that were able to win battles against overwhelming odds by exerting moral force over an entire nation.

As a visitor reaches the end of the hall, however, a corner turns to a jarring, discordant sight. Two familiar faces stare out from a wall-size monument that seems strangely out of place. The faces are Malcolm X and Elijah Muhammad, leaders of the Nation of Islam. Aside from one of King himself, there are no other portraits of similar dimension in the museum. It is clear that its creators intended to establish these men along with King as spiritual avatars of the civil rights cause.

For one old enough to have supported King, such a view seems incomprehensible. At the time of these struggles, Malcolm X was King's great antagonist in the black community, leading its resistance to the civil rights hope. The Black Muslim publicly scorned King's March on Washington as "ridiculous" and predicted the failure of the civil rights movement King led because the white man would never willingly give black Americans such rights. He rejected King's call to non-violence and his goal of an integrated society, and in so doing earned the disapproval of the American majority that King had wooed and was about to win. Malcolm even denied King's racial authenticity, redefining the term "Negro"—which King and his movement had used to describe themselves—to mean "Uncle Tom."

King was unyielding in the face of these attacks. To clarify his opposition to Malcolm X's racism, King refused to appear on any platform with him, effectively banning Malcolm from the community of respect. The other heads of the principal civil rights organizations, the NAACP's Roy Wilkins and the Urban League's Whitney Young, joined King in enforcing this ban. It was only in the last year of Malcolm's life, when the civil rights cause was all but won, and when Malcolm had left the Nation of Islam and rejected its racism, that King finally relented and agreed to appear in the now- famous photograph of the two that became iconic after their deaths.

This very reconciliation—more a concession on Malcolm's part than King's—might argue the appropriateness of Malcolm's place in a civil rights museum. Malcolm certainly earned an important place in any historical tribute to the struggle of the descendants of Africans to secure dignity, equality, and respect in a society that had brought them to its shores as slaves. His understanding of the psychology of oppression, his courage in asserting the self-confidence and pride of black Americans and his final conversion might make him worthy of inclusion in the temple of a man who was never a racist and whose movement he scorned.

But what about Elijah Muhammad? What is a racist and the founder of a hate cult doing in a monument to the civil rights movement and Martin Luther King? In contrast to Malcolm's portrait, Elijah Muhammad's is a truly perverse intrusion. The teachings of Elijah Muhammad mirror the white supremacist doctrines of the Southern racists against whom King and the civil rights movement did battle. According to Elijah's teachings, white people were invented 6,000 years ago by a mad scientist named Yacub, in a failed experiment to dilute the blood of human beings who at the time were all black. The result was a morally tainted strain of humanity—"white devils" who went on to devastate the world and oppress all other human beings, and whom God would one day destroy in a liberating Armageddon. Why is the image of this bizarre racist blown up several times life-size to form the iconography of a National Civil Rights Museum? It is as though someone had placed a statue of Nathan Bedford Forrest in the Lincoln Memorial.

After leaving the museum, it occurred to me that this image reflected a truth about the afterlife of the movement King created, whose new leaders had squandered his moral legacy after his death. This decline is reflected in many episodes of the last quarter-century: the embrace of racist demagogues like Louis Farrakhan and Al Sharpton; the indefensible causes of Tawana Brawley, O.J. Simpson, the Los Angeles race rioters and numerous others; the Million Man March on Washington, organized by the racist leader of the Nation of Islam and cynically designed to appropriate the moral mantle of King's historic event.

The impact of such episodes is compounded by the silence of black civil rights leaders over racial outrages committed by African-Americans against non-black groups—the anti-Korean incitements of black activists in New York, the mob attacks by black gangs on Asian and white storeowners during the Los Angeles riot, the lynching of a Hasidic Jew by a black mob in Crown Heights, and a black jury's acquittal of his murderer. The failures of civil rights leaders like Jesse Jackson, Kweisi Mfume and Julian Bond to condemn black racists, or black outrages committed against other ethnic communities, have been striking in contrast to the demands such leaders make on the consciences of whites— or to the moral example set by King when he dissociated his movement from the racist preaching of Malcolm X.

The moral abdication of black civil rights leaders is integrally related to their close association with a radical left whose anti-white hatreds are a by-product of their anti-Americanism. As a result of this alliance, ideological hatred of whites is now an expanding industry, not only in the African-American community but among white "liberals" in elite educational institutions as well.[1] Harvard's prestigious W.E.B. Du Bois Institute, for example, provided an academic platform for lecturer Noel Ignatiev to launch "whiteness studies," an academic field promoting the idea that "whiteness" is an oppressive "social construct" which must be "abolished."

---

[1] Jim Sleeper, *Liberal Racism*, Viking, 1997.

The magazine *Race Traitor* is the theoretical organ of this academic cult, emblazoned with the motto: "Treason to Whiteness is Loyalty to Humanity." This is hardly a new theme on the left, echoing, as it does, Susan Sontag's equally perverse claim that "the white race is the cancer of history." (Sontag eventually expressed regrets about her remark, not because it was a racial smear, but out of deference to cancer patients who might feel unjustly slurred.) According to the *Race Traitor* intellectuals, "whiteness" is the principal scourge of mankind, an idea that Louis Farrakhan promoted at the Million Man March when he declared that the world's "number one problem ... is white supremacy." Consequently, according to *Race Traitor*, "the key to solving the social problems of our age is to abolish the white race." The new racism expresses itself in slogans directly out of the radical Sixties. According to the Whiteness Studies revolutionaries, "the abolition of whiteness" must be accomplished "by any means necessary." To underscore that this slogan means exactly what it says, the editors of *Race Traitor* have explicitly embraced the military strategy of American neo-Nazis and the militia movement, and call for a John Brown-style insurrection that would trigger a second American civil war.

These attitudes promote a widespread denigration of Jews, Arabs, Central Europeans, Mediterranean Europeans, East Indians and Armenians—who are multi-ethnic and often dark-skinned, but who for official purposes (and under pressure from civil rights groups) are designated "white." Unlike anti-black attitudes, which are universally decried, and would trigger the expulsion of their purveyors from any liberal institution in America, this racism is not only permitted but encouraged, especially in the academic culture responsible for the moral and intellectual instruction of tomorrow's elites.

An anthology of the first five years of *Race Traitor* has been published by Routledge, a prestigious, academic-oriented publishing house, and was the winner of the 1997 American Book Award. Its jacket features praise by Harvard professor Cornel West, who writes: "*Race Traitor* is the most visionary, courageous journal in America." West's featured role as a speaker at the Million Man March and his coziness with Farrakhan have done nothing to tarnish his own academic reputation, his popularity with students or his standing in the civil rights community. The same is true of Afrocentrist racists like Derrick Bell and the late John Henrik Clarke, who have also been honored voices among the academic elites for decades, often running entire departments. By contrast, a distinguished Harvard scholar, Stephan Thernstrom, who is white, was driven out of his classroom by black student leftists who decided that his lectures on slavery were politically incorrect because they didn't reflect prevailing leftist prejudices.

In recent decades, anti-white racism has, in fact, become a common currency of the "progressive" intelligentsia. Examples range from Communist professor Angela Davis, who recently told an audience of undergraduates at Michigan State that the number-one problem in the world was white people, to Nobel laureate Toni Morrison, whose boundless suspicions of white America amount to a demonization almost as intense as Elijah Muhammad's. In her introduction to an anthology about the O.J. Simpson case, *Birth of a Nation 'Hood,* for example, Morrison compared the symbolic meanings of the O.J. Simpson case to D.W. Griffith's epic celebration of the Ku Klux Klan, insinuating that white America acted as the KKK in pursuing the guilty Simpson for the murders of Ron Goldman and Simpson's ex-wife.

With university support, *Race Traitor* intellectuals in the field of "whiteness studies" have produced an entire library of "scholarly" works to incite hatred against white America, against "Euro-American" culture, and against American institutions in general. Thus, according to the editors of *Race Traitor:* "Just as the capitalist system is not a capitalist plot, race is not the work of racists. On the contrary, it is reproduced by the principal institutions of society, among which are the schools (which define 'excellence'), the labor market (which defines 'employment'), the law (which defines 'crime'), the welfare system (which defines 'poverty'), and the family (which defines 'kinship'). . . ." Left-wing racists, like the editors of *Race Traitor,* characterize the presence of whites on this continent as an unmitigated catastrophe for "peoples of color" and an offense to everything that is decent and humane. In the perspective of these race radicals, white America is the "Great Satan." In academic cant, they replicate the poisonous message of the black racists of the Nation of Islam.

I once occupied the other side of the political divide, but my views on race have not changed over the years. I opposed racial preferences and double standards when segregationists supported them in the 1960s, and I oppose them now. I believed then that only a government neutral towards racial groups was compatible with a multi-ethnic democracy. I believe that today. Where my views have changed is in the appreciation I now have for America's constitutional framework and its commitment to those ideals. America's unique political culture was indeed created by white European males, primarily English and Christian. It should be obvious to anyone with even a modest historical understanding that these antecedents are not incidental to the fact that America and England led the world in abolishing slavery and in establishing the principles of ethnic and racial inclusion. Or that "people of color" are attempting to immigrate to our shores in large numbers in order to take advantage of the unparalleled opportunities and rights our society offers them, as theirs do not.

The creation of America by Protestant Christians within the framework of the British Empire has afforded greater privileges and protections to all minorities than any society extant. European-American culture is one that the citizens of this nation can take enormous pride in, precisely because its principles provide for the inclusion of cultures that are non-white, non-Christian and ethnically diverse. That is why America's democratic and pluralistic framework remains an inspiration to people of all colors all over the world, from Tiananmen Square to Haiti and Havana. This was once the common self-understanding of all Americans and is still the understanding of those who have not been seduced by the worldview of the progressive left.

The left's war against "whiteness" and America's democratic culture is in many respects the Cold War come home. The agendas of contemporary leftists are updated versions of the ideas of the Marxist left that supported the Communist empire. The same radicals who launched the social and political eruptions of the 1960s have now become the politically correct faculties of American universities. With suitable cosmetic adjustments, the theories, texts and leaders of this left display a striking continuity with the radicalism of thirty and sixty years ago. Their goal remains the destruction of America's national identity and, in particular, of the moral, political and economic institutions that are its social foundation.

In the heyday of Stalinism, the accusation of "class bias" was used by Communists to undermine and attack individuals and institutions with which they were at war. This accusation magically turned well-meaning citizens into "enemies of the people," a phrase handed down through radical generations from the Jacobin Terror in revolutionary France through the Stalinist purges in Russia and the blood-soaked cultural revolutions of Chairman Mao. The identical strategy is alive and well today in the left's self-righteous imputation of sexism, racism, and homophobia to anyone who dissents from its party line. Always weak in intellectual argument, the left habitually relies on accusation and defamation to promote its increasingly incoherent worldview.

It is not that no one else in politics uses such tactics; it is just that the left uses them so reflexively, so recklessly, and so effectively. In the battle over California's Civil Rights Initiative, which outlawed racial preferences, the left's opposition took the form of a scorched-earth strategy whose purpose was to strip its proponents of any shred of respectability. The chief spokesman for the anti-discrimination initiative, Ward Connerly, himself an African-American, was accused of anti-black racism, of wanting to be white, and of being a bedfellow of the Ku Klux Klan. The left invited former Klan member David Duke to California to forge the nonexistent connection, paying his expenses for the trip. During the Initiative campaign, NAACP and ACLU lawyers who debated its proponents relied almost exclusively on charges of racism and alarmist visions of a future in which African-Americans and women would be deprived of their rights. In their TV spots, the anti-Initiative groups actually featured hooded Klan figures burning crosses to stigmatize Initiative supporters. A tremulous voice-over by actress Candace Bergen linked Ward Connerly, California Governor Pete Wilson, and House Speaker Newt Gingrich with the KKK, claiming that women would lose all the rights they had won, and blacks would be thrown back to a time before the Civil Rights Acts if its proponents succeeded. They even suggested that maternity leaves for pregnant women would become illegal if the law was passed.

The years since the passage of the California Civil Rights Initiative have refuted every one of the left's dire predictions. Women have not lost their rights, and blacks have not been thrown back to the segregationist era. Even the enrollment of blacks in California's higher education institutions has not significantly dropped, although demagogues of the left—including President Clinton—have used a shortfall in black admissions at the very highest levels of the system (Berkeley and UCLA) to mislead the public into thinking that an overall decline in black enrollment has taken place. One year after the Initiative's adoption, enrollment had significantly fallen at only six *elite* graduate, law, and medical school programs in a higher-education system that consisted of more than seventy-four programs total. Yet there have been no apologies or acknowledgments of these facts from Candace Bergen, the NAACP, the ACLU, People for the American Way, or the other groups responsible for the campaign against the Civil Rights Initiative, or for the inflammatory rhetoric and public fear-mongering that accompanied it.

When an article of mine on racial issues was published in *Salon* magazine, it was attacked by award-winning African-American novelist Ishmael Reed, who suggested that I did not really care about what happened to blacks. Reed's not-so-subtle imputation, that I was a racist, was typical of the way leftists approached any disagreement over policy that touched on race.[2] In a futile attempt to forestall such attacks, I had cited the opinions of black conservatives in my article in support of my theses. The left's response was to dismiss them as "inauthentic" blacks, "sambos," "neocons" and "black comedians." For leftists, the only good black was a black who parroted their party line.

There is no real answer to such patronizing attitudes and nasty attacks. Nonetheless, I will repeat the response I made to Ishmael Reed. I have three black granddaughters for whom I want the absolute best that this life and this society have to offer. My extended black family, which is large and from humble origins in the Deep South, contains members who agree and who disagree with my views on these matters. But all of them understand that whatever I write on the subject of race derives from a profound desire for justice and opportunity for all. It springs from the hope that we can move towards a society where individuals, not groups, are what matter, and race is not a factor at all.

---

[2] A chapter in David Horowitz, *Hating Whitey and Other Progressive Causes*, Spence, 1999.

Clarence Page's Race Problem, and Mine

C larence Page is a well-known television African-American commentator, Pulitzer Prize-winning columnist for the *Chicago Tribune,* and author of the recent book *Showing My Color.* An adolescent in the civil rights era, Page could be taken as a symbol of that era's success. Unlike many of his radical peers, he has forcefully dissociated himself from the separatists of the Million Man March and is not ashamed of expressing hope in the American dream. Yet, in *Showing My Color,* Page has written what amounts to an apologia for those same bitter and unappreciative voices that call into question the legacy of Martin Luther King. Consequently his book is also a prime example of the problematic racial attitudes of black intellectuals in the post-King era.

Page takes the title of his book from a parental admonition frequently heard during his youth: "Don't be showin' yo' color." Showing your color, he explains, "could mean acting out or showing anger in a loud and uncivilized way." More particularly, to him it means playing to stereotype. In other words, "showing your color" really means showing your *culture*—a critical point that escapes him. The title, he explains, "emerged from my fuming discontent with the current fashions of racial denial, steadfast repudiations of the difference race continues to make in American life." Having failed to make the distinction between cultural differences

Heterodoxy, May/June 1996, http://www.discoverthenetworks.org/Articles/May-June%201996.pdf .

and color differences, Page goes on to defend affirmative action racial preferences and attack the "'color-blind' approach to civil rights law," lamenting the way the words of Martin Luther King have been "perverted" by supporters of the "color-blind" view.

Page's book begins inauspiciously with a personal anecdote with which he intends to establish that racism is, indeed, a "rude factor" in his life and—by extension—the lives of all black Americans. Unfortunately for his case, the anecdote is fifty years old, involving a trip to segregated Alabama in the fifties, where he encountered water fountains marked "colored" and "white." It does not occur to him that outrage over an event that took place nearly half a century ago has exhausted its shelf life. Page does acknowledge that such moments are probably behind us, but goes on to argue—as the post-King civil rights activists are prone to do—that a subtle and invisible set of power relationships continues to produce the same results: "Social, historical, traditional and institutional habits of mind that are deeply imbedded in the national psyche ... work as active agents to impede equal opportunity for blacks."

The politically correct term for these invisible factors is "institutional racism," which Page explains this way: "[Racism] is not just an internalized belief or attitude. It is also an externalized public practice, a power relationship that continually dominates, encourages, and reproduces the very conditions that make it so useful and profitable." This mystical formulation, without any concrete evidence to the real world, is not surprisingly phrased in a language redolent with Marxist clichés. On the other hand, Page is also capable of a more complex understanding of the dilemmas we face. He may think of himself as a "progressive," but there is a conservative inside him struggling to get out: "Conservatism resonates familiarly with me," he writes in a chapter called A Farewell to Alms, "as I think it does with most black Americans."

"We vote liberal, for liberalism has helped us make our greatest gains. But in other areas, we swing conservative. We want to believe that hard work will be rewarded.... We want to believe in the promise of America."

It takes courage for Page to defend his conservative instincts, especially in view of the intimidating pressures within the black community to make public figures like him observe racial solidarity on crucial political issues. Page does not hesitate to point out that the anti-Semitic ravings of Louis Farrakhan and other spokesmen for the Nation of Islam created the public climate in which a Yankel Rosenbaum could be lynched in Crown Heights a few years ago, and in which his killer could be acquitted by a jury of blacks. Yet Page remains a political liberal and Democrat, he claims, because of Republicans' alleged assumption that "racism is no longer a problem" and that "government programs and agencies must be trimmed, even when those programs and agencies offer the last slender thread of protection the grandchildren of America's black slaves have against further slides back into oppression."

To support this dire view, Page points to conservative opposition to minimum-wage laws, affirmative action employment policies, and welfare aid to mothers with dependent children. But a deeper cultural dimension to Page's differences with Republicans is evoked by sentences like this: "Klan membership dropped sharply in the early 1980s, according to researchers for the Anti-Defamation League and other Klan-watching groups, as many found a new, satisfying voice and vehicle in Republican Party politics. Enter David Duke." But this is almost as far-fetched as recalling the segregated water fountains of a distant past. Duke's influence, unlike Farrakhan's, doesn't reach outside Louisiana or into the chambers of Congress. Duke has been publicly condemned by the Republican Party leadership, including three former Republican presidents, something Page neglects to mention.

This lapse into partisan race-baiting prompts me to show my own color. I am a Jewish Republican, who nearly fifty years ago marched in support of Harry Truman's civil rights legislation and have been active in civil rights struggles ever since. Moreover, I can produce a personal anecdote of anti-Semitism that, unlike Page's encounter with segregated facilities as a child, is actually current. My fiancée is a non-Jewish woman who has been confronted by several friends who have said to her, "How can you marry a Jew?" Prejudice exists, but there is no need to make more of it than it deserves.

The level of Jew-hatred in America actually is higher today than it has been in my entire lifetime, thanks not only to the poisonous rants of Louis Farrakhan but also to the collusion of large sections of the black intelligentsia in legitimizing his viewpoint for African-Americans. It is black anti-Semites who have legitimated public anti-Semitism in a way that no other group in America could. Nor does it seem that Jews or other minorities can feel as protected today by the American mainstream as blacks. When Marlon Brando launched an attack on Hollywood Jews on a Larry King show and went on to talk about "kikes," "chinks," and "niggers," it was only the "N-word" that got bleeped by the CNN censors. "Institutional racism," if we want to grant that mythical construct a modicum of reality, can cut more than one way.

Anti-Semitism has real-world consequences for Jews, just as surely as racism does for blacks. For example, a Jew knows not to seek a career in the auto business without taking into account the fact that Jews are few and far between in the auto industry and almost invisible at executive levels. I have stood in the living rooms of Grosse Pointe mansions and felt the disdain caused by my ethnicity. But this does not lead me or my fellow Jews to call for government-enforced preferences for Jews or to seek the source of this prejudice in the institutional heart of the nation.

For a voting liberal, Page has an unusually broad familiarity with conservative writers, and his readings are mostly respectful. It is not surprising, therefore, that his defense of affirmative action is often shrewd, even if his arguments remain unconvincing. Like other defenders of an indefensible policy, Page begins by denying that affirmative action is what it is: "Despite myths to the contrary, affirmative action is not intended to promote people who are not qualified. It is intended to widen the criteria for those who are chosen out of the pool of the qualified." Unfortunately for this argument, there are a plethora of examples that prove just the opposite.

Journalist Roger Wilkins was made University Professor of History at George Mason University despite the fact that he had no qualifications as a historian, never having written a scholarly monograph. Wilkins was chosen, it happens, over my friend Ronald Radosh, who at the time had been a history professor for twenty years, had published widely in scholarly journals, and had also written several highly respected books in his field. Nor is Wilkins an isolated case. Julian Bond's failed political career has led for no apparent reason other than the politics of race to concurrent professorships at two universities (Virginia and Maryland), also in history. Cornel West and Angela Davis hold two of the highest-paid and most prestigious university chairs in America, despite their intellectual mediocrity (in Davis's case, compounded by her disreputable career as a Communist Party apparatchik and lifelong apologist for Marxist police states). Indeed, the weakness of the affirmative action case is exposed by the very fact that its most intensely contested battlefields are elite universities, which rank among the nation's most liberal institutions.

Page actually defends the beleaguered affirmative action programs at the University of California with the argument that enrollment levels of blacks are expected to drop when affirmative action is ended. Would Page have us believe that the admissions departments of liberal universities like the University of California are infested with angry whites conspiring to keep black enrollment down? Or with built-in "institutional biases" that exclude blacks? The reality is that since 1957, when the California regents adopted their famous "Master Plan," every single California resident, regardless of race, who graduates from high school with certain achievements has been *guaranteed* a place in the university system. Matriculation from various points in the system, starting with community and junior colleges to positions at Berkeley and UCLA (its academic pinnacles), are based on grade-point averages and achievement tests, and these alone.

In defending policies under which racial preferences trump achievements, Page compares them to the "geographical diversity" criteria of the Ivy League schools, commenting, "Americans have always had a wide array of exotic standards for determining 'merit.'" Page doesn't seem to realize that "geographical diversity" criteria were introduced to *restrict* the enrollment of Jews rather than to provide affirmative action programs for students from Wyoming and Utah. Page even quotes, without irony, a friend who said he was convinced he got into Dartmouth because he was the only applicant from Albuquerque: "I'm sure some talented Jewish kid from New York was kept out so I could get in."

When I was a student at Columbia in the Fifties, the geographical diversity program was in place and the Jewish enrollment was 48 percent. That was the Jewish quota. As Jews we were well aware of the anti-Semitic subtext of the geographical program and talked about it among ourselves. But we did not launch protests or seek government interventions to abolish the program. Once the principle of Jewish admission was accepted, even residual (or "institutional") anti-Semitism could not keep Jews, who constituted only 3 percent of the population, from flooding the enrollment lists of Ivy League schools. Liberals like Clarence Page support affirmative action because they are in a state of massive denial. The problem of low black enrollment at elite universities is not caused by racist admissions policies. It is caused by poor academic performance among blacks.

In defending affirmative action policies, Page reveals the underlying element in most expressions of "black rage" these days. This is the displacement of personal frustrations, the unwillingness of many blacks to go through the arduous process that other ethnic minorities have followed in their climb up the American ladder. Thus Page opens his chapter on affirmative action with a personal anecdote. As a high school graduate in 1965, he applied for a summer newsroom job but was beaten out by a girl who was less qualified and younger, but white. Shortly after that, the Watts riot occurred and he was hired. Page's comment: "You might say that my first job in newspapers came as a result of an affirmative action program called 'urban riots.'" This is a thinly veiled justification for criminal behavior and a familiar cliché of the Left: white people respond fairly to blacks only when they have a gun to their heads. Thus Malcolm X, who scorned the civil rights movement—in a 1963 speech he referred to "the recent ridiculous march on Washington" because he believed, wrongly, that Americans would never give blacks their rights—is seen in retrospect by many black intellectuals as its author because his violent racism scared whites into yielding. But what is immediately striking in Page's reflection is that he doesn't pause to consider that this was his first job application and that it was only for a summer position. Perhaps the men doing the hiring wanted to have a girl around the office for a couple of months. This would be an unprofessional rationale for the hiring, but not racist. Nor would it require a riot to remedy.

Page gives no thought to the possibility that he would have been hired eventually anyway. Recognizing that significant changes take time is not the same as saying that they require force to implement. Was it the threat of riots or of affirmative action laws that eventually made black athletes dominant in leagues whose owners often do not rank among the socially enlightened? Or that allowed black cultural artists to achieve an equally dominant position in the popular music industry? How did Oprah Winfrey, a black sharecropper's daughter from Mississippi, become mother-confessor to millions of lower-middle-class white women (and a billionaire in the process) without affirmative action? Page has no answer. And he doesn't even address the most striking implication of his anecdotal encounter with racism as a youth: The kind of discrimination that upset him then has, in affirmative action, been systematized and elevated to a national policy.

The primary reason most conservatives oppose affirmative action is one that is given almost no attention by progressives eager to attribute base motives to their opponents. Racial preference is an offense to the core values of American pluralism, which depends on individual rights and the neutrality of government toward all its communities. Affirmative action is a threat to inclusiveness, because privilege is established as a group right and enforced by legal coercion. Affirmative action— which is in practice, despite all denials, a system of racial preferences—is a threat to what Felix Frankfurter identified as "the ultimate foundation of a free society ... the binding tie of cohesive sentiment." Affirmative action based on principles like geographical diversity constitutes no such threat, but policies based on race do. Racial preferences are a corrosive acid, eating at the moral and social fabric of American life. Every time a black leader refers to the paucity of blacks on the faculty of Harvard or in the upper reaches of corporate America, the automatic presumption is that white racism is responsible, not factors contributing to individual merit or the lack thereof. The legal concept of "racial disparity" employs the same assumption. The idea that government must compel its white citizens to be fair to its minority citizens presumes that white America is so racist it cannot be fair on its own account. This involves supporters of affirmative action in an illogic so insurmountable it is never mentioned: If the white majority needs to be forced by government to be fair, how is it possible that the same white majority—led by a Republican president named Richard Nixon—created affirmative action policies in the first place?

There is no answer to this question because, in fact, affirmative action was not created because of white racism. It was created because of widespread black failure to take advantage of the opportunities made available when legal segregation was ended. Since the politics of the left are premised on the idea that social institutions determine individual outcomes, this failure had to be the result of institutional rather than individual factors. Whites led by Richard Nixon accepted this fallacious argument and, because they did not want blacks to be second-class citizens, created affirmative action programs.

If affirmative action works, as Page implies, it does so in ways he does not mention. Its primary achievement is to have convinced black Americans that whites are so racist that some external force must compel their respect and, secondarily, that blacks need affirmative action in order to gain equal access to the American dream. The further consequence of this misguided remedy has been to sow a racial paranoia in the black community so pervasive and profound that even blacks who have benefited from America's racial opportunities have been significantly affected in the way they think. How significantly is revealed in the almost casual way the paranoia surfaces: "'Black is beautiful' was the slogan which made many white people nervous, as any show of positive black racial identification tends to do." Does it? The television mini-series *Roots* was one of the most significant milestones of positive black racial identification—an epic of black nobility and white evil purporting to represent the entire history of American race relations. It was not only produced and made possible by whites, but also voluntarily watched by more whites than any previous television show in history. Conversely, most of the negative stereotypes of blacks in today's popular culture are the work of black stars and directors like Martin Lawrence and Spike Lee and the "gangsta rap" industry, which celebrates black sociopathic behavior.

In gauging the size of the chip ominously perched on black America's shoulder, few measures are so choice as the following passage from Page's book:

> Black people may read dictionaries, but many see them as instruments of white supremacy. They have a point. Dictionaries define what is acceptable and unacceptable in the language we use as defined by the ruling class [sic].... The dictionary's pleasant synonyms for "white" ("free from moral impurity ... innocent ... favorable, fortunate ...") and unpleasant synonyms for "black" ("... thoroughly sinister or evil ... wicked ... condemnation or discredit ... the devil ... sad, gloomy or calamitous ... sullen ...") are alone enough to remind black people of their subordinate position to white people in Anglo-European traditions and fact.

In fact, white lexicographers had nothing to do with identifying Clarence Page and his racial kindred as "black" in the first place. When Page and I were young, blacks were called "Negroes" and had been called that or "colored" for hundreds of years. The word Negro has no such negative connotations, moral or otherwise. It was Malcolm X who first embraced "black" as a term of pride, and made "Negro" a term to connote the white man's pliant black, the "Uncle Tom." After Malcolm's death, Stokely Carmichael and the new radical civil rights leadership aggressively took up the label with the slogan "Black Power" and demanded that "black" be used as a sign of respect. Accommodating whites complied. For more than a generation now, the majority of whites have ardently wished that black America would finally get what it wanted from them—and be happy about it.

When all the layers are peeled from the discussion of "racism" in *Showing My Color,* we are left with a disappointing residue of hand-me-down Marxism:

> Modern capitalist society puts racism to work, wittingly or
> unwittingly. It populates a surplus labor pool of last-hired, first-
> fired workers whose easy employability when economic times
> are good and easy disposability when times go bad helps keep all
> workers' wages low and owners' profits high.... Racism is one of
> many non-class issues, such as busing, affirmative action, or flag
> burning, that diverts attention from pocketbook issues that
> might unite voters across racial lines.

This is simple-minded, sorry stuff, unworthy of Clarence Page or any other intellectual (black or otherwise). The problem with the black underclass is not that it is underemployed, but that it is unemployable. Blacks who have fallen through society's cracks don't even get to the point of being "last-hired." The flood of illegal Hispanic immigrants into areas like South Central Los Angeles, displacing indigenous blacks, shows that the jobs exist but that the resident black population either won't or can't take them, or are not hired for some reason other than their minority status.

The fact that one in three young black males in America is enmeshed in the criminal justice system—a fact that Page doesn't begin to confront—doesn't help their employability. Once again, the category of race provides a convenient pretext for a massive denial of problems that have very little to do, specifically, with racial prejudice.

In fact, the racial conflict in America is being driven not by economics or even white prejudice, but by radical political agendas— by Clarence Page's friends on the far left like Manning Marable, Ronald Takaki and Michael Lerner, all of whom have provided blurbs for Page's book. The very phrase "institutional racism"— necessary because there are so very few overt racists available—is, of course, a leftist invention. It is also a totalitarian concept. Like "ruling class," it refers to an abstraction, not a responsible individual human actor. You are a class enemy (or, in this case, a race enemy) not because of anything you actually think or do, but "objectively"—because you are situated in a structure of power that gives you (white skin) privilege. Page is astute enough to see that if racism is defined as an institutional flaw, "it does not matter what you think as an individual" and therefore such a definition offers "instant innocence" to the oppressor. But he is not shrewd or candid enough to see that it imputes instant guilt as well. While absolving individual whites, it makes all whites guilty.

The belief in the power of institutional racism allows black civil rights leaders to denounce America as a racist society, when it is actually the only society on earth—black, white, brown or yellow—whose defining creed is *anti*-racist; a society to which blacks from black-ruled nations regularly flee in search of opportunity and refuge. But the real bottom line is that the phantom of institutional racism allows black leaders to avoid the encounter with real problems in their own communities which are neither caused by whites nor solvable by the actions of whites.

The problem with the discontent now smoldering inside America's privileged black intellectuals, so well expressed in *Showing My Color*, is that it can never be satisfied:

Nothing annoys black people more than the hearty perennial of black life in America, the persistent reality of having one's fate in America decided inevitably by white people. It is an annoyance that underlies all racial grievances in America, beginning with slavery, evolving through the eras of mass lynchings and segregated water fountains, and continuing through the age of "white flight," mortgage discrimination, police brutality, and the "race card" in politics.

In Page's view, the unifying and ultimate goal of all black reformers, whether radicals like bell hooks or conservatives like Clarence Thomas, is "black self-determination." What Clarence Page and blacks like him want is "to free the destiny of blacks from the power of whites." But outside of Africa and some Caribbean countries, this is obviously an impossible goal and those who advocate it must know this. (Does Page want to go back to Stokely Carmichael's ridiculous demand in the Sixties for blacks to be given Mississippi?) The goal is precious to them precisely because it can never be realized and thus, to turn one of Jesse Jackson's slogans on its head, keeps rage alive. Those who push for "black self-determination" in the American context are destined to be frustrated and angry and to look on themselves as "oppressed." The irony, of course, is that America's multiethnic society and color-blind ideal—the equality of all citizens before the law—provides the most favorable setting for individuals to enjoy freedom and the opportunity to determine their destinies, even if they happen to be members of a minority. Ask Jews. For two thousand years, Jews of the Diaspora have not been able to free their destiny from the power of gentiles. But in America, where they are a tiny minority, they have done very well, thank you, and do not feel oppressed except, perhaps, by black demagogues like Farrakhan and company.

3

Black History Lesson

Fifty years ago this spring, Jackie Robinson broke the color bar in baseball. The events that followed provide a lesson that many civil rights leaders seem to have forgotten. Following Robinson's historic breakthrough, as everybody knows, other black athletes followed his example and professional basketball and football also became multiracial sports. Over the years, however, there were many doubters that these gains were possible or that the revolution would continue. The doubters said whites would never accept more than a few black players; there would always be quotas to limit the number of blacks. Whites, they said, would never allow blacks to become managers or quarterbacks or the owners of clubs. Most ominously, they said that if blacks became the majority of the players in professional basketball, for example, whites wouldn't go to see the games.

History has shown that on all counts the doubters were wrong. Blacks did become quarterbacks and managers and general managers. Superstars like Isiah Thomas and Magic Johnson became owners. So thoroughly did blacks come to dominate sports that were once the exclusive province of whites that in basketball today almost 90 percent of the starting players are black. When the NBA All-Star Game was played last year, it was televised to 170 countries worldwide, and nine out of the ten starting players were black multimillionaires, with contracts totaling $50 million,

February 24, 1997, http://archive.frontpagemag.com/Printable.aspx?ArtId =24416; http://www.salon.com/1997/02/24/horowitz970224/.

$80 million and even $100 million. Despite this overwhelming tide of color in the sport, 80 percent of the paying customers are still white.

The most telling point in the history just summarized is the following neglected fact: This was all accomplished without government intervention and without affirmative action. There were no government policies or official guidelines laid down for owners of athletic teams, no EEOC investigators hovering around stadiums or summoning owners to court; no lawsuits filed by NAACP lawyers, no consent decrees ordered by federal judges, no heavy government hand compelling owners to redress "past injustice." Only two things were required to launch this momentous change in America's race relations: a single white businessman with a vision, and a public to support him.

That man was Branch Rickey, the owner of the Brooklyn Dodgers. It was Branch Rickey and Branch Rickey alone who decided to hire Jackie Robinson and make baseball a multiracial sport. To complete the process, a second element was indispensable: the good will of the white fans. If whites had turned away from the game because of the presence of black players, Rickey's efforts would have come to naught. But the crowds kept coming. Other owners, needing the best players to transform their clubs into winning teams, and seeing that the fans would accept players of any race, followed suit. And that was how the face of America's sports industry was changed: through an open market and competition.

Sports club owners are not the most enlightened segment of the population, and neither perhaps are sports fans themselves. But they have shown over half a century they are not racists either. Given the choice, they will accept black Americans, recognize their achievements and even worship them as popular icons and heroes, rewarding them like kings in the process.

So tolerant is the real America that, in 1997, Dennis Rodman, a black transvestite with orange and sometimes green hair, can earn millions of dollars a year, be sought after for product endorsements and become an idol to white American youngsters. These are facts that need to be remembered at a time when so many civil rights leaders dwell only on the negative aspects of our racial present and past.

The corrosive effect of affirmative action policies that insist on government-ordered race preferences is to make America forget this history, and to convince black Americans that without government coercion and court decrees, they cannot get the justice they deserve. It is to convince them that whites are irredeemably racist and that black success depends on government agencies forcing whites to be fair. This is a perverse argument and I leave it to armchair psychologists to figure out why it is apparently so persuasive.

Jackie Robinson was able to break the color bar and enter the major leagues because he was better than most of the players at the time. The injustice of his exclusion was obvious first to one man and then to all. Americans are by and large a fair-minded people. As we commemorate Black History Month, it's time for us all to acknowledge this fact.

4

Farrakhan and the Right

Considered by many conservatives as the great hope of the Republican Party, Jack Kemp has a strange weakness for America's premier black racist, Louis Farrakhan. On a campaign stop in Harlem during his 1996 vice-presidential campaign, Kemp praised Farrakhan as a "wonderful" supply-side role model for inner-city blacks, without mentioning Farrakhan's racial venom against whites or his pathological obsession with Jews.

Kemp was prompted to embrace Farrakhan by his eccentric friend Jude Wanniski, a Wall Street economic advisor whose supply-side theories are highly influential in some conservative circles.[1] But the two went much further earlier this month at Wanniski's annual gathering for clients and admirers in Boca Raton, Florida. Lured by such stars as Kemp, conservative columnist Robert Novak and key legislators like Sen. Christopher Dodd, D-Conn., and Rep. John Kasich, R-Ohio, chairman of the House Budget Committee, approximately 100 Wall Street and industrial movers and shakers came to hear a 90-minute talk by the gathering's main attraction, Minister Farrakhan.

The Kemp-Wanniski agenda in Boca Raton was to introduce representatives of the white establishment to the "new" Farrakhan, a

---

http://www.salon.com/1997/03/20/news_351/.

[1] See also "Kemp Praises Farrakhan For His Focus on Family," Jerry Gray, *New York Times*, September 10, 1996, http://www.nytimes.com/1996/09/10/us/kemp-praises-farrakhan-for-his-focus-on-family.html.

smooth-talking advocate of inner-city "self-reliance"—a nostrum dear to the hearts of some conservative theorists—and to promote reconciliation with the fanatic and his gullible followers. Novak, who moderated the event, described Farrakhan as "a man trying to transcend his past."

While Farrakhan was supposedly undertaking that effort, his followers were distributing hundreds of thousands of copies of the March issue of his newspaper, *The Final Call*, to black communities across the nation. The issue accuses whites of "lynching" O.J. Simpson and insinuates that Jewish manipulators of the media deliberately scheduled NBC's airing of *Schindler's List*, the Academy Award-winning film about the Holocaust, during Black History Month as an insult to African-Americans. It also reprints an article by the late Elijah Muhammad about the coming "fall of America"—a fall ordained by God because of this nation's irredeemable wickedness—and prints a message that Libyan dictator Moammar Gaddafi sent to Farrakhan's recent Saviors' Day Convention in Chicago.

What attracts these white conservatives—who presumably don't read *The Final Call*—to Farrakhan? Like the Marxists of a bygone era, Kemp and Wanniski are convinced that economics is destiny, even in the poorer segments of the black community. Convinced that "enterprise zones" will cure America's inner-city problems, they regard anyone who adopts such market-oriented solutions with favor. What they perhaps did not know was that only weeks earlier, Farrakhan had re-launched his crusade for an independent and separate black state to be carved out of America. This, it is true, would be a self-reliant entity, but one premised on the belief that white America is irretrievably racist—a belief that repudiates everything Kemp presumably holds dear.

If Louis Farrakhan wants to convince the objects of his venom that he is interested in reconciliation, he does not need Jack Kemp, Jude Wanniski or Robert Novak to act as interpreters for him. Any day Farrakhan wants to show that he has changed his malevolent tune, he can do so very simply and all by himself. He can begin by repudiating the creed that he preaches: that white people are "blue-eyed devils" created by a mad scientist named Yakub, that they are guilty of monstrous crimes against humanity and are therefore slated for destruction by God in order that the world may be saved. Then he can stop his publication and distribution of "The Secret Relationship Between Blacks and Jews," which is the Nation of Islam's home-grown version of the Protocols of the Elders of Zion, portraying Jews as the diabolical and conspiratorial enemies of blacks through history.

Until Farrakhan repudiates his abhorrent preaching, it is shameful for American conservatives to lend him credibility and support.

5

*A Washer Woman
Shall Lead Them*

As someone who helped to create the radical New Left in the '60s and became a conservative in the '80s, I am often asked to explain how it is possible to make such a 180-degree turn. I have tried to answer this in a 450-page autobiography.[1] But there is a short answer as well. I abandoned the agendas of the left because they do not work. Socialism, big government and economic redistribution have proven disastrous to the very people whom the left proposes to "liberate."

I still believe in the "liberation" of blacks, minorities and the poor, as I did in the 1960s. Only now I believe in their liberation from the chains of "liberalism" and the welfare state—from permanent dependence on government handouts, from perverse incentives to bear children out of wedlock, from inverted ethics that imply it is better to receive than to give, and worse, to receive without reciprocity or responsibility and above all without work. The doctrines of the left teach those who have fallen behind in the economic scramble to blame others for their failure. This attitude stimulates resentment and deprives its holders of the power to change their condition. The left insists on race preferences, thus delivering the message to minorities that they cannot compete unless the system is rigged in their favor. This reinforces the sense of group inferiority, which is the essence of racism.

March 31, 1997, http://www.salon.com/1997/03/31/horowitz970331/
http://www.newsrealblog.com/2011/01/21/an-old-black-washer-woman-shall-lead-them/print/.
[1]David Horowitz, *Radical Son: A Generational Odyssey*, Free Press, 1997.

Leftist doctrine proposes double standards of intellectual, moral and professional competence, teaching minorities that they can get away with less. It is a crippling philosophy for those it claims to help, and a not-so-subtle expression of racial arrogance on the part of those are behind it. Under "liberalism" no one is responsible. Instead, something called "society" is the root of all evil. If a criminal strikes a prey, "society" is the root cause of his wickedness; if a person is poor, "society" has made him so. If conservatives seek to hold people responsible for their condition, it is out of a mean-spirited impulse to blame the victims. How could there possibly be all this opportunity conservatives talk about when America is saturated with racism and oppression?

I used to believe all this nonsense, but then I arrived at a world-view based on what I have recently come to call the Oseola McCarty principle. Oseola McCarty is a 75-year-old African-American cleaning woman from Mississippi. From her working life she was able to accumulate enough savings to donate $150,000 to a student scholarship program at the University of Southern Mississippi. In short, a black woman living in the most racist and poorest state in the union (almost half her life under segregation) could earn enough money washing other people's clothes to save $150,000 and give it away. If Oseola McCarty can do that, what American black or white cannot?

Oseola McCarty's example tells us that the poverty problem in America is not about lack of opportunity or jobs, or about racism. Poverty is about individual failure. It is about family dysfunction, character disorder and self-destructive behavior. That is what Oseola McCarty's achievement means. It is no surprise that, while most self-appointed spokesmen get tongue-tied when asked if African-Americans have gained anything from the civil rights revolution of the last 30 years, Oseola McCarty has no hesitation. She says the world is a "much, much better place" than when she was a child. So it can be for anyone liberated from the philosophy of the left. The new mantra would be this: Spare us from the kindness of those who would cripple us with excuses for attitudes and behaviors that can only hold us back and eventually destroy us. Keep us from the charity of those who would chain us to their benevolence with lifetime handouts. Spare us the compassion of saviors who secretly despise us, who think that we cannot compete on our merits or live up to the moral standards they expect of themselves.

This is the creed of true equality. It has just taken me a long time to understand that.

6

Alternative to Affirmative Action

President Clinton's much-awaited statement on race has come and gone and, as usual with this president, no one on either side of the argument is convinced that anything was said at all. Perhaps this reveals something about the general state of the nation—our inability to speak clearly, unambiguously and directly about the issue of race.

The president chose a University of California campus in San Diego as the site for his pronouncement in order to focus attention on California's ban on racial preferences and what he described as the drop in enrollment rates resulting from that ban. According to university officials, African-American admissions to UC's Boalt Hall law school, one of the most prestigious in the nation, dropped by 85 percent as a result of the new policy. But African-American enrollment *throughout the whole University of California system* actually increased. What the president chose not to discuss was the way in which the results at an elite institution like Boalt completely undermine the defenders of the affirmative action/racial preference policies that are now—thanks to Proposition 209—illegal in California. During the arguments over the California Civil Rights Initiative, opponents had claimed that race was only one of many factors and an insignificant one at best in awarding affirmative action slots at the university. Now it is clear that affirmative

June 23, 1997, http://archive.frontpagemag.com/Printable.aspx?ArtId=24401; http://www.salon.com/1997/06/23/horowitz970623/.

action is a system of racial preferences and racial discrimination and nothing more.

The president calls for a conversation about race, but what he really wants is a conversation about racism, and about white racism exclusively. His response to California's rejection of racial preferences is that we must not "re-segregate" higher education. As though re-segregation was not already an accomplished agenda of the left; as though black separatists and their liberal allies were not the leaders of the movement; as though there were not separate black dorms and black graduations sanctioned by progressive university administrators; as though there were not special orientations for incoming black freshmen and expensive invitations to black racists like Khalid Muhammad, Louis Farrakhan, Kwame Ture, Professor Griff, Sister Souljah, Leonard Jeffries, Tony Martin, Frances Welsing, etc., etc., to speak before black student unions and Pan African student associations and incite racial hatred against whites.

Lacking any interest in addressing the real problems of racial division in America, what the president did was to offer a challenge to those of us who remain faithful to the vision of the civil rights movement and reject government discrimination. To those who oppose affirmative action, the president said, "I'll ask you to come up with an alternative. I would embrace it if I could find a better way."

There is such an alternative. It's called *study*. Study hard. If you want to get into an elite law school, that's what you need to do. The alternative to rigging the standards, Mr. President, is to teach one's children the value of an education in the first place. It is to stick around after conception to help children enter a difficult and demanding world. It is to give up the blame game and look at your own responsibility for where you are. It is to tell your children that getting educated is not "thinking white." It's thinking.

How is it helpful to African-Americans to tell them that it is not their failure when they do not meet standards that others do, but the fault of white racists who want to keep them down? This is a lie and everybody knows it. African-Americans are failing because they are not prepared by their families and their culture to succeed. If race or poverty were real concerns of the University of California, its administrators would not be excluding Vietnamese and Cambodian children (who do meet the standards) in order to make room for African-American and Hispanic children (who do not).

It's time for a president of the United States to stand up and be proud of the fact that in America minorities are no longer barred because of race from America's best universities, or indeed from any American university. Racial handwringing by guilt-ridden whites does not help the disadvantaged. On the contrary, it is an obstacle to their progress. It contributes to what is now a massive denial of the problems that minority communities create for themselves. And by contributing to the delusion that others who have been successful control the destinies of those who are not, it takes from them the power to change their fate.

7

Progressives Support Racial Divisions

A Clinton task force has unanimously recommended against adding the category "multiracial" to the government census forms which now list four official race categories: white, black, American Indian/Alaskan Native, and Asian/Pacific Islander. According to news reports on this development, "The recommendation marks a victory for traditional civil rights and ethnic advocacy groups, including the NAACP and the National Council of La Raza, which were pitted against the newer multiracial advocacy groups." Welcome to the Alice-in-Wonderland world of America's racial politics.

Begin anywhere: Asians (to pick only one of those official categories) are not a race. The National Council of La Raza (The Race) is an ethnic advocacy group, but neither the Hispanic nor the Latino ethnic constituency it claims to represent is really an ethnicity. They are language groups. Moreover, the terms Latino and Hispanic cover not only different but polarized ethnicities, nationalities and races (e.g., the Mexican Indians of Chiapas and their European-descended Hispanic oppressors). Finally, neither the NAACP nor La Raza can be said to be much concerned for civil rights these days, judging by their advocacy of racial and ethnic preferences and the zeal they have shown in opposing the civil rights claims of multiracial Americans.

August 3, 1997, http://archive.frontpagemag.com/Printable.aspx?ArtId=
24395; http://www.salon.com/1997/07/18/horowitz970718/.

The multiracial latecomers to the debate have discovered that there is no room for them at the civil rights table. Despite creating their own advocacy institutions modeled on what's become of the civil rights struggle, including a march on Washington to protest their "under-representation," they have come up virtually empty in their quest for a census box. There is not going to be a Tiger Woods band in the American rainbow, at least not this year; no designation for the one-quarter white, one-eighth black, one-quarter Thai, one-quarter Chinese, one-eighth Indian American. Of course, the administration liberals didn't fail to throw a crumb in the direction of the multiracials: namely, the ability to check off multiple boxes if they should so choose.

A spokesperson for the multiracial coalition named Susan Graham, president of a group called Project Race, welcomed this "victory" but insisted that her troops would continue to pursue the multiracial category: "As it is, my children cannot be multiracial children. My children can be 'check-all-that-apply' children and I do not consider that fair."

It's not really about fairness, Susan. It's about a racial/ethnic spoils system, which is the sorry mess that civil rights advocacy has become in America since the death of Martin Luther King. The stakes here, of course, are not rights but entitlements: the set-asides, grants, voting district lines and other government (and now private) handouts that serve as payoffs to the racial/ethnic grievance-mongers. Otherwise, who could be against a multiracial census category, which if adopted would embody the celebrated American mosaic?

Actually, I would be against it. I say this not only as a veteran of the once venerable civil rights struggle, but as the grandfather of three beautiful granddaughters who would qualify for the box that will not appear on your next national census and thus would not qualify for the affirmative action perks, the special even-if-you-don't-really-need-them scholarships, and the minority even-if-you-have-to-subcontract-them-to-someone-who-is-actually-qualified-to-do-the-job contracts.

Of course, my granddaughters will be able to fill a preferred racial box anyway and qualify for all these perks if they just tick off the category which includes that part of their racial/ethnic chromosomes (in their case, black) that make the Clinton liberals and other social engineers of the new American apartheid feel good about themselves. I use the word "apartheid" advisedly, because apartheid in its origins was nothing more than an affirmative action program for the Boer minority, who were oppressed by the English.

The current multiracial census fiasco ought to set off alarm bells to the nation, that we are headed down a terribly wrong path. We have already become a race-conscious society in a way that would have been unthinkable just a generation ago, when the phrase "without regard to race, color or creed" was still invoked whenever anyone wanted to describe American pluralism. Will the present path lead us down the road to deeper and more bitter racial divisions, ugly struggles over diminishing racial spoils, increasing civil conflict and eventually a South African future? Or perhaps just further into the realm of the ridiculous and the just plain stupid? I have no idea. But you can check one of the above.

8

Johnnie's Other O.J.

Ifirst heard the name Geronimo Pratt in the early 1970s during a late night conversation with Huey Newton, the "Minister of Defense" of the Black Panther Party, now deceased. Pratt was the leader of the Los Angeles branch of the Party and had been convicted of a robbery-murder that occurred on December 18, 1968. A young elementary school teacher named Caroline Olsen and her husband, Kenneth, were accosted by two gunmen on a Santa Monica tennis court, and were ordered to lie down and give up their cash and jewelry, which they did. But as the predators left the scene, one of the gunmen emptied his .45 caliber weapon into their prone bodies, wounding Kenneth Olsen and killing Caroline. Nearly two years later, Geronimo Pratt was charged with the murder and subsequently convicted despite the efforts of a young attorney on the make named Johnnie Cochran.

It was not just the murder conviction that made Pratt a figure of interest, since other Panthers had gone to jail for criminal offenses as well. Pratt was special because Newton and the Party had hung him out to dry. Even though he was "Deputy Minister of Defense," and ran the Los Angeles Party, there were no "Free Geronimo" rallies organized on his behalf, as there had been for Huey and other Panthers like Ericka Huggins and Bobby Seale. In fact, Huey and the other Panther leaders—Seale, David Hilliard and Elaine Brown—flatly denied Pratt's alibi that he was at a

September 1, 1997, http://archive.frontpagemag.com/Printable.aspx? ArtId=22335.

Panther meeting in Oakland at the time of the murder. It was this denial that sealed Pratt's fate.

There were reasons why Huey would do this. He had expelled Pratt from the Panthers shortly after the murder of Caroline Olsen because of his support for an anti-Newton Black Panther faction led by Eldridge Cleaver. This more violent wing of the Party had accused Newton of selling out the "armed struggle." To show their authenticity, Cleaver's followers had formed the "Black Liberation Army," which had already launched a "guerilla war" in America's cities, conducting a string of armed robberies and several murders in the process. A Vietnam War veteran, Pratt had been the Party's "military expert." As head of the Los Angeles chapter, he had fortified its headquarters for a shootout with police, deploying machine guns and other automatic weapons in a firefight in which three officers and three Panthers were wounded. At the beginning of August 1970, when Pratt was kicked out of the Party, another member of his violent faction, Jonathan Jackson, marched into a Marin County courthouse with loaded shotguns and took hostages in an episode that cost the lives of a federal judge, Jackson, and two of his cohorts. Pratt had supported Jackson and his plan to use the hostages to liberate his brother from San Quentin, where he was waiting trial for murder.

The evening Huey and I talked about Geronimo, he explained to me that Pratt, a decorated Vietnam veteran, was also psychotic (the word he used); he had not only committed the Santa Monica murder but actually enjoyed violence for its own sake. Huey attributed Pratt's aberrant behavior to his war experience, although he had not known Pratt prior to his military discharge. And that was the way it remained for me for twenty-five years, as I was discovering that Huey himself was a cold-blooded killer and the Panthers a political gang that had committed many robberies, arsons and murders. By the time Johnnie Cochran brought Pratt's case before the general public, I was almost ready myself to give him the benefit of the doubt. Perhaps some other Panther had killed Caroline Olsen and used Pratt's car to commit the crime, as his supporters maintained. Perhaps the murder weapon, a distinctive .45 caliber model used in the military and identified by several witnesses as belonging to Pratt, had actually belonged to someone else, as he maintained.

But there was a detail from that conversation with Huey that I could never forget and yet never quite believe either. Pratt was so crazy, Huey told me, that "he couldn't get an erection unless he was holding a knife in his hand." This detail would surface in the aftermath of Pratt's release last June by Orange County Superior Court Judge Everett Dickey. Dickey had agreed with Cochran that the prosecution had wrongfully concealed from the original jury the information that their key witness, a former Panther named Julius Butler, had acted as a police and FBI informant. It was Butler who had identified the .45 as Geronimo's weapon and—even more damning—had claimed that Pratt boasted to him that he had killed Caroline Olsen. It was Butler—and the adroit use Cochran made of him—that led Pratt to be granted a new trial and be hailed by Cochran and a compliant press as a hero and a victim of injustice.

In the tapestry of Johnnie Cochran's political career, the case of Geronimo Pratt forms a central thread. A young Johnnie Cochran, just setting out on his law career, had been Pratt's counsel in the original trial. By his own account, it was the Pratt case that radicalized him, persuading him that America's criminal justice system was unfair to black men. It showed him, too, that his failure to play the race card had led to the conviction of his client. He resolved never to make this mistake again. When decades later Cochran took on the legal battle that made him famous, he told O.J. Simpson, "I'm not going to let happen to you what happened to Geronimo Pratt." After getting Simpson off, he recalled the solemn promise he had made to the imprisoned Pratt: that he would never rest "until you are free."

As in the Simpson case, the indictment of law enforcement as a racist conspiracy was the heart of the Cochran appeal that eventually freed Geronimo Pratt. Of course, the public climate had already been so turned against law enforcement by the racial left that all Cochran had to show was that Julius Butler, the prosecution's chief witness, had contacts with the police prior to the trial in order to taint the verdict. It was this use of the race card, along with that odd comment Huey had made to me over twenty years earlier, which led me to inquire into the decision to give Geronimo Pratt a new trial and free him.

To understand the flimsy construction of the argument that prompted Judge Dickey's decision, one need only look at the court's lengthy rejection of an almost identical appeal Pratt's lawyers made in 1980. At that time, Pratt's petition was supported by a blue-ribbon *amici curiae* list which included Congresswoman Maxine Waters, Congressman Pete McCloskey, San Francisco mayor Willie Brown, the ACLU, the president of the California Democratic Council, and the chair of the Coalition to Free Geronimo Pratt. The central claim made by Pratt's defenders had not changed in twenty years:

> A totally innocent man has languished in [prison] since mid-1972.... He was sent there as the result of a case which was deliberately contrived by agents of our state and federal governments.... [His] conviction was the result of a joint effort by state and federal governments to neutralize and discredit him because of his membership in the militant Black Panther Party ...[1]

This time the press bought the argument whole. But the facts, summarized in the earlier opinion from the court record, reveal this argument to be fiction. All the information that follows was easily available to reporters, but none of it made its way into the reams of newsprint that described the second trial and celebrated Pratt's release.

In the judicial opinion that released Pratt, his accuser Julius Butler is dismissed as a police informer. But it was not until August 10, 1969, about seven months and three weeks after the

---

[1] In Re Pratt, Docket No. 37534, Court of Appeals of California, Second District, Division One, *Leagle*, December 3, 1980, http://www.leagle.com/decision/1980907112CalApp3d795_1840.

murder of Caroline Olsen, and more than a month after he had been expelled from the Black Panther Party, that Julius Butler made his first voluntary contact with any law enforcement official. He then met with Sergeant Duwayne Rice of the Los Angeles Police Department and gave him a sealed envelope. The envelope was addressed to Rice and had the words "Only to be opened in the event of my death" printed on the outside. Butler did not reveal the contents of the envelope to Rice. The envelope was then put in a locked safe where it remained for 14 months after this meeting, while the murderer was on the loose.

When Butler's envelope was finally opened, 14 months after his meeting with Rice and 22 months after the murder, the letter inside was for the first time read by police. It described a factional struggle in the Black Panther Party and said that the writer was fearful because of threats on his life made by Geronimo Pratt and other Panther leaders, including Roger Lewis, whose nickname was "Blue." The letter offered "the following Reason I feel the Death threat may be carried out"—namely that Geronimo and the other Panthers "were Responsible for Acts of murder they carelessly Bragged about":

> No. 1: Geronimo for the Killing of a White School Teacher and the wounding of Her Husband on a Tennis Court in the City of Santa Monica some time during the year of 1968.
>
> No. 2: Geronimo and Blue being Responsible for the Killing of Capt. Franco [a Panther leader] in January 1969 and constantly stating as a threat to me that I was just like Franco and gave them No Alternative but to "Wash me Away."[2]

This was and remains the most important incriminating evidence linking Geronimo Pratt to the tennis court murder. Yet it is not even addressed as an issue in the Court's decision to accept Johnnie Cochran's appeal. In a recorded prison interview with

---

[2]Ibid.

attorneys for the state, Roger "Blue" Lewis also testified that Geronimo Pratt had killed Caroline Olsen and that the murder weapon was his. Eyewitnesses identified Pratt at the murder scene, and at an attempted robbery committed moments before. Neither Pratt nor his attorneys have denied that the car driven by the murderer belonged to Pratt. Still, no other piece of evidence is as incontrovertible and unimpeachable as the letter from Julius Butler contained in the sealed envelope.

Although Butler is accused by Cochran of being a police and FBI informant working with law enforcement to frame Pratt, he did not give this envelope to the FBI. In fact, he had never had a single contact with the FBI up to this time. Nor did he just give the envelope to the Los Angeles Police Department. He gave it to a friend—a policeman whom he trusted, and who was black.

When Julius Butler handed the envelope to Duwayne Rice on August 10, 1969, FBI agents observed the transfer. Three days later, on August 13, the FBI approached Butler and questioned him for the first time. Butler refused to answer their questions about what was in the envelope and told them nothing about its incriminating contents. The FBI then went to Rice to get him to give up the envelope. Rice was also uncooperative. The FBI threatened him with prosecution for obstruction of justice and withholding evidence. Even in the face of these threats, Rice held firm. He would neither open the envelope nor turn it over to the agents. It took the FBI another fourteen months, until October 20, 1970, under circumstances to which I will turn in a moment, to get Rice to give up the letter so that they could open it themselves and read Butler's testimony that Geronimo Pratt had killed Caroline Olsen.

In addition to their accusations that Butler was an informer, Pratt's defenders speculate that the prosecution of Pratt was the result of a "Cointelpro" conspiracy by the FBI to "neutralize" leaders of the Black Panther Party. Their references, typically vague, are meant to insinuate foul play. But they are irrelevant. By the time of the Pratt trial, the FBI's "Cointelpro" program had been terminated. Moreover, Pratt was no longer even a Panther. He had been expelled three months earlier, in August 1970. (The official "declaration" of his expulsion, complete with the charge that he had threatened to assassinate Newton, was not made public until his arrest.)

On December 4, 1970, two months after the letter was opened, Pratt was indicted by a grand jury on one count of murder, one count of assault to commit murder and two counts of robbery. He was arraigned in April 1971 and was convicted a year later, on July 28, 1972. Throughout the trial, Pratt maintained that he was in Oakland at the time of the murder for a meeting with Panther leaders. During the trial, and for nearly twenty years thereafter, the Panther leaders—Bobby Seale, David Hilliard and Elaine Brown—denied Pratt's story and left him to his fate. It was their decision to change their story that led to the new and successful appeal.

In the 1980 court opinion denying Pratt's original appeal, the conspiracy theory is succinctly refuted: "First, it is noted that Julius Butler did not give the letter to the FBI but to a trusted friend (Sergeant Rice) for safekeeping only to be opened in the event of his death.... Second, logic dictates that if the FBI with the aid of local law enforcement officers had targeted Pratt and intended to 'neutralize' him by 'framing' him for the December 18, 1968, murder of Caroline Olsen, they would not have waited over 14 months after the letter was handed to Sergeant Rice to have the contents of the sealed letter disclosed."

The circumstances under which Butler's letter was finally opened are actually even more troublesome for the conspiracy argument. The FBI agents who had observed Butler transferring the sealed envelope walked over to Sergeant Rice after Butler had left and demanded that he turn over the envelope to them. Rice refused. Then, as a precaution, he gave the envelope to yet another black police officer, Captain Edward Henry, who put it in his safe deposit box, still sealed. Rice told no one of this move, in order that the FBI would not know its location. What next transpired is best told in Sergeant Rice's own words:

Soon after this incident [the initial demand for the letter from the FBI], the FBI threatened to indict me for obstruction of justice for refusing to turn over the letter to them. Some time during the next year I was involved in a fight with a white Los Angeles police officer. Due to this fight, and other allegations against me, I became the subject of an internal police investigation. During this investigation I was questioned by the Los Angeles Police Department regarding what Julius Butler had given me and ordered to turn it over to the police department. When I refused, I was threatened with being fired for refusing a direct order.[3]

It was this investigation of Rice by the LAPD's Department of Internal Affairs that led to the opening of the letter. Internal Affairs had actually become suspicious that Rice was subversive and sympathetic to the Panthers because of his relationship with Butler. The FBI was also pressuring Butler about his involvement in the Black Panther Party and a possible firearms violation. (Butler had purchased an illegal submachine gun in October 1968, while still a Panther, and did not want to reveal the name of the person he had given it to—another puzzling attitude for someone who was no more than a "paid informant.")

The questioning of Butler by the FBI, after he was observed delivering the envelope to Sergeant Rice, is the principal source of the false impression successfully promoted by the Cochran team that Butler was on the payroll as an informant for the agency. In the records of the seven FBI interviews with Butler, however, the only mention of Pratt is "that Pratt had a machine gun was common knowledge" and that "Pratt also had a caliber .45 pistol." There is no mention of the crucial fact, still hidden in the sealed envelope, that Pratt had boasted of killing a white schoolteacher and wounding her husband on a Santa Monica tennis court in 1968.

---

[3] Ibid.

In fact, an exhaustive review of the FBI records by a deputy attorney general of California states categorically: "Prior to [Pratt's] indictment [for the crime] in December 1970, there are no FBI documents connecting [Pratt] with the tennis court murder." Pratt's indictment was based on the evidence in the sealed envelope Julius Butler gave to Rice. It was opened at Butler's request in October 1970–22 months after the murder took place—because, as he put it, the FBI was "jamming" him. In turning down Pratt's 1980 appeal, the court noted that "It would be unnatural for the FBI not to be inquisitive about the contents of the sealed envelope once aware of its existence."

The appeal that secured Pratt's release in May 1997 adds only minor details to the original rejected 1980 appeal. It basically cites recent information, voluntarily turned over by prosecutors, which seems to amplify the claim that Butler had some kind of involvement with law enforcement after the sealed envelope was delivered to Sergeant Rice. The principal new claim was the existence of an "informant" card that the district attorney's office voluntarily turned over to Cochran's team. When I asked one of the original prosecutors about this, he maintained that the informant card was insignificant. "When you take someone to lunch you have to provide a chit for the lunch," he explained. "'Informant' is a convenient category, and that's all there is to it." There is a record of Butler's contacts with the FBI following its agents' observation of the encounter with Sergeant Rice. Butler's response to agents' questions was always that he was no longer with the Party and wasn't able to give them an informed opinion.

But no matter how one parses the language of these reports or interprets "informant card," none of the evidence brought forward by Cochran in any way alters the picture of Julius Butler's relations to law enforcement as outlined above. Butler did not take his charges against Pratt to the police but strenuously withheld them for nearly two years, until forced by the Internal Affairs investigation of Rice to give them up.

Johnnie Cochran has called Julius Butler a "conniving snake" and "liar" and "police informant." As in the Simpson case, he has had great success with this line of attack before a credulous and ill-informed public and press. Los Angeles Urban League President John Mack was only one of many who swallowed the Cochran line whole. At the time of Pratt's release, Mack told the *Los Angeles Times:* "The Geronimo Pratt case is one of the most compelling and painful examples of a political assassination on an African-American activist."

Cochran's brief for Pratt follows the pattern of the Simpson defense: an attack on law enforcement as a racist conspiracy out to "get" his client. A principal problem for Cochran has been the fact that Butler is black, and that until Cochran's charges he was a responsible and respected member of the community, a lawyer and a church elder. As part of Cochran's assault on Butler's character, he has alleged that Butler carried a grudge which was the result of thwarted ambition. Specifically, Cochran claims that when Alprentice "Bunchy" Carter, the leader of the Los Angeles Panthers, was killed by a rival gang headed by Ron (Maulana) Karenga in a shoot-out at UCLA a month after the Olsen murder, Pratt rather than Butler was made head of the Party and Butler didn't forgive him.

Once again, however, the facts do not substantiate the Cochran thesis. If jealousy was the motive, why not go to the police immediately? Why hand over a sealed letter and wait 22 months until long after you have become so disillusioned with the Panthers that your jealousy, if not cooled, has become an irrelevance?

In fact, Butler did not even deposit his insurance letter into the safekeeping of Sergeant Rice immediately after the murder. He did so only after being relieved of his Panther duties in July 1969, and then physically threatened by Pratt and his lieutenants, who were conducting a purge in the Party's ranks in the wake of the murder of Bunchy Carter. The cause of Butler's conflict with Pratt was not envy, but a growing concern about the Party's direction. In the sealed letter, Butler wrote:

During the year of 1969 I began to notice the party changing its direction from that set forth by Huey P. Newton, and dissented with some theorys [sic] and practices of the So. Calif. Leadership. During the months of June and July 1969 I more strongly critisized [sic] these Leaders, because I felt they were carelessly, and foolishly doing things that didn't have a direction benificial [sic] for the people. I also critisized [sic] the Physical Actions or threats to Party members who were attempting to sincerly [sic] impliment [sic] programs that oppressed people could respond to.[4]

The incident that most depressed Butler was the pistol-whipping of a 17-year-old Panther named Ollie Taylor, who was suspected of working for Karenga's gang. The incident led to "false imprisonment" and "assault with a deadly weapon" charges against Butler, Geronimo Pratt and Roger Lewis. Butler's feelings about this incident were so regretful that he pled guilty to the charges in the case. Pratt was also tried but the juries were hung 10–2 and 11–1 for conviction.

According to Butler, Pratt masterminded the torture-interrogation of Taylor, holding a cocked weapon at Butler's head while ordering him to beat the suspect. Under oath at his own trial, Pratt not only denied leading the interrogation but claimed that the beating had taken place before he arrived and that he reprimanded Butler, telling him this wasn't the Panther way to deal with suspects. He then relieved Butler of his position in the Party's security force and placed him under house arrest. At trial, the victim Ollie Taylor confirmed Butler's version of the events and flatly contradicted Pratt's story.

Reading Butler's testimony about the Ollie Taylor incident, I had a jolt of recognition that resolved any remaining doubt I may have had as to the integrity of Butler's account, not only of these matters but of those regarding the behavior and guilt of Geronimo

---

[4] Ibid.

Pratt. For it was in examining Butler's testimony that Huey's story about the eroticism of violence in Pratt's psyche resurfaced with riveting force:

Q. Was Ollie Taylor in the room at this time?
A. Yes.
Q. Okay.
A. Ollie Taylor was sitting in the middle of the room, and I was sitting next to Ollie Taylor, and I was trying to talk to Ollie Taylor on the basis of 'Give as much information about yourself to clear yourself,' and Geronimo stated to me that the shit he was talking was a bunch of bull shit, and I looked over and he cocked the hammer on the pistol.
Q. Where was the pistol pointed, if at all?
A. It was actually right between me and Ollie Taylor, because I was sitting side-by-side with Ollie Taylor.

Then I noticed that Geronimo had an erection, and he stated, "If you don't move, I'll blow your head off," and he said "Furthermore, I think maybe you're siding with him," so he told me to slap Ollie Taylor.

He say, "You interrogate," so I did it in the pretense of trying to—at that time I was frightened of Geronimo's behavior, very seriously frightened. *I had never seen a man with an erection....* (emphasis added)[5]

Before Butler could complete the sentence, his attorney interrupted with an objection that the course of inquiry was irrelevant. But as far as I was concerned, the sentence didn't need to be finished. Here were two different figures, both close to Pratt but otherwise far separated by distance, status, and motivation, who remarked on the erotic charge that violence had for him.

Despite the persuasive evidence of Pratt's guilt as contained in the sealed letter, and despite the persuasive evidence in the handling of the letter showing that Butler was not part of a police or

---

[4] Ibid.

FBI conspiracy to frame Pratt, Cochran's conspiracy theory prevailed. On May 29, 1997, Judge Dickey granted Pratt a new trial and immediate release from his current confinement. Dickey concluded that "this was not a strong case for the prosecution without the testimony of [Julius] Butler," and that it was reasonably probable that Pratt could have obtained a different result "in the entire absence of Butler's testimony," or had the prosecution revealed Butler's contacts with law enforcement.

Reading Judge Dickey's opinion is a depressing experience for anyone concerned about American justice. The salient reason cited for overturning the original verdict is that the prosecution concealed the "fact" that "[Butler] had been, for at least three years before the trial, providing information about the Black Panther Party and individuals associated with it to law enforcement agencies on a confidential basis." On the evidence provided in the court records, this statement by the Judge is misleading and irrelevant. Julius Butler had absolutely no contact with the FBI or law enforcement prior to his delivery of the sealed letter to Sgt. Rice on August 10, 1969, seven months after the murder and less than two years before the trial. The letter's identification of Pratt as the killer of Caroline Olsen was available to the jury and was a centerpiece of the court proceeding, a fact not even addressed in Dickey's opinion. Nor is the whole history of Butler's withholding of the incriminating document despite efforts by the FBI and the police to pry it from him. These would seem to establish beyond a reasonable doubt that Julius Butler was not an informant and was not cooperating with the FBI, the police, or the prosecutors of Geronimo Pratt prior to Pratt's arraignment for the murder. Moreover, Butler's testimony at the trial is entirely consistent with the information contained in the incriminating letter and with his behavior throughout the case.

Why didn't justice prevail in this matter? Why was a murderer set free? The answer lies in the tenor of the times, in which the testimony of officers of the law has become more readily impeachable than the testimony of criminals. As in the O.J. Simpson trial, the appeals process in the Pratt case was turned by Johnnie Cochran into a class action libel against the FBI, the police, the prosecution and its chief witness. And as in the Simpson case, Johnnie Cochran's fictional melodrama won out over the politically incorrect truth.

9

When "Civil Rights" Become Civil Wrongs

During the darkest days of the Cold War, the Italian writer Ignazio Silone predicted the final struggle would be between the communist believers and the ex-believers. A similar conflict seems to be shaping up among civil rights activists. Last month, Jesse Jackson chose the anniversary of Martin Luther King Jr.'s famous 1963 March on Washington to lead a march across the Golden Gate Bridge against California's Proposition 209. Passed last year, Prop. 209 prohibits race-based hiring and recruiting in government jobs and state colleges. Jackson's symbolism was clear: support for race-based regulations is now the focus of the civil rights cause.

One immediate problem for this stance is that the architect and principal spokesman for Prop. 209, Ward Connerly, is also a veteran of King's movement. It is no mere coincidence that Connerly's measure is called "The California Civil Rights Initiative," or that its text is carefully constructed to conform to both the letter and spirit of the landmark Civil Rights Acts of 1964 and 1965.

The split in the ranks of civil rights veterans is over conflicting assessments of the movement's success. How much racial progress has been made since the federal government embraced the civil rights agenda? What is the best way to overcome the racial inequalities that still persist? For the anti-209 marchers, little has changed. Whatever gains blacks have made have been

September 15, 1997, http://archive.frontpagemag.com/Printable.aspx? ArtId=24389; http://www.salon.com/1997/09/15/horowitz970915/.

limited and have been forced upon recalcitrant whites. Without greater government efforts, existing inequalities will morph into new injustices as bad as before. Making government race-neutral, as the pro-209ers propose, would encourage historic prejudice to reassert itself in all its malignity. Eliminating affirmative action, both Jesse Jackson and President Clinton have warned, is to invite the "re-segregation" of American life.

Yet consider these unruly facts comparing social advances made by African-Americans before and after affirmative action policies were put in place:

> In 1940, 87 percent of American blacks lived below the poverty line. By 1960, five years before the Civil Rights acts and 10 years before the first affirmative action policies, the figure was down to 47 percent. That was a greater and more rapid decline than took place over the next 35 years, when the black poverty rate came down to 26 percent. In 1940, only 5 percent of black men and 6.4 percent of black women were in middle-class occupations. By 1970, the figures were 22 percent for black men and 36 percent for black women, larger again than the increases that took place in the 20 years after affirmative action was put in place, when the figures reached 32 percent and 59 percent respectively.

These figures come from a new scholarly work, *America in Black and White,* by two civil rights veterans, Stephan and Abigail Thernstrom, who have reconstructed the history of racial progress and conflict in the postwar era and examined the impact of affirmative action solutions. Black poverty, the Thernstroms show, has little to do with race, and its solution will not be affected by affirmative action set-asides. Such policies have had the net effect not of employing greater numbers of blacks or raising their living standards, but of shifting black employment from small businesses to large corporations and to government. A far more effective anti-poverty program would be to promote black marriages. Currently, 85 percent of poor black children live in fatherless families, while the poverty rate for black children

without fathers is nearly six times that for black children with
two parents.

In higher education, the rate of gain for blacks in college enrollments was greater before the implementation of affirmative action
policies. Between 1960 and 1970 enrollments increased from 4 percent to 7 percent of the total college population, greater than in the
decades that followed. Enrollments rose from 7 percent to 9.9 percent between 1970 and 1980, and to 10.7 percent between 1980
and 1994. In 1965, before affirmative action, blacks were only
about half as likely to actually graduate college as whites. In 1995,
the figure was exactly the same.

In 1995, only 1,764 black students nationwide (1.7 percent of
all blacks who took the test) scored as high as 600 on the verbal
SATs; the math scores were even worse. By comparison, 64,950
white students (9.6 percent of all whites who took the test) scored
600 or higher on the verbal SATs. But under affirmative action
guidelines, those same black students have been recruited by
Berkeley, Harvard and similar elite schools, where the average
white student (and the average Asian) had scores at least 100
points higher. At Berkeley, the gap is nearly 300 points. Predictably, blacks drop out of Berkeley at nearly three times the rate
of whites.

This is but one example of the collateral damage—to blacks—
of affirmative action policies. African-Americans are being put in
college programs that far exceed their abilities and qualifications,
a sure prescription for fanning the flames of resentment and prejudice. As the Thernstroms ruefully observe, the college that comes
closest to equality in actually graduating its students is Ole Miss,
one of the last bastions of segregation in the South. Integrated
now, Ole Miss is resistant to the new racial duplicity in admissions standards. The result: 49 percent of freshmen whites graduate, and so do 48 percent of blacks.

On the basis of what actually has happened, increasingly some
civil rights supporters on the left have begun to conclude that affirmative action is not only having little or no effect on the income

and education gaps, but is actually destructive to the people it is supposed to help. It is creating black failure, while stirring the resentment of other groups that see themselves displaced on the basis of race from their hard-earned places of merit. "Liberalism no longer curbs discrimination. It invites it. It does not expose racism; it recapitulates and, sometimes, reinvents it." Those are not the words of some Confederate flag-waving demagogue from below the Mason-Dixon line; they are the words of another veteran of the civil rights movement, Jim Sleeper, a columnist with the *New York Daily News*, and they are taken from his new book, *Liberal Racism*, which examines the toxic effects of well-intended liberal programs like affirmative action.[1]

So does the wheel of history turn.

---

[1] "Why Liberals Can't Think Straight about Race," Jim Sleeper, *Salon*, August 19, 1997, http://www.salon.com/1997/08/19/race970818/.

10

An Academic Lynching

L ino Graglia is a 67-year-old Sicilian-born American who was an attorney in the Eisenhower Justice Department and has been teaching constitutional law at the University of Texas in Austin for 33 years. A stiff-necked Catholic conservative, he passionately holds to a belief that some would call fundamentalist: if representatives of the sovereign people choose to enact a law that is not contradicted by the actual text of the Constitution, then that law is constitutional. Period. Without judicial review.

Last week, the president of his university, the chancellor and 51 of his law school colleagues denounced him. State legislators, including the chairman of the Hispanic Caucus, described him variously as a Klan supporter, a racist and "academic riff-raff." The *Houston Chronicle* condemned him as an "embarrassment" and the local NAACP and three student groups charged him with "racial harassment." Jesse Jackson urged 5,000 cheering campus demonstrators to boycott his classes and "turn him into a moral and social pariah."

Graglia's crime? As usual in these intellectual *auto-da-fés:* telling an uncomfortable truth. In Graglia's case the truth was that affirmative action is an attempt to conceal or wish away the unwelcome fact that currently blacks and Mexican-Americans are not academically competitive with whites and Asians. Graglia made the remarks in a speech to Students for Equal Opportunity, a

September 22, 1997, http://archive.frontpagemag.com/Printable.aspx? ArtId=24388; http://www.salon.com/1997/09/22/horowitz970922/.

campus organization for which he was the faculty advisor. The topic of the meeting was the Hopwood case, which recently ended affirmative action at the university.

The views that inspired the attacks were hardly new for Graglia. Twenty years ago he wrote a book called *Disaster by Decree: The Supreme Court Decisions on Race and the Schools.* In it, he frequently refers to affirmative action programs as a "fungus" and a "fraud." His latest remarks on the subject were almost tepid by comparison, leaving Graglia totally unprepared for the public hanging that followed them.

Out of a faculty of more than 1,000 professors, only two have been willing to come forward to defend the character of a man who has taught alongside them for three decades, and whose dean, on reviewing his personal file, stated that there were no grounds for disciplinary action. Despite the ferocious claims of the attackers, the dean added, "The record does not justify a charge that he discriminates against his students and others on the basis of race or ethnicity." Even the *Houston Chronicle* conceded, "No one has offered any evidence that Graglia treats minority and white students differently."

What then provoked such a lynch-mob atmosphere? In the original newspaper story about the speech, Graglia was quoted as saying, "blacks and Mexican-Americans can't compete academically with whites." While such a statement is a factual summary of the test scores, the statement might be considered racist if it meant that by nature these minorities can't compete. But it didn't. The *Chronicle* reporter asked Graglia what he thought caused the gap in performance on standardized tests. Graglia answered that he didn't know. When asked whether he thought the cause was "genetic or cultural," Graglia said he thought it was cultural, suggesting that perhaps academically underachieving groups put less emphasis on academic achievement and do not necessarily consider academic failure "a disaster." Later, Graglia explained how, in his own Sicilian upbringing, academic achievement was given less emphasis than among many Jewish households he knew. He cited various studies that seemed to show "that blacks and Mexican-Americans spend much less time in school. They have a culture that seems not to encourage achievement. Failure is not looked upon with disgrace."

Similar points were made in a recent *U.S. News & World Report* story on the differing academic attainment of white and black students in the schools of Little Rock, Ark., and elsewhere across the country: "In some cases ... it is black parents themselves who steer their children away from honors classes or don't fight to keep them enrolled. Black students say there is also peer pressure not to take honors classes." So Graglia is not alone in his beliefs, and not on the wrong side of the facts. Why then is this distinguished professor of law now a pariah in his own community? Because the witch-hunting atmosphere on college campuses around the issue of affirmative action is as intense today as fears of communism in the McCarthy era. Graglia is being strung up for saying an obvious but discomforting truth: blacks, Hispanics and other minorities designated for affirmative action preferences are not competing intellectually on standardized tests.

Graglia also said something else before the Students for Equal Opportunity: "Racial preferences are the root cause of virtually all the major problems plaguing American campuses today. They result in a student body with two groups, identifiable by race, essentially in different academic ballparks. An inability to compete successfully in the game being played necessarily results in demands that the game be changed, and thus are born demands for black and Hispanic studies and 'multiculturalism.' Little is more humiliating to the racially preferred than open discussion of the conditions of their admission. Concealment and deception are therefore always essential elements of racial preference programs and thus is born insistence on political correctness and the need [to suppress] 'hate speech.'" No doubt this exposure of the depredation inflicted by progressives is sufficient cause for a public hanging.

Choke Your Coach,
Become a Cause

Imagine that a white player in the National Basketball Association had first tried to strangle his black coach and then threatened to kill him in front of the whole team. Suppose that this white player had previously threatened a teammate with a gun and a two-by-four. Suppose that the NBA, responding to this conduct, had suspended the white player for a year and that his team had terminated his contract. How many public figures do you think would step forward to defend the culprit? How many mayors of major cities would speak out in his behalf, as San Francisco Mayor Willie Brown did in the case of Latrell Sprewell, even suggesting that "Maybe the coach deserved to be choked"? How many famous white lawyers would claim, as Johnnie Cochran did, that there had been a "rush to judgment" and a "disparity in treatment," implying that the white player was being punished only because his victim was black?

Here's another exercise: Imagine that a white football star with a history of brutality and jealous rages toward his black wife was suspected in the savage murder of her and a friend. Suppose he attempted to flee, with a passport and money in his possession, toward the Mexican border. Suppose his blood was found all over the crime scene, and the blood of his dead wife on his clothes, his car and at his home. Suppose that a 911 recording of an earlier incident with her screaming that he was going to kill her was played

December 15, 1997, http://archive.frontpagemag.com/Printable.aspx?
ArtId=24380; http://www.salon.com/1997/12/15/nc_15horo_3/.

in court and to the whole country. What are the chances that a white jury would acquit him in less than an hour? Or that the white population would cheer such a verdict, rather than hang its head in shame? Yet all this transpired in the O.J. Simpson case with a black committing the murders and fellow blacks the miscarriage of justice in setting him free.

Or, imagine that a convicted felon and parole violator named Rodney King had been white. That he had led the law on a high-speed chase, throwing cops off his back when finally stopped and otherwise physically resisting arrest. How much attention would have been paid to the fact that the police got overly rough with him? Would the president of the United States have called for the cops to be tried and, when they were acquitted, re-tried until they were sent to jail? Would a white Rodney King have been given $3 million in compensation by a contrite Los Angeles and made a poster boy for police brutality and injustice by the nation as a whole?

These exercises show what is missing from the current dialogue on race: a candid discussion of the way white America has been overreacting to the shame of its receding racial past, and then of the way race has become such an all-purpose excuse for much of black America that many prominent black figures don't seem to be able to leave home without it. Are blacks failing to keep up educationally with Asians and whites? "Institutional racism" must be to blame. Are blacks committing crimes out of all proportion to their representation in the population? The racist criminal justice system is responsible. Are a few high-paid black thugs threatening to bring down a sport that black athletes like Michael Jordan had elevated to such a magnificent level? That's just talk by racist white owners and officials rushing to judgment with disparate punishments leveled against blacks.

Such candor is absent because the so-called dialogue has been framed by people for whom there is only one acceptable conclusion: blacks are victims and whites are to blame. That is why the chairman of the president's commission on race excluded Ward

Connerly, a pre-eminent critic of affirmative action, from the panel. That's why President Clinton himself would brook no disagreement with his view that affirmative action was a good thing during a town hall meeting on race in Akron, Ohio. Few dare to suggest that affirmative action has become racial payback. Opposing affirmative action is to blame the victim, which of course no decent person would do.

Those dominating the national dialogue can't accept that America has moved far beyond the bad days of segregation in the South and institutionalized racial injustice. This is the 1990s, with black multimillionaires like Sprewell constituting 80 percent of the NBA players, black millionaire mayors like Brown calling the shots in major American cities and black millionaire lawyers like Johnnie Cochran commanding national audiences.

And the rest of America knows it. The overwhelmingly negative reaction to the Sprewell affair and to the ludicrous comments by people like Mayor Brown suggest that the rest of America, including liberal sportswriters and commentators, may at last be ready to say out loud that they have had it up to their ears with the blame-game and the self-flagellation. And in no small part because they realize such attitudes only make things worse.

The Sprewell affair shows that we are approaching the end of an era, which is the best news about race yet.[1] White America has changed. All blacks no longer look alike. Even ordinary Americans, sports fans for instance, no longer look at blacks as the anonymous Other, the inscrutable menace or the universal victim. White America can tell the difference between a Latrell Sprewell and a Michael Jordan, a Rodney King and a Martin Luther King. There's hope in that.

---

[1] This proved far too optimistic.

12

"Liberals" Want
a Racial Monologue

In an editorial comment on President Clinton's "racial dialogue" initiative, *The New York Times* cites an academic's
claim that blacks were not frank in the dialogue because they
knew that if they charged whites with racism "that sort of bluntness would end the conversation" and whites did not "want to
talk openly about their suspicions that blacks may be genetically
inferior."[1] Far from explaining why Clinton's dialogue on race cannot get off the ground, this "analysis"—racist in itself—is the core
of the problem. Clinton liberals think the real racial problem—the
only racial problem—is *white* racism. Their idea of a racial dialogue is for blacks to express displeasure at a *status quo* that
denies them equality, while whites, who are presently in denial,
come to their senses and recognize that they are racists. That is
why Clinton has stacked his race commission with racial leftists,
excluding such key opponents of affirmative action as Ward Connerly. That is why, when Clinton invited Abigail Thernstrom to
his town meeting, he did so solely for the purpose of bullying her
into submission:

> "Abigail, do you favor the U.S. Army abolishing the affirmative
> action program that produced Colin Powell? Yes or no?" When

---

December 18, 1997, http://archive.frontpagemag.com/Printable.aspx?
ArtId=24379.
[1] "The Honest Dialogue That Is Neither," Felicia R. Lee, *New York Times,*
December 7, 1997, http://www.nytimes.com/1997/12/07/weekinre-
view/the-nation-the-honest-dialogue-that-is-neither.html.

Thernstrom responded that she didn't think affirmative action preferences were responsible for Powell's success, Clinton retorted: "Well, Colin Powell thinks they were."

This was two lies in one. In his memoir, Powell says that his success was *not* owed to affirmative action preferences. In fact, the U.S. Army has no affirmative action program of the kind opposed by Connerly and Thernstrom.

The reason there won't be *a dialogue on race* at this time is not because there is only one reasonable, moral side to the issues but because liberals are unable to face the fact that there is another. Liberals are in a state of profound denial about the realities that fuel the racial issue, in particular the current failure of some sections of the black community to meet the standards that have been set for everyone else. The liberal view is premised on the belief that the white community must be held responsible for black failures.

An example of this liberal denial was on display in a recent *Los Angeles Times* article in which civil rights activist Roger Wilkins described the "essence" of the position taken by affirmative action opponents as the belief "that the civil rights movements of the 1950s and '60s left us with a degree of racism so negligible that the only things now threatening our racial tranquility are race-conscious remedies, particularly affirmative action." To dispel this benighted attitude, Wilkins reminds us that "real gaps in income, wealth, education, health, housing opportunities and employment still remain, at all education levels, and are especially acute for the least skilled. And, tragically, more than 40 percent of black children are growing up in poverty."[2]

This is the way liberals think: if there is a gap between blacks and whites that is detrimental to blacks, then whites must be to

---

[2] "Arguing Over 'Means,' We Forget 'Ends,'" Roger Wilkins, *Los Angeles Times*, December 7, 1997, http://articles.latimes.com/1997/dec/07/opinion/op-61539.

blame. But the facts show otherwise. Statistics show that six out of seven children raised by single mothers will be poor regardless of race. Eighty-five percent of black children who are poor are living in single-parent families. In other words, there is no poverty gap once individual behavior is taken into account. The same can be said for virtually every other disparity marshaled by liberals to demonstrate the "institutional racism" alleged to be responsible for the failure of some blacks.

These are the realities that liberals cannot face: blacks are underrepresented at elite universities because their test scores are abysmal. Blacks are incarcerated in prisons in staggering numbers because they commit crimes in staggering disproportion to their representation in the population. Those blacks who are chronically unemployed are unemployed not because there are no jobs nor because they are barred from jobs, but because they are unemployable: They do not seek work as avidly as other groups do; they make their neighborhoods too dangerous for businesses; and they do not acquire the educational skills and work habits necessary for employment.

These are the hard truths that the Clinton liberals don't want to face. But they need to be faced if the black underclass is going to take advantage of the same opportunities that a thriving black middle class already has embraced. That is what a real dialogue on race would address. And that is why Clinton's initiative is only a dialogue of the deaf.

13

Hate Crimes Are Multicultural, Too

Two weeks ago, a young man named Matthew Shepard was tortured and left to die on the high plains of Wyoming simply because he was gay.[1] On June 7th, a black man named James Byrd, Jr. was attacked in Texas. Both crimes produced outpourings of public grief and rage, in editorial comments and from political pulpits across the nation. These were appropriate if extraordinary responses to crimes against ordinary citizens, whose untimely deaths would otherwise have been unremarkable. It was the fact that the perpetrators and victims were set apart by communal bigotries, of which the crimes appeared to be particularly violent expressions, that made the acts seem so important.

The enhanced sense of human depravity that colored the public reactions to these incidents lies in our shared conviction that their nature as "hate crimes" made them an outrage to the nation's sense of self, as well as a threat to its communal future. Well and good enough. These responses are signs of health in the body politic, the presence of a will to summon the better angels of our nature, and to keep at bay the savagery that lurks beneath the surface of any civilized society.

October 26, 1998, http://archive.frontpagemag.com/readArticle.aspx?ArtId=24303
[1] A book written in 2013 by a gay journalist suggests that this was not the case—that Shepard was actually killed by a gay hustler, high on methamphetamines, who set out to rob him. See Stephen Jimenez, *The Book of Matt: Hidden Truths About the Murder of Matthew Shepard*, Steerforth, 2013.

But these expressions did not exhaust the public response to the two crimes. While libertarians and conservatives looked on in dismay, a coalition of radical and liberal activists, led by Congressman Barney Frank and other gay spokesmen, held a press conference on the Capitol steps in Washington to pressure Congress into passing a bill that would extend existing federal hate-crimes legislation to cover the categories of gender, sexual orientation and handicapped status, and to make all such crimes easier to prosecute. They were joined in the call by President Clinton.

Meanwhile, others raised legal concerns about the civil liberties issues of the proposed legislation. Probing the intentions of any perpetrator, and especially those whose victims are already targets of community prejudice, poses troubling issues; for example, the temptation offered to aggressive prosecutors to postulate such intentions where none might exist. In a sobering column, George Will recalls a recent example of perverse legal reasoning when applying a hate-crime standard. In 1989, a white female jogger was raped and beaten into a coma by a gang of black and Hispanic youths on a "wilding" rampage. The act was not deemed a "hate crime" by prosecutors, and the perpetrators did not suffer enhanced penalties under the law, because they also assaulted Hispanics that evening. They got more lenient treatment because of the catholicity of their barbarism. Of course, the act they committed—rape—could itself be characterized as a hate crime.

In the emotional atmosphere created by the murder of Matthew Shepard, the left has once again found its political oxygen. Temporarily thrown by feminist hypocrisies around the Clinton scandal, the left has recovered its balance with the prospect of once again rallying behind society's victims and against their victimizers. This politics of the left is what George Will calls "a sentiment competition," which is "less about changing society than striking poses." The proposed multiplication of hate-crime categories, which stipulate that some crime victims are more important than others, would be what Will calls "an imprudent extension of identity politics." It would work against, not for, the principle of social tolerance.

A little more than a year before the attack on James Byrd in Texas, three white Michigan youngsters hitched a train-ride as a teenage lark. When they got off the train, they found themselves in the wrong urban neighborhood, surrounded by a gang of armed black youths. One of the white teenagers, Michael Carter, aged 14, was killed. Dustin Kaiser, aged 15, was brutally beaten and shot in the head, but eventually survived. The fourteen-year-old girl (whose name has been withheld) was pistol-whipped and shot in the face after being forced to perform oral sex on her attackers.

Though the six African-Americans responsible for the deed were arrested and convicted, their attack was not prosecuted as a "hate crime." More to the point, most of the nation never knew that the crime had taken place. The few papers that reported the incident nationally did so on their inside pages. There was no public outrage expressed in national editorials or in the halls of Congress. Beyond the Michigan region, the stories often failed to mention the races of the participants at all. The crime took place on July 21, 1997, but among readers of these sentences there will not be one in a hundred who has even heard of it. That is because as a hate crime it was, in a sense, politically incorrect. To notice that black people, as well as whites, can be responsible for vicious crimes of hate is improper. Hate crimes can only be committed by an oppressor caste; therefore what happened in Michigan was not a hate crime at all.

Two years ago, the most celebrated "trial of the century" was about a black man accused of murdering two whites in what was apparently an act of blind rage. The idea that O.J. Simpson might have murdered his wife and a stranger because they were white was never even hinted at by the prosecution, while the defense turned the case into a circus of racial accusations against whites.

The crude truth is that it is not okay in America to hate blacks, but it is okay in our politically correct culture to hate white people. Entire academic departments and college curricula are based on this idea. White people are the oppressors of minority communities and cultures. According to progressives, that is America's "true" legacy. There is even an academic field of "Whiteness Studies" to parallel Black Studies and Women's Studies. But the parallel is an inverted one. Blacks are celebrated in Black Studies and women are championed in Women's Studies. Whiteness Studies, on the other hand, are devoted to the claim that whites construct the idea of race to enable them to oppress others. In other words, Whiteness Studies are about how whites are evil.

Hollywood understands this rule of progressive etiquette. A new film, *American History X*, will for the umpteenth time feature white neo-Nazis as the villains of a morality play about racial bigotry. A few years ago, a sensational mass-murder trial in Miami spotlighted a black cult leader named Yahweh Ben Yahweh, who required his cult members to kill whites and bring back their ears as proof of the deed. There was no Hollywood scramble for the rights to the Yahweh cult story, and few Americans are even aware that it ever took place. Last week, a German tourist was shot to death in Santa Monica, California, in front of his wife and children. The trigger for the killing seems to have been his failure to understand the English commands of his attackers. This crime was committed by two African-American men and one African-American woman, though one would never know this from reading the *Los Angeles Times* or AP accounts. (I had to verify their racial identities by calling the Santa Monica police department directly.) The word "hate crime" never surfaced in connection with the deed, either in the press accounts or in editorial commentaries that followed. Now, suppose that three whites had gone to a Hispanic neighborhood to rob inhabitants and had murdered a Hispanic immigrant because he could not speak English. Does anyone imagine that the press accounts would hide the identity of the attackers, or that the question of whether it might be a hate crime would never come up?

According to U.S. Department of Justice figures, in 1993 there were 1.4 million violent crimes of interracial violence nationwide. Eighty-five percent of them were committed by blacks against whites. A white is fifty times more likely to be the victim of a violent crime committed by a black person than the other way around. Not surprisingly, the first hate-crime conviction to be appealed to the Supreme Court involved a black perpetrator and a white victim. The politically righteous, who are pushing the current legislation, will be in for some surprises should the law they are proposing go into effect.

How many of the interracial crimes of violence committed by blacks and other minorities are actually hate crimes? In fact, there is no real way to tell. Of course, the leftist university has a ready answer for the question: only whites can be racist. The alleged reasoning is that, in our society, only whites have power. This is an obvious absurdity that only an intellectual could believe. Forget the thousands of public officials great and small, police chiefs, judges, administrators, members of Congress, petty bureaucrats, corporate executives and military officers who are now drawn from the ranks of minorities. At the most elemental level, a black street criminal with a gun has the power of life and death over an unarmed law abiding citizen of any race or color.

The doctrine that only whites can be racist is itself racist, an encouragement to hate white people. Yet it has now apparently spread to the secondary-school system. Last week, a Seattle father called in to a national radio talk show, which I happened to be on, and told the audience that his son's class in junior-high school had been discussing the hate-crime concept because of the Shepard killing. During the discussion, the teacher informed the class that only heterosexual whites could be racists. Responding to this idea, the caller's son brought up the savage beating of Reginald Denny during the Los Angeles riots by a group of black gang members. Surely, he suggested, this was a hate crime. But his teacher corrected him. Even though Denny was pulled from his truck solely because he was white, and then beaten to within an inch of his life, he could not be the victim of racial poisons. The attempted murder of Reginald Denny was actually an act of rebellion by people who were themselves the victims of a white racist system, and therefore the act they committed could not be considered a hate crime.

That is why I will not join Barney Frank and the left in promoting politically correct hate-crime legislation that will create more specially protected categories among us as a kind of human "endangered species" act. Sorting Americans into distinctive racial, ethnic, and gender groups, while designating whites and heterosexuals their "oppressors," makes the so-called oppressors into legitimate targets of hate. It thus becomes a way of exacerbating rather than correcting the problem.

It is time to go back to the wisdom of the Founders who wrote a constitution without reference to ethnic or gender groups. They did so in order to render us equal before the nation's system of laws. It was an imperfectly realized ideal, but that should be no excuse for abandoning it. We need to end the vicious libels of political correctness that have intruded into our mainstream culture with their message of anti-white racism. The vast majority of white people do not hate or oppress black people, just as the vast majority of heterosexuals do not hate or oppress gays. We need to single out those individuals who do—whatever their race or gender—and condemn them. But we also need to go back to the task of treating all Americans as individuals first, and as members of groups only secondarily, if at all.

14

One Who Will Not
Be Missed

Stokely Carmichael (1941–1998)

Kwame Ture, aka Stokely Carmichael, is dead of prostate cancer at the age of 57. Jesse Jackson, who was with him in Africa at the last, claimed Carmichael for the radical Sixties. "He was one of our generation who was determined to give his life to transforming America and Africa," Jackson eulogized; "he rang the freedom bell in this century."

The truth is otherwise. Kwame Ture was not a good man, did not advance the cause of freedom, and the world will not miss him. A West Indian immigrant to America, a child of middle-class privilege, Carmichael hated his adopted country from youth through age, and never bothered once to acknowledge the immense advantages and personal recognition it undeservedly gave him.

As "Stokely Carmichael," his chief claim to fame was to lead young Turks in the civil rights movement in pushing Martin Luther King aside and dismissing him as an "Uncle Tom." In 1966 Carmichael emerged as the chief spokesman for the "black power" movement, which replaced King's goals of non-violence and integration with agendas of political violence and racial separatism. In 1967, when Israel was attacked by six Arab nations, Carmichael proclaimed, "The only good Zionist is a dead Zionist,"

November 17, 1998, http://archive.frontpagemag.com/Printable.aspx? ArtId=24298.

and became the first prominent American figure since Senator Bilbo in the 1940s to spew anti-Semitic bile into the public space.

The following year, Carmichael began a campaign to promote armed warfare in American cities and was briefly made prime minister of the Black Panther Party for his efforts. Ever the racist, Carmichael tried to persuade the Panthers to break off their alliances with whites but failed. This led to his expulsion from the party and a ritual beating by his erstwhile comrades. Shortly thereafter, Carmichael left the United States for Africa in a self-imposed exile.

In Africa, he changed his name to Kwame Ture, thereby honoring two dictators (Kwame Nkrumah and Sékou Touré) who caused untold misery to their own peoples. He took up residence in Guinea as the personal guest of Touré, its paranoid dictator, whose reputation was built on the torture-murders of thousands of his subjects. Some 250,000 Guineans were driven into exile during Carmichael's stay there, with no apparent protest from this champion of freedom.

Returning to the United States in the late Eighties, he took to the lecture circuit as a racial hate-monger, attacking Jews, whites, and America to approving audiences on American university campuses. In the end he found a fitting refuge in the racial sewer of the Nation of Islam as a protégé of its Jew-baiting, America-hating, racist cult leader Louis Farrakhan. Carmichael's farewell shot was to accuse "the forces of American imperialism" of causing the prostate cancer that would have killed him sooner if it had not been for the creative medical contributions of so many Jews, whites and Americans.

[*2014 Note:* A laudatory biography of Carmichael appeared recently, which carefully avoids any confrontation with the unpleasant facts mentioned above. It was written by Tufts professor Peniel Joseph, and reflects the disturbing consensus that now exists within the world of academic African-American Studies and the black intellectual establishment generally in regard to this anti-American, anti-Semitic, racist. This is what Harvard professor

Charles Ogletree wrote about Peniel's shameful book and Carmichael: "With *Stokely: A Life*, Peniel Joseph has produced a thoroughly impressive volume on the life and legacy of Stokely Carmichael, an often under-appreciated and poorly understood giant of the civil rights movement and African-American history. Joseph's book is richly researched, masterfully executed, beautifully written, and will surely work as a vital testament to confirm the place of Kwame Ture, aka Stokely Carmichael, as one of the most powerful voices we have ever produced." Ogletree's enthusiasm for Carmichael was shared by leading black intellectuals as disparate as Michael Eric Dyson and Henry Louis Gates, both of who provided blurbs for Joseph's sycophantic and dishonest portrait of Carmichael's career. For an account of the degradation of the American university that has led to this intellectual collapse, see Volume VII of this series, *The Left In the University*.]

PART III

Racial Correctness

The Race Card

(co-authored with Peter Collier)

W hen it was revealed that Lionel Cryer, the male juror who flashed O.J. Simpson a black-power salute right after the verdict in his murder trial, was once a member of the Black Panther Party, the Simpson case finally found its context. That black fist called up a host of Sixties memories, among them the ghostly voice of criminal-hero Eldridge Cleaver, who taunted the white world in his autobiography, *Soul on Ice:* "I'm perfectly aware that I'm in prison, that I'm a Negro, that I've been a rapist.... My answer to all such things lurking in their split-level heads, crouching behind their squinting bombardier eyes is that the blood of Vietnamese peasants has paid off all my debts." By the same corrupt reasoning, it is not hard to imagine O.J., his consciousness now raised to new heights by his new political advisers, thinking, if not saying, that Mark Fuhrman has paid off all his.[1]

In addition to Cleaver's hallucinatory voice and the gestural politics it spoke for, in the complex background of the Simpson criminal trial stands another trial that took place nearly thirty years ago and troubled the American criminal-justice system even more profoundly—and permanently—than O.J.'s did. The defendant then was Cleaver's co-conspirator, Black Panther leader Huey

---

June 14, 1999, http://archive.frontpagemag.com/Printable.aspx?ArtId=22654.

[1] Fuhrman was a police officer who testified as a witness for the prosecution and was discredited by defense attorneys when it was revealed that he had used the word "nigger" in discussing a film script.

Newton, charged with murdering a white policeman in Oakland. There was no question that Newton had been present at the scene, or that he had threatened to kill a policeman in the past. There was a compelling timeline, a wealth of physical and forensic evidence, and even a black eyewitness to the crime. But as framed by Newton's attorney, Charles Garry, the issue was not whether Newton did it but whether "the system" had conspired to put yet another proud black male in jeopardy. In putting the system on trial instead of the defendant, Garry joined up with the Zeitgeist and invented the wheel that would be rolled adroitly over truth and common sense by a generation of legal demagogues from William Kunstler to Leonard Weinglass. Garry's innovation, and the radical racial themes he imported into the criminal-justice system, were part of an inheritance that ultimately passed also to Johnnie Cochran.

A young attorney with wide-lapel, lime-green suits and a luxuriant Afro, Johnnie Cochran was a sometime prosecutor, political fixer and aspiring member of the Tom Bradley machine in Los Angeles during the Seventies. By his own testimony, one event changed him forever—his decision to take on the case of Elmer "Geronimo" Pratt, a black Vietnam vet who returned home from the war with a knowledge of munitions and explosives and became the head of the Black Panther Party's underground "army."[2]

In a case that would have eerie resonance with the Simpson affair twenty-six years later, Pratt murdered a white couple in 1968 on a Los Angeles tennis court. Cochran entered the case and offered a defense based on the assertion that his client had been set up by FBI agents who had maliciously corrupted evidence and suborned witnesses. The theory did not play as well as it would one generation later, when racial paranoia was more widespread; Cochran had a richer, more mediagenic client and a more immediately vulnerable

---

[2] See "Johnnie's Other O.J." in Part I, Chapter 8, above.

enemy in the Los Angeles Police Department. Pratt was convicted, but the experience stayed with Cochran. He says that shortly after joining the defense team, he told O.J. about what had happened to Geronimo and pledged, "I will not let this happen to you."

Cochran could say this with some confidence because his own "life experience" (a term he told Oprah Winfrey he preferred to race) told him how deeply the radical thinking of the Sixties had penetrated Southern California's black community, where racism—as his own meteoric career attests—is less onerous than at any other time in American history, but is nonetheless an explanation invoked with an almost addictive fervor for any adverse behavior or social outcome affecting black people. A beneficiary of the changes of the last thirty years, Cochran saw how they could be used in the O.J. defense in a way that was not possible when he took the case of Geronimo Pratt.

Cochran learned, for instance, from Huey Newton, who had always insisted on white attorneys and juries. Newton knew that he could impress whites by his self-constructed political myth of the outlaw rebel, a man in "primitive revolt" against the social oppression exemplified by the guardians of that injustice, the racist police. While this tactic was very successful, he still feared a jury of his black peers because he knew they would recognize him for the street hustler he was. Johnnie Cochran did not want O.J. to have a jury of his peers either. Brentwood millionaires would not buy the defense he planned to use to get his client off. He needed a panel representative of the black 'hood, which he felt was now ready to believe the myth he planned to create—that his client was a crossover artist who had taken his act into the white world but who, for all his charisma, had ultimately been rejected there because, when push came to shove, race overwhelmed even the power that comes from wealth and celebrity. Cochran was betting on the polarization and radicalization that had overtaken the black community in the last thirty years and so destroyed its center of gravity that it believed without question the notion that racism in America was worse than ever.

The system had been put on trial continually since 1967, most recently in the riot following the Rodney King verdict, and Cochran saw that it could be put on trial again in what, on the surface, was a less promising case even than Geronimo Pratt's. He knew the race card would trump the prosecution's full house of evidence. "Send a message," he urged the jury in his summation—not "Seek the truth" or "Do what is just," but "send a message" to the system and to the LAPD, which is the system's most visible and most disgusting symbol. And Lionel Cryer's black-power salute showed that the message—"It's payback time"—had gotten through. That this message hit home outside the courtroom could be seen in the representative reaction of Benny Davis, a black store owner in Los Angeles, who said after the verdict was announced, "Yeah, he did it. About time a brother got away with something around here."

If it is true, as member of O.J.'s legal team Robert Shapiro said, that the race card was dealt from the bottom of the deck all during the proceedings that freed his client, it is also clear that the race card was played long before the trial began and Mark Fuhrman became the shadow defendant for his out-of-court racial remarks. From the outset, white officials in the Los Angeles County district attorney's office behaved like the characters in *The Manchurian Candidate*, who enter a state of mesmerized suggestibility whenever a Soviet control agent gets out a deck of cards. In the movie it was the Queen of Hearts that triggers this response, but in the Simpson trial it was the race card.

It was the threat of black riots, like those that followed the Simi Valley trial of the policemen who beat Rodney King, that caused District Attorney Gil Carcetti to file the Simpson case downtown—a world apart from Brentwood and O.J.'s real life. This fateful decision, which more than anything else determined the outcome of the case, was followed by Garcetti's capitulation to a pretrial delegation of black leaders (including Johnnie Cochran) who demanded that the death penalty, itself a presumed symbol of institutional racism, not be invoked.

The race card was on the table in the DA's office when the prosecution left ten of its peremptory challenges unused and impaneled a jury with members who had been revealed during *voir dire* to be clearly sympathetic to Simpson. It is not hard to imagine what race cards were played when eleven jurors of color in the deliberation room finally confronted a sixty-one-year-old white woman who was a potential holdout.

This woman's daughter said afterward that her mother tearfully told her she thought O.J. was guilty and then added, "But Fuhrman!" And indeed Mark Fuhrman was like Voltaire's God: If he hadn't existed, Johnnie Cochran would have had to invent him. Even if it were true that Fuhrman was a racist with violent intentions, these intentions are probably no more violent than those acted out by O.J. in his repeated assaults on his ex-wife Nicole. The infamous tapes of Furhman's conversations with a television writer suggest how Fuhrman might deal with gangsters, crack heads, and lowlifes in South Central Los Angeles, but they do not predict very well how he would deal with a well-connected black millionaire sports legend in Brentwood. And in fact, when Fuhrman showed up at the Rockingham estate during one of O.J.'s earlier rampages against Nicole, he cut Simpson slack instead of taking him in, as he should have. Thus, for all the sound bites and fury about Fuhrman's alleged racism, one might say that so far the only proven victim of his less-than-admirable behavior as a cop has been the dead white wife, Nicole Brown Simpson.

Fuhrman's kid-glove treatment of O.J. was a preview of the red carpet initially rolled out for him by the LAPD itself after the murders. At a time when it was supposed to be planning a strategy to "get" Simpson, the police failed to identify him as an immediate suspect and then left him free and unwatched—after notifying him of his arrest!—allowing him to attempt an escape televised on national TV. The idea that Fuhrman and his pals could have conceived an on-the-spot conspiracy to frame Simpson—a plot then ratified by the highest levels of the LAPD in the few minutes allotted—is about as credible as the notion that AIDS is a white plot against black Americans, that the government has a secret program which intentionally funnels crack into the ghetto, or any of the other lurid conspiracy theories that spread like a plague in the radicalized black subculture.

Johnnie Cochran's playing of the race card in O.J. Simpson's criminal trial helped accentuate the condescension and double standards that have come to distinguish discussions of race in America. Fuhrman's romance with the word "nigger" was treated as if it were the worst thing that had ever been said in contemporary American history. In point of fact, slurs exist across the racial board. But because Fuhrman is white, his use of the N-word has stigmatized him and made him a hunted as well as a haunted man. The Reverend Jesse Jackson used the H-word—hymie, as in Jew, a word Jackson has occasionally uttered in public discourse in such a way as to make it clear he is forcing himself to omit the modifying adjective "dirty"—and yet he remains showered with honors, perhaps the most respected figure in the African-American community.

There was also something fishy about the way the Los Angeles police were stigmatized in this trial. By the time the verdict was delivered, they were being routinely discussed as if they were the Gestapo, not only by the defense but also by the media and the man in the street. In fact, far from being an Aryan monolith capable of implementing genocidal conspiracies on a moment's notice, the LAPD is 43 percent nonwhite, with a black chief and a black commissioner. In 1994 the LAPD took one million calls, gave out 400,000 traffic tickets, and made 150,000 arrests. All this activity generated 139 complaints of "officer discourtesy" and 168 complaints of "excessive force." Of these, only 22 and 8, respectively, were found upon examination to have merit.

Johnnie Cochran's fantasies of living in a racist police-state obscured the fact that in Los Angeles and other major cities in America, the issue is not lawless white cops but remorseless black criminals. It is not racism that has trapped one out of three young black men in the criminal-justice system. It is not racism that makes black males, only six percent of the population, commit almost 50 percent of all violent crimes. If racism were to blame, blacks would not be the chief victims of black criminality, three times as likely to be robbed as whites and seven times as likely to be murdered. In Los Angeles County there are 1,142 street gangs, which account for much of the city's violence. There are many poor whites in Southern California. But of the street gangs, 1,132—99 percent—are nonwhite. These young men of color control South Central like homicidal warlords, murdering people because they come from the wrong block, wear the wrong colors, or—like the three-year-old white girl whose family made a wrong turn in their car—are the wrong color.

Domestic violence is an important issue in this country—some 50 percent of female homicide victims are killed by past or present husbands and boyfriends. But it was apparently not an issue for the Simpson jurors, one of whom, the egregious Brenda Moran, played a subtle race card of her own in a post-trial news conference, when she contemptuously dismissed as "a waste of time" the prosecution's effort to show that O.J.'s battering of Nicole provided a motive for the murder. This statement, and the visceral disgust with which it was delivered, were so extreme as to invite speculation. Was this a black woman's rage at those iconic blonde goddesses like Nicole, who are said to steal away black men like Simpson and Johnnie Cochran? Or was it the scorn of an African-American woman who comes from a community where domestic violence is both routine and truly violent and who knows, therefore, what real battering is all about?

The Simpson affair has been treated as a great celebrity case in the tradition of the trials of Dr. Sam Sheppard, convicted of killing his wife, or Bruno Hauptmann, convicted of kidnapping the Lindbergh baby. This it certainly was. But it was far more a political trial whose antecedents are Charles Garry's defense of Huey Newton or William Kunstler's defense of Larry Davis—the drug king who shot nine policemen attempting to arrest him but was acquitted because Kunstler convinced the jury that the police had been out to "get" yet another black man who was acting in "self-defense."

The real story in the Simpson case was not the defendant or even the defense attorney, but the jury itself. What were regarded as extremist slogans in the sixties—All black males are victims! All prisoners are political prisoners!—became the jury's key intellectual assumptions. The jury closest in spirit to the one that decided the O.J. case was the one that judged Lemrick Nelson, a black man who murdered a Hasidic Jew in Crown Heights in 1992. In that case, Yankel Rosenbaum was run down by a crowd of blacks chanting, "Kill the Jew!" The killer was caught with the murder weapon and the blood of Rosenbaum on his person; he was identified by the dying man and he confessed to his captors in jail. But taking the Garry-Kunstler-Cochran line of defense, his lawyers argued that Lemrick Nelson was the victim of a police conspiracy and frame-up. A jury of nine blacks and three Puerto Ricans acquitted him. Afterward, in their version of Lionel Cryer's black-power salute, the jurors gave a party for the murderer to celebrate his release.

The Simpson jury could be sequestered from the public, but not from the resentment and blame that have spread through the black community like addictive substances in recent years. Nor could it be sequestered from the developing phenomenon of black racism, which feeds off paranoia and irrationality. It was no accident that the Los Angeles courtroom was filled with subliminal reminders of the tension between black radicals and the Jews who were their strongest allies in the heyday of the civil rights movement. Reminders of that inflamed relationship, which has come to be a barometer measuring the decline of race relations in America, were present in the appearance of anti-Semitic Fruit of Islam soldiers who functioned as Cochran's praetorian guard; in the fact that a Jew was one of the victims, and that the verdict was read on the eve of Yom Kippur; in "genocidal racist," the bizarre neologism that Cochran used to describe Fuhrman; and in Cochran's cynical comparison of Fuhrman to Hitler, which took Holocaust revisionism to a new low.

By the time the verdict was read, Louis Farrakhan had become a ghostly presence in this trial. Initially, Farrakhan had scornfully dismissed O.J. as one of those black men who become trivial and inauthentic in their lapdog attempts to be accepted by the white world. (The buffoonish Simpson had once joked weakly that he could never embrace Islam because he liked bacon too much.) Yet, by the end of the trial, acting through Cochran, Farrakhan had in effect offered the defendant a safety net and a place to go when the white world of celebrity rejected him.

Transfigured by the racial solidarity that is now the highest good in the black community, the presumably sadder but wiser Simpson will realize where he truly belongs. He will become a brother returned to the fold, a civil rights martyr, someone who might well show up as a celebrity figure at some future event like the Million Man March held in 1995. Indeed, like the Simpson verdict itself, Farrakhan's march provides the mirror for a civil rights establishment so debased by radical strategies, double standards, and shameless appeals to white guilt that it has become an exercise in self-parody. When Johnnie Cochran appeared before the Congressional Black Caucus and compared the Simpson trial to the *Dred Scott* case and the *Brown v. Board of Education* decision, there was not even a murmur of dissent.

Over the last three decades, the moral voices of the black community were first muted and then drowned out, as dissent from the desperate search for psychological and fiscal entitlements now euphemistically termed the "civil rights agenda" was ruthlessly crushed. In the wake of the trial, writer Richard Rodriguez commented sadly that the two hundred years of moral capital stored up by the civil rights movement had been squandered to acquit O.J. He is only partially correct. That capital has actually been wasted incrementally all along the long march down the mountain—from the summit Martin Luther King, Jr. achieved into the fever swamps of today—as racial hate-mongers like Farrakhan and charlatans like Al Sharpton have replaced King and Medgar Evers; as lying delinquents like Tawana Brawley, who falsely claimed to have been abducted and abused by whites, have replaced true victims like Emmett Till, a black adolescent brutally murdered in Mississippi in the Fifties by whites who believed he had whistled at a white woman; as figures like the ever-corrupt Marion Barry, the felon Rodney King, the thug Damian Williams, the cop-killer Mumia Abu-Jamal, and now O.J. Simpson himself have all been embraced as heroes of the struggle, as worthy of admiration as Rosa Parks. This inability to discriminate right from wrong and heroes from perpetrators suggests that the so-called civil rights movement has not only lost its moorings and morality, but in some sense its mind as well.

The system that Huey Newton put on trial nearly three decades ago has been attacked so often in the intervening years that its immunity has been destroyed and it is now prey to every exotic racial agenda that comes along. In the case of O.J. Simpson, black radicals got the payback they've been asking for since the Newton trial. But its cost will continue to be paid—by all of us—in the years ahead. All during the year before the verdict, black leaders kept saying that O.J. couldn't get a fair trial. The tragedy of the outcome—the acquittal of a brutal murderer—is that they were right.

2

Guns Don't Kill Black People, Other Black People Do

D escribing itself as an organization of "half a million adult and youth members [who] are the premier advocates for social justice and equal opportunity," the National Association for the Advancement of Colored People launched a new civil rights crusade at its annual convention last month. NAACP president Kweisi Mfume announced plans to file an injunctive class-action suit against gun manufacturers "to force them to distribute their product responsibly." Mfume cited the disparate impact of gun violence among young black males. An NAACP press release cited statistics showing that African-American males between the ages of 15 and 24 are almost five times more likely to be injured by firearms than white males in the same age group. "Firearm homicide has been the leading cause of death among young African-American males for nearly 30 years."

Am I alone in thinking this a pathetic, absurd, and almost hilarious demonstration of political desperation by the civil rights establishment? What's next? Will Irish Americans sue whiskey distillers, or Jews the gas company? That last analogy only works, of course, for those who think the Holocaust was a self-inflicted wound. In fact, black leaders have already accused white and Korean liquor vendors of "invading" black communities and intoxicating their inhabitants. Boycotts have followed these charges, and anti-white, anti-Korean race riots as well.

August 16, 1999, http://www.salon.com/1999/08/16/naacp/; http://
archive.frontpagemag.com/Printable.aspx?ArtId=24294.

But who forces alcohol down reluctant throats? Who, exactly, is using those guns irresponsibly, making young black males almost five times more likely to be victims than whites? Why does the NAACP even make the comparison between gun deaths of blacks and whites if not as a racist insinuation that whites are somehow the *cause* of those "disproportionate" violent deaths, just as whites are often the implied *cause* of other social pathologies that afflict the African-American community? In the sociology of the left, there cannot be a wound the black community inflicts on itself which is not ultimately the responsibility of malicious whites. To think otherwise would be to "blame the victim." Only mean-spirited conservatives would even think of doing that.

These are the facts: While blacks make up only twelve percent of the population, they account for more than 46 percent of total violent crime and more than 90 percent of the murders of blacks. It is young black males, not whites or gun manufacturers, who are responsible for the disproportionate gun deaths of young black males. A gun—do I really have to spell this out?—is an inanimate object. It takes a human to pull the trigger. Firearms don't kill people. Sociopaths do. If young black males abuse firearms in an irresponsible and criminal fashion, why should the firearms industry be held accountable? Why not the parents of the shooters? Why not the shooters themselves?

Unfortunately, as a nation we have become so trapped in the melodrama of black victimization and white "oppression" that we are in danger of losing all sense of reality. If blacks are oppressed in America, why isn't there a black exodus? Why do all those black Haitians want to come here? To be oppressed? In the grip of a politically inspired group psychosis, we find it the path of least resistance to collude with demagogic race-hustlers in supporting a fantasy in which African-Americans are no longer responsible for anything negative they do, even to themselves.

If blacks constitute just under half the prison population, for example, one cannot be allowed to insinuate that the black community might have a problem when it comes to raising its children as law abiding members of society. Oh no. Such a statistic can only be explained by the racism of a criminal-justice system that is incarcerating too many blacks. Nonsense like this is proposed daily by the entire spectrum of the so-called civil rights leadership, from the racist bloviator Al Sharpton to the urbane Urban League president Hugh Price. In the intimidating atmosphere that this consensus creates, to suggest the obvious—that too many blacks are in prison because too many blacks commit crimes—is to be identified as an apologist for racism and perhaps a racist oneself.

The NAACP's anti-gun lawsuit comes on the heels of the crusade to defend crack dealers because 90 percent of them are African-American and their sentences are considered "too harsh." This insipid campaign was launched by Jesse Jackson at the Washington march of race-hater Louis Farrakhan. That 90 percent of crack cocaine dealers are black cannot be seen, of course, as a moral stain on those crack dealers or as a massive social problem for the community that produces them. It can only be the result of a white legal system that stigmatizes crack as a more dangerous and more culpable drug than powder cocaine. Forget that the heavier penalties were originally demanded by black leaders who claimed that crack was associated with street violence in the black community, while the white criminal-justice system did not care enough about its destructive consequences to make the penalties harsh. That was then, this is now. And now, lessening the sentences that were previously raised has become a crusade for "social justice" that overshadows the need to combat the crime wave itself. Because racial oppression is the main enemy, the villainy of the crack trade is transformed into yet another symbol of white malfeasance.

This kind of race-baiting has now intruded into the presidential contest as a means of smearing the Republican candidate, George Bush, who is distinguished by his outreach to minority communities and by his support among blacks. Is there a vast left-wing conspiracy that sees Bush's black support as a political threat? Of course there is. Precisely because Bush is perceived as a candidate who can break the vicious stereotyping of Republicans as anti-black, he has to be smeared. Thus Bush was labeled "Governor Death" in a Christopher Hitchens column that appeared in *Salon* on August 10, 1999. The clear implication of Hitchens's attack was that Bush colludes in a racist justice system in Texas that executes blacks in disproportionate numbers. "Perhaps you wonder if capital punishment is unevenly applied, as respects race and class, in the state of Texas," wrote Hitchens. "Wonder no longer. Just read the Amnesty report *Killing With Prejudice: Race and the Death Penalty in the USA.*"

I read the Amnesty report. Maybe Christopher should, too. The Amnesty report *does not even mention racial or class statistics in Texas* and could not possibly be used to draw such a conclusion. Moreover, a perusal of the report reveals no self-evident truths, even nationally. It is slovenly and inflammatory. Under the heading "Racist Representation of Indigent Defendants," it offers this evidence: "Gary Burns, black, executed in Indiana on 20 November 1997, was described to the jury by his white attorney as an 'insignificant, snivelly little street person.'" End of example. What is this supposed to prove? Maybe the attorney was trying to suggest that someone else must have done the dirty work that his client was too weak to be guilty of. Who can tell from this example? Most of the Amnesty report consists of unsystematic and frustratingly brief snippets of cases like this, along with a sprinkling of unanalyzed statistics that are arrayed to serve Amnesty's political agenda.

It is true that the number of blacks executed in Texas (and nationwide) is greater than their proportion in the population. But it is also true that the proportion of black murderers far exceeds the proportion of blacks in the population. According to the Bureau of Justice Statistics 1996 report (released May 1999), blacks commit 54 percent of the homicides in America even though they constitute only 12 percent of the population. An individual black male is eight times more likely to commit murder than an individual white male. Thus, in the most equitable system imaginable, a black male would be more likely than a white male to be executed for murder. In fact, however, convicted white murderers are more likely to be executed for their crimes than convicted black murderers. In 1996–1997, whites accounted for 62 percent of the convicted murderers executed in Texas. According to statistics provided by the Justice Department, the proportion of whites presently on death row compared to the total white population is almost four times that of the comparable proportion of blacks on death row in terms of the total black population. Whatever these statistics prove, they do not prove that the American justice system is systemically biased against blacks.

Actually, the Amnesty report does not explicitly claim that there is a racial bias against African-American *defendants* in murder cases (although its implications are clearly that). The reason is that most studies of racial sentencing, including the Baldus study—the one most frequently invoked by anti-death penalty activists—have found "neither strong nor consistent" evidence of discrimination directed against black defendants because of race.[1] But the desperation to prove white turpitude is so great that instead of celebrating this as a triumph of civil rights reform in the law, the race-baiters merely shift their focus to a new victim class—those who have committed capital crimes and are scheduled for execution.

The statistic with which Amnesty opens its case is this: "Of the 500 prisoners executed between 1977 and 1998, 81.8 percent were convicted of murdering a white person, even though blacks and whites are the victims of homicide in almost equal numbers nationwide." What the Report's raw statistic fails to take into account is that the death penalty is only imposed in aggravated circumstances, which can include the violence of the crime, whether it is committed in the course of another crime, or whether the

---

[1] Randall Kennedy, *Race, Crime and the Law*, Vintage, 1998, pp. 158, 329.

perpetrator has a prior criminal record of violent crimes. All these factors are ignored in the Amnesty report. It so happens that black felons commit 43 percent of aggravated assaults, 66 percent of (armed) robberies, 27 percent of rapes and 85 percent of interracial crimes of violence, mainly against whites (this last figure from a Justice Department report for 1993). Since juries generally don't demand the death penalty for crimes of passion, where the victim is known to the killer, and since blacks are far more likely to commit violent crimes against whites than whites are to commit such crimes against blacks, the disparity that offends the Amnesty report has a basis in facts that may not imply a racial bias on the part of prosecutors and juries. The report does not even acknowledge this as a problem.

The defense of criminals as a civil rights cause is only an extreme manifestation of what has apparently become the very essence of the civil rights movement. Do black children fail to achieve in school? White oppression explains their failure. Any other explanation would blame the victims. Poor black academic performance cannot be seen as a failure of black families to educate their children, or of the black community to support educational values, which are often referred to derisively as "thinking white." Black failure can only be the result of some lingering residue of the white perfidy involved in slavery and segregation. Call it "institutional racism."

Of course, those who invoke the phantom of "institutional racism" are too sophisticated to claim that there are actual racists embedded in our liberal education establishment who refuse to admit black children to legally integrated schools, or refuse to teach them when they get there. Instead, the concept of "institutional racism" is designed to encompass an entire *system* of oppression that invisibly conspires to keep black children down. It may do so through culturally rigged tests; or through the failure to provide black role models in positions of authority; or by underfunding schools in black neighborhoods; or as a result of the pervasive negative pressure exerted by an environment of poverty that cannot be countered with a mere six hours of school. Compulsory pre-school is already being proposed by Democrat candidate Al Gore and the political left as a new "right" and social cure-all.

In reality, the failure of African-American children to make the educational grade cannot be explained by *any* of the above factors. Statistics analyzed by *The New York Times* dispel the poverty argument by establishing that impoverished white children whose parents earn less than $10,000 a year score higher on standardized SAT tests than black children whose parents earn more than $70,000.[2] None of the above arguments, moreover, can explain why Vietnamese children who are poor and discriminated against, whose schools are under-funded, who are culturally at a greater disadvantage than blacks and have even fewer "role models" to inspire them, still manage to be educationally competitive.

While the oppression theme dominates public discourse, no attention can be paid to the real problems that hold African-American children back. There is a symbiosis between the political mumbo jumbo of the Kweisi Mfumes and Jesse Jacksons (abetted mightily by patronizing white liberals) and the seemingly intractable social problems of the black community. The myth of racial oppression, invoked to explain every social deficit of blacks, is an exercise in psychological denial. Crying racism deflects attention from the actual causes of the problems that afflict African-American communities and denies them the power to change their fate.

Nearly 70 percent of black children are born out of wedlock. A child raised in a single-parent, female-headed household is five and a half times more likely to be poor than a child of any color born into a two-parent household. Seventy percent of youth violence is committed by males from female-headed households, regardless of race. If the NAACP and other black leaders want to end the terrible scourge of gun violence committed by young inner-city blacks,

---

[2] July 4, 1999.

they should launch a campaign to promote marriage and family formation in the African-American community; they should issue a moral plea to the community to stigmatize fathers who abandon their children and parents who have more children than they can afford. Instead of waging war against law enforcement agencies and supporting destructive racial demagogues like Al Sharpton, they should support the Rudy Giulianis and other champions of public safety, whom they now attack. They should campaign for a tripling of police forces in inner-city areas to protect the vast majority of inhabitants who are law abiding and the true victims of the predators among them. But to take these remedial steps would require rejecting the bogus charge of white oppression. It would mean abandoning the ludicrous claim that white America and firearms manufacturers are the problems afflicting African-Americans. It would mean taking responsibility for one's own communities instead.

Why do the NAACP and the civil rights establishment perpetuate this myth of white oppression? Because the same individuals reap great moral, psychological, and material rewards for doing so. Blaming others for the failures and offenses that are your own responsibility is a predictable human behavior. When it is reinforced, as it is in this case, by a patronizing white liberal establishment, its payoffs can be irresistible. There are material rewards as well. Racial ambulance-chasing has allowed Jesse Jackson to live the life of a multi-millionaire and catapulted Kweisi Mfume and others like him into the social and political stratosphere. Unfortunately, they have made their successes off the backs of the truly afflicted and disadvantaged African-Americans their demagoguery leaves behind.

To take one example: *The Shape of the River*, by William Bowen and Derek Bok, studied the effect of affirmative action policies at 28 elite colleges. According to Bowen and Bok, 86 percent of the African-American beneficiaries of racial preferences at those colleges came from households that were already middle-class or affluent, while 64 percent had at least one parent who had been to college, a figure *six times* greater than the proportion for all college-age black youths. In other words, without the race card so adeptly played by organizations like the NAACP, the already-privileged families of the black middle-class would have had to forego the government-provided additional privileges that the continuing specter of white oppression justifies. Among these are free tuition, rigged entrance requirements, artificially inflated salaries, set-aside front companies and a variety of extortions, from the outrageous sums provided to collegiate black student associations to the ransoms paid by Texaco and other companies to forestall potentially damaging racial boycotts and often groundless discrimination suits. The continued suffering of disadvantaged black communities and the continued under-par performance of black school children is a price the well-heeled civil rights establishment is apparently willing to pay to keep their hope alive of continuing guilt tributes from their all-too-accommodating white "oppressors."

3

Time Magazine's *Attack*

[N]OTE: The preceding article "Guns Don't Kill Black People—Other Black People Do," elicited a scathing response from Jack White, a black columnist for *Time* magazine, who attacked me as a "bigot" for writing it. *Time* accompanied the White column with a photograph of me, captioned "Real Live Bigot." I wrote the following letter to Walter Isaacson, then *Time*'s editor-in-chief, who invited me to meet with him and his editorial board. The letter is long and detailed because I felt isolated and vulnerable, and needed others to know my activities and views in behalf of racial equality, lest White's slander stick. My sole defender at the time with a large audience was Matt Drudge, who posted this letter on the Drudge Report.

When I met with the *Time* editorial board, Issacson conceded that White's characterization was false, and apologized for being out of town when it was set in print, and said he would not have approved it if he had been. But he also maintained that his hands were tied by the National Association of Black Journalists who would defend White, and by his responsibility as editor to stand by his staff. Consequently, he was not going to print my letter or an editorial apology. I wasn't persuaded by this argument but told him that I did understand that if he criticized White he would be attacked as a racist too. I think everyone in the room understood that this was the real reason they would not repudiate White's

September 1 1999, http://archive.frontpagemag.com/Printable.aspx?ArtId=22632; http://www.salon.com/1999/08/25/response/.

slander. Isaacson, who was respectful of my work, did offer to have my new book, *Hating Whitey & Other Progressive Causes*, reviewed by *Time.* I thought to myself, this was something *Time* should have done in any case. But I accepted the offering. The review was written by Lance Morrow, who was also present at the meeting. Morrow defended the integrity of my views on race matters, describing my book, which included the article about guns, as having "an indignant sanity" on matters of race. All things considered, I considered myself lucky to have come out of this in one piece. It should be said that Walter Isaacson was generous to me in subsequent years, providing blurbs praising my books *The End of Time* and *A Point in Time.*]

Walter Isaacson
Time & Life Building
Rockefeller Center
New York, NY 10020

Dear Mr. Isaacson,
In a column authored by Jack White in your August 30 issue, your magazine has committed an outrage against myself and my family, which I appeal to you to redress. As you know, the exercise of freedom of the press comes with a responsibility not to abuse its power and crush unequal individuals with statements that are defamatory and libelous. Jack White's column in your August 30 issue, which features my image and describes me as "A Real, Live Bigot" is a hateful racial lie.[1]

I understand from years of personal experience that the political arena can be rough. I certainly expected some strong reactions to the article I wrote for *Salon* magazine on August 16 ("Guns Don't Kill Black People, Other Black People Do"). But there is not a shred of evidence in White's column or in the entire record of my

---

[1] "A Real, Live Bigot," Jack E. White, *Time*, August 30, 1999, http://www.time.com/time/magazine/article/0,9171,991864,00.html.

very public career that would justify calling me a racial bigot. If there were, *Salon*'s editors would not have published the piece and would not have hired me as a regular columnist for their magazine, which White describes as "otherwise one of the Internet's most humane and sophisticated websites." *Salon*'s editors have known me personally for thirty years, and therefore are aware that one aspect of my career that has remained consistent is my steadfast commitment to equal rights for African-Americans and for all Americans.

In a lifetime of public activity, as an author and activist, I have never written or spoken a word—or committed an act—that any reasonable person could call "bigoted." Nor has your columnist found a single comment in my article that would justify the hateful headline with which you have stigmatized me to millions of Americans.

I began my political career at a demonstration in 1948 in support of Harry Truman's Fair Employment Practices Commission, which sought to end employment discrimination against African-Americans in the federal government. For fifty-one years since that demonstration, I have fought for equal rights for black Americans and for all Americans. As a young activist in Berkeley in the 1960s, I picketed Woolworth's for CORE, and played a small role in the civil rights movement led by Martin Luther King that extended America's constitutional protections to black Americans. It is true that my politics have generally become more conservative since the 1960s. But my attitude towards racial equality and integration has not changed. On innumerable occasions, in articles I have written and in speeches I have given from public platforms, I have expressed my continuing dedication and commitment to the values and goals of the civil rights movement led by King. In all the time that has elapsed since that era, I have never once repudiated my belief in the basic dignity of all people of whatever ethnic or racial group.

Two years ago I raised half a million dollars to conduct a TV ad campaign on behalf of an African-American talk-show host in Los

Angeles named Larry Elder whose show was under attack.[2] The station manager at the Disney affiliate KABC-Los Angeles had cut Elder's hours, hired a replacement, and threatened to fire him. As a direct result of my campaign, Elder's ratings increased by 30 percent, his hours were restored, and the station manager was fired. Today, Larry Elder is the number-one drive time talk-show host in the Los Angeles media market.

Last year I organized a conservative conference in Arizona, which *The New York Times* called the alternative to the Clinton Renaissance Weekend and which was attended by the chair and co-chair of the Republican Party along with more than a dozen Republican senators, congressmen, and elected officials. My featured speakers included Newt Gingrich, John McCain, Fred Thompson, and Rudy Giuliani. I also invited five African-American friends of mine—Congressman J.C. Watts, Operation Hope chairman John Bryant, Los Angeles Civil Rights Commission president Joe Hicks, Oakland NAACP president Shannon Reeves, and Larry Elder—to speak at this event, specifically to tell Republicans that they were not doing enough for African-Americans and other minorities who are disadvantaged, and that the Republican Party was not doing enough to reach out to minority constituencies in general.

In 1996, I was a member of the Exploratory Committee to Draft Colin Powell for President. This year, I undertook my own campaign to draft Eloise Anderson for Senate in my home state of California. Eloise Anderson is an African-American, and a former welfare mother, who headed the Human Services Department in the Pete Wilson Administration. She is speaking, along with African-Americans J.C. Watts, Shannon Reeves, and Lt. Governor Joe Rogers of Colorado at this year's "Weekend" event, which will be held over Labor Day in Colorado Springs.

---

[2] "An Unfair Attack Against a Fair-minded Man," Larry Elder, *Jewish World Review*, October 1, 1999, http://www.jewishworldreview.com/cols/elder100199.asp.

Presently, I am engaged in a nationwide campaign to get the Republican Party to champion the cause of poor people and minorities. I have written a booklet outlining this proposal that has already been distributed to 35,000 Republican officials and party activists with endorsement letters from a dozen state party chairmen. The chief political strategist for the Bush presidential campaign, Karl Rove, has called my booklet "the perfect pocket guide to winning on the political battlefield" and made it required reading for the entire Bush campaign staff. Part Two of the final section of the booklet, which is devoted to "Reshaping the Republican Party," is sub-titled: "Give Minorities, Poor People, and Working Americans a Shot at the American Dream."

I have created a charity organization called Hollywood Concerned that is dedicated "to helping charities that benefit minorities and poor people." We are currently serving more than twelve inner-city charities in the Los Angeles area that help homeless children and youth at risk who are mainly Hispanic and African-American. One of the most destructive aspects of your slander is the damage it will do to our efforts to help these children.

It could reasonably be said that there are few conservatives who have been as active and outspoken as I am in trying to persuade Republicans to embrace the cause of African-Americans and other minorities, to be more active in their concerns about the plight of citizens of our inner cities, and to become a more inclusive organization reflecting the multi-colored and multi-ethnic face of America.

All these facts are publicly known and were readily available to your reporter. In the course of the "interview" he conducted with me in preparation for his column, Jack White indicated that he had consulted my website *FrontPage Magazine* where my *Salon* article appears in a version that restores three paragraphs the editors had cut for reasons of space. If White had the least interest in reporting the truth about me and my beliefs, he could have found out about Hollywood Concerned, the Larry Elder campaign, the Arizona and Colorado conferences, and he could have read the booklet I have written about the Republican Party, since all are available on the same website.

But White did not care about the truth. Instead, he caricatured me as a racial bigot, and wrote a column that disregards the facts in order to perform a character assassination dressed up as commentary. In the process he has made me and my family the target of racial resentments and angers from who knows what sources. You and your headline writers have abetted this destructive agenda.

It is true that I have a polemical style that may provoke some strong reactions in others, and that certainly had an effect on your columnist. But as I explained to Jack White during our interview, I created this rhetorical style to match that of black leaders like Jesse Jackson, Kweisi Mfume, and Al Sharpton, when they are busily framing their indictments of white Americans and other ethnic groups, and even entire industries, for the problems that afflict some African-American communities.

The subject of my style was the focus of one part of the interview that Jack White seriously distorted in his column. I told Jack White that liberals had a habit of patronizing black people by not telling them what they really felt. I gave as an example the failure of white editorialists to be critical of the NAACP's suit against gun manufacturers for violence that inner-city blacks perpetrate on each other. I said: "White people generally are intimidated from telling black people the truth in a blunt manner." Jack White asked me: "Why then do you think that *you* can talk to black people that way?" I answered: "Because I earned the right to do so in the Sixties." Here is how White distorted my answer:

> "Last week Horowitz told me that he had earned the right to talk down to blacks 'because of all I did in the '6os.'"

Jack White's animus towards me is one thing; *Time*'s failure to exercise responsible editorial control over its columnist is another. The question I ask you is: "How do I get my reputation back?" What do I tell my African-American daughter-in-law or my three granddaughters when they ask me why an otherwise reputable magazine like *Time* would pillory their grandfather as a racial bigot, putting me in a category alongside deranged hate-mongers? How, as a public figure, do I carry on the quest for a frank and honest dialogue over race if I am stigmatized with a label like this, which I have done nothing to deserve? Why would anyone else attempt to engage in candid talk about race, seeing what has happened to me?

I hope you will consider the gravity of what you and your columnist have done. I hope you will print this letter and feature it, in article form, as a response to the malicious slanders that appeared in your magazine. I hope you will accompany it with an editorial apology for the damage you have done, and thus afford me the same rectification that you would any other victim of racial injustice.

Sincerely,
David Horowitz

4

Walk in My Shoes

One of the letters responding to my *Salon* column about black racism and denial ("Guns Don't Kill Black People—Other Black People Do") was from an angry Chicago reader named Alice Huber, who introduced herself as an African-American woman married to a white man.[1] According to Mrs. Huber, I was indeed a "bigot," as columnist Jack White had said.[2] Moreover, I was "the worst kind." I had earned the label "racist" by suggesting that blacks might no longer be "oppressed" as a group in America, and by questioning whether white racism was the immediate or principal cause of problems afflicting black youth like violence and educational failure. I earned it by "trotting out my 'black family'" and mentioning the anguish White's lies might cause them. I guess it's inconvenient to have a "bigot" who not only does not hate blacks, but is flesh and blood with individual blacks whom he might actually love.

Almost as damning in Mrs. Huber's mind was my claim to solidarity in the struggle for equal rights. "Horowitz says he earned the right to talk to blacks 'honestly,'" Huber wrote, "because of the '60s. Personally, I don't care how many marches he went to, how much money he dropped in a civil rights bucket, how many times he sang 'We Shall Overcome' with guest celebrities;

September 13, 1999, http://archive.frontpagemag.com/Printable.aspx?ArtId=24299; http://www.salon.com/1999/09/13/racism_4/.
[1] See above, Chapter 2, *Guns Don't Kill Black People, Other Black People Do.*
[2] See above, Chapter 3, *Time's Attack.*

Horowitz is not black, and he has no right to tell me or any other person of color how to pursue issues pertaining to our communities."

This attitude is not original with Mrs. Huber but will be familiar to anyone who has engaged African-Americans over issues of race in recent decades. "If you don't walk in my shoes, you can't feel my pain." The conclusion that is supposed to follow from this observation is usually presented as self-evident: "If you can't feel my pain, you can't tell me how I should deal with it."

This was indeed the text of many a political sermon when objections were raised to the Million Man March because it was organized and led by an anti-Semitic racist. "Don't tell us what leaders to choose or what marches to join," was the response of many otherwise sensible black commentators. It was a "black thing," a matter of community pride. "We're not listening when white people tell us what to do anymore." "We're not letting you choose our leaders." Indeed, marching behind such an unpalatable figure was itself a way of emphasizing black independence, the degree to which African-Americans had liberated themselves from the tutelage of former masters.

The same attitude was operative during the O.J. Simpson trial, when black leaders showed not the slightest embarrassment at the fact that African-American communities all over the nation, in a demonstration of striking insensitivity, cheered the acquittal of the accused. Imagine the reaction of black leaders if white communities had cheered the release of a white defendant accused of murdering his black wife and a black stranger, particularly if the white defendant had no serious alibi, was confronted by overwhelming circumstantial and DNA evidence, and had a record of beating his black spouse prior to her death. A triumphal response to the acquittal in such a case would have been taken as evidence of racism. But in the case of an accused black murderer, the response of the African-American community was: we don't care what you think or what you feel. We know what we feel and that is all that matters. If our response is insensitive, so what? We are going to be the judges of what is right or wrong for us, and no one—least of all any white person—is going to tell us how to behave. Imagine if the colors had been reversed!

This cold-hearted calculus is a central theme of what is now generously described as "black separatism." It is an attitude that is deep and widespread in the African-American community, and needs to be looked at more carefully in light of reports that it is now on the rise. A recent poll by the NAACP reported that over 40 percent of blacks and 50 percent of whites now accept the doctrine of racially separate but equal. There should be no surprise here, given the official sanction of segregation for blacks in universities, the most "liberal" institutions in our culture. Whites have their own segregationist impulses, but the license that black leadership has given to separatism among the educated classes can hardly have been without effect. Perhaps out of guilt, perhaps out of lack of serious caring, whites have been willing to go along with what the African-American community wants in these matters, without regard to their own standards of what is appropriate or moral or good. If blacks want to march *en masse* behind a racist kook like Farrakhan, fine. If they want racially segregated graduations and racially segregated dormitories and racially specific curriculums in our schools, that's okay. If they want to bring back the segregationist standard of "separate but equal" anywhere in our national life, that must be all right as well.

Meanwhile, as we divide along racial lines and increasingly surrender the ability to speak with a communal voice, we are losing the fundamental idea of what it means to be American. This is the idea that all—regardless of race, color or creed—are created equal before the community's law. The founders did not say whites. The words "black" and "white" do not appear in the Constitution. The fact that they used the common generic term "men" obviously did not mean just the male gender, either. The Constitution not only does not specifically exclude women from its Bill of Rights; it does not use the words "male" or "female" at all.

The implications of separatism are fundamentally subversive of the American idea, and also of the moral ideal that has been responsible for the liberation of blacks from their oppression. If the white majority could not feel blacks' pain, they would not have responded as they did to the injustices they or their ancestors had inflicted, which had brought many of them material advantages.

It is, of course, not just whites who cannot feel blacks' pain in the sense implied in the statements above. The fact is that nobody can feel any pain but one's own. This paradox is a timeless theme of Western epistemologists going back to Descartes, who believed that the only certain reality is the interior knowledge we have of our own feelings and thoughts. *Cogito ergo sum.* But this solipsistic viewpoint, and the relativist perspective that follows would—if taken to its logical extreme—mean the end of any ethical outlook, of the possibility of any appeal to morality or conscience, and thus of the possibility of any society—let alone a multi-ethnic one like ours—surviving the essential anarchy of the human condition.

How can any morality exist if you have to actually be in others' shoes to feel their pain? How can we know that slavery is wrong if we have not been slaves? Or that discrimination is wrong if we have not been discriminated against? How can we feel compelled to do unto others as we would have them do unto us, if there is no commonality between us? Yet the very idea of that kinship in our common humanity is what motivated Wilberforce and other white Christians to end the African slave trade that blacks and Arabs had started. How could they (or we) know or feel that an injustice had been done to others if those others are so alien that we cannot identify with them?

Or take this a step further: How can blacks presume to tell whites what is right or wrong for them—which is after all what the entire civil rights discourse has been about in this country—if being different disqualifies anyone from making such statements? How can blacks appeal to the conscience of whites in seeking to be treated as equals, if the very concept of a common humanity that underpins the principle of equality is rejected by them? *How can blacks expect justice from us, if we cannot expect it from them?* If we cannot imagine what it is like to be them, what is it that they are appealing to in us when they ask for justice and respect? "There but for the grace of God go I," is the fundamental ethical intuition. If we cannot imagine ourselves in the place of others, what sympathy can we have for them? What kinship can we feel? How can we regard them as brothers and sisters under the skin?

We can't. And that is the problem that those who employ the separatist argument must provide an answer to. Nonetheless, there is a kernel of truth in the separatist complaint. Life experiences are different and differences can be important. Existential differences undoubtedly form the basis of many intellectual disagreements, and provide the ground of our pluralistic identity. But the basis of our American identity is an injunction to accept these differences in order to overcome them: *E pluribus unum;* out of many cultures and many ethnicities, one.

It is crucial to the moral community we strive to inhabit that our differences have a limit, and that they be checked against sympathies that are evident. If I show care for you, I probably have a capacity to empathize with your experience and understand who you are. It is your ability to recognize this, and to listen to me as a friend (as well as my ability to listen to you) that forms the basis of our ability to coexist with each other in a democratic framework. If you ignore me and my concerns, on the other hand, you invite a similar response.

Taking this a step further, if you show hostility to me, I probably am not going to care as much about you as I might have, and even be tempted to reciprocate the hostility. A significant amount of the hostility anyone experiences is often self-induced. The hostility that black separatism projects towards non-blacks is, not surprisingly, a proximate cause of the lack of sympathy that is often returned by them to blacks. In recent decades, there has been a palpable decline in the sympathy that other Americans feel for the agendas of the civil rights movement. This is directly related to the growth of separatist feelings and ideas in the African-American community, and the perversion of civil rights agendas into separatist grievances.

The civil rights movement Martin Luther King led was based on the old ethics and the old integrationist philosophy. It was supported by 90-percent majorities in the Congress and the overwhelming majority of the white population. The same cannot be said for the "civil rights" policies of the current African-American leadership. There will not be a lot of support for the NAACP's recently announced suit against gun manufacturers. Similarly, racial preferences, which are considered the *sine qua non* of a civil rights position these days, are rejected by majorities among non-African-Americans almost as large as those that had supported the original civil rights agenda proposed by Martin Luther King. Recognizing this fact, African-Americans have to ask themselves whether this is the result of racist attitudes on the part of whites or whether it is a failure of their own leadership to articulate worthy goals.

If Mrs. Huber and Jack White want to call a "racist" someone as committed to civil rights issues as I am, just because I disagree with their assessment of some racial grievances, they must bear responsibility for the decreasing power of the term itself. In fact, the term "racism" has lost a great deal of its sting in recent decades through its abusive use by separatist demagogues. If Jack White, a prime offender in these matters, had written his slander for the *Village Voice* or the *Amsterdam News,* no one would have paid any attention or cared. The reason is that those journals have so abused the term by applying it frivolously to political opponents, only their own constituencies find their usage credible anymore. It is only the authority of *Time* that gives White's slanders their weight. If *Time* continues to publish racial rants like his, its own credibility will diminish.

Drawing inspiration from the separatist ideas of Malcolm X, the present leaders of the African-American community have squandered the moral capital that Martin Luther King accumulated, undermining in the process the civil rights cause they claim to support. Ask yourself which current African-American civil rights leader has any significant respect among communities that are not black or politically to the left. Certainly not Kweisi Mfume, Julian Bond or Jesse Jackson, whose moral authority among most Americans is virtually nil. Under this abysmal leadership, the African-American community is in danger of isolating itself and reviving its own segregation, a somber thought indeed.

5

Cornel West:
Affirmative Action Baby

There are many African-American scholars who are making major contributions in their fields; Cornel West of Harvard is not one of them.[1] In spite of this—even because of it—West is a star in an academic firmament that is progressively left and politically correct. In addition to his professorships in theology and African-American Studies at Harvard, he has been on the faculties of Yale, Princeton and the University of Paris. His income is in the six-figure range, and his books are required texts in college curricula across the nation. Only 46 years old, West has been called—if only by his publisher—"the pre-eminent African-American intellectual of his generation." His work has elicited White House invitations and more requests as a speaker, blurb-writer, and distinguished guest than any individual could possibly fill. In a market in which it is increasingly difficult for genuine scholars to get an academic monograph into print, West has written or edited twenty books issued by commercial publishers—sixteen in the last ten years alone. Even more remarkable, except for two thin volumes of rambling opinions on issues of the day, none of West's books sells sufficiently to justify the commercial support his work has received. They are put into print (as one of his publishers informed me) as "prestige" publications to bring credit to the house.

October 11, 1999, http://www.salon.com/1999/10/11/cornel/
[1] Among them are Thomas Sowell, Walter Williams, Henry Louis Gates, Randall Kennedy, Orlando Patterson, Stephen Carter, William Julius Wilson, and Glenn Loury.

West's first book, published when he was 29 (and old enough to know better), was titled *Prophesy Deliverance! An Afro-American Revolutionary Christianity.* There followed *Prophetic Fragments, The American Evasion of Philosophy, The Ethical Dimensions of Marxist Thought, Prophetic Thought in Postmodern Times, Prophetic Reflections, Keeping Faith* and *Restoring Hope.*

If the subject matter implied by these titles suggests intellectual airiness, their style recalls a Jesse Jackson riff without the rhymes. Thus we learn from notes West has supplied for the new *Cornel West Reader* that "prophesy" (which appears to be his academic specialty) means injecting Marxist clichés into religious dogmas: "These introductory remarks to my second book, *Prophetic Fragments* (1988), convey my moral outrage at the relative indifference of American religion to the challenge of social justice beyond charity." The excerpt from the book that appears in the *Reader* is more explicit: "The principal aim of *Prophetic Fragments* is to examine and explore, delineate and demystify, counter and contest the widespread accommodation of American religion to the political and cultural status quo."

A few years ago, Leon Wieseltier wrote a cover feature for *The New Republic* on West's oeuvre, called "The Decline of the Black Intellectual." West's productions were, in Wieseltier's mortifying words, "monuments to the devastation of a mind by the squalls of theory." Surveying the corpus of West's academic work, Wieseltier concluded that the Alphonse Fletcher, Jr. University Professor at Harvard was an intellectual empty suit whose writing was "noisy, tedious, slippery ... sectarian, humorless, pedantic and self-endeared," and whose works were "almost completely worthless." Gertrude Stein's famous quip about the city of Oakland applies perfectly to West: "there is no there there."

Ironically, it is the very emptiness, even incoherence, of his intellectual persona that West has turned into a career virtue. One of the early catalysts of his rise into the cultural stratosphere was his plea for racial harmony. As a Marxist black radical he was almost unique in saying that it was not appropriate for other black militants to hate all whites and Jews. Yet he has endorsed the radicals grouped around the magazine *Race Traitor*, which calls for the "abolition of whiteness," and is a vocal apologist for two of America's most notorious black race-haters. West is a friend to Louis Farrakhan, the most influential anti-Semite in America. Recently, as Bill Bradley's advisor on blacks, he encouraged the presidential candidate to meet with Al Sharpton (whose own senatorial candidacy West supported). This is the same Sharpton who incited black anti-Semites to boycott a Jewish-owned store in Harlem, which was then torched by a deranged member of the group and set on fire, with seven people killed.

The text of the *Cornel West Reader*, itself a holograph of his iconic place in the PC culture, reads like the diary of an ingénue—breathless with discoveries both real and imagined, particularly the discovery of self. It is as though Georgie Porgie, reincarnated as a Harvard don, had stuck in his thumb and pulled out this plum: "I am a Chekhovian Christian." But what is this? What does it mean? Looking for tangible meaning in West's prose is a discouraging exercise, a bit like looking for a breath of fresh air at the bottom of the sea:

> I am a Chekhovian Christian ... By this I mean that I am
> obsessed with confronting the pervasive evil of unjustified suffer-
> ing and unnecessary social misery.

In other words: What a good boy am I! If we ask why *Chekhov,* and not some other author, however, all we get is a blast of hot air: "I find the incomparable works of Anton Chekhov—the best singular body by a modern artist..." Or, as specifically as West can manage: "[Chekhov's] magisterial depiction of the cold Cosmos, indifferent Nature, crushing Fate and the cruel histories that circumscribe desperate, bored, confused and anxiety-ridden yet love-hungry people, who try to endure against all odds, rings true to me." But what has this to do with Chekhovianism as a genus of Christian faith? It turns out to be above West's mental ceiling to confront the question his juxtaposition begs: How can a Christian universe informed by love and the prospect of redemption be squared with the cold Chekhovian Cosmos, an "indifferent Nature [and] crushing Fate"? Don't strain too many gray cells attempting to answer this.

These philosophical wafflings are accompanied by an intellectual status-seeking worthy of Molière: "Despite my Chekhovian Christian conception of what it means to be human—a view that invokes pre-modern biblical narratives ... I stand in the skeptical Christian tradition of Montaigne, Pascal, and Kierkegaard ... My Chekhovian Christian viewpoint is idiosyncratic and iconoclastic. My sense of the absurdity and incongruity of the world is closer to the Gnosticism of Valentinus, Luria, or Monoimos ... My intellectual lineage goes more through Schopenhauer, Tolstoy, Rilke, Melville, Lorca, Kafka, Celan, Beckett, Soyinka, O'Neill, Kazantzakis, Morrison, and above all, Chekhov.... And, I should add, it reaches its highest expression in Brahms's 'Requiem' and Coltrane's 'A Love Supreme.'" Hard to surpass this as self-parody.

Growing up as a precocious black child in the radical 1960s, West became a black militant activist, president of his senior high-school class, and an inevitable target of liberal uplift. At seventeen he was recruited to Harvard, where his political militancy convinced him that he had more to tell his professors than they had to teach him. He was determined, as he informs us, to press the university and its intellectual traditions into the service of his political agendas and not to have its educational agendas imposed on him. "Owing to my family, church, and the black social movements of the 1960s, I arrived at Harvard unashamed of my African, Christian, and militant de-colonized outlooks. More pointedly, I acknowledged and accented the empowerment of my black styles, mannerisms, and viewpoints, my Christian values of service, love, humility, and struggle, and my anti-colonial sense of self-determination for oppressed people and nations around the world."

This was a crucial moment for what could have been a promising student—the confrontation of a brash but also impressionable youth with a 300-year-old educational institution dedicated to passing on the intellectual traditions of a 3,000-year-old civilization. It was a system that had shaped generations before him. Yet, it was a system that failed Cornel West as its liberal ramparts collapsed before his militancy. In the years West was a student at Harvard, traditional disciplines were being broken down and destroyed, intellectual authority assaulted and deconstructed, and the university transformed into a quasi-political party. New disciplines and even entire institutions were created—ideologically committed Black Studies and Women's Studies departments, paganized theology schools, Marxist and post-Marxist curricula in English and humanities departments. The old and tested rules of scholarship were rejected. Instead of educating and disciplining their intellectual tyro, Harvard and its liberal faculties encouraged his shallow ideological prejudices. It was the PC thing to do for the oppressed. Cornel West's aborted education was a case of what Shelby Steele has analyzed as liberal whites looking for moral absolution and radical blacks looking for the easy way up—and who could blame them or West for that? As a result, the once-promising student never learned the difference between an intellectual argument and a political posture, between a genuine intellectual inquiry and a search for answers that were ideologically correct.

The Cornel West Reader is a testament to the intellectual vacuum that a progressive education creates. The trappings of intellect are in place, the canonical names invoked, the capsule histories recalled, the theories broadly rehearsed. But behind the footnotes and the Latinate prose, the vulgar mind of the activist is feverishly at work. A discourse is produced in which political posturing invariably triumphs over thought.

West's intellectual ruin is not an isolated case. There is a whole generation of racially favored intellectual water flies—bell hooks, Michael Eric Dyson, Robin D.G. Kelley, Patricia Williams, to name a few—whose cultural elevation is not only unrelated to any serious intellectual achievement but has eliminated the possibility of one. For them, as for West, the pathos lies in what might have been. The left-wing university culture has stripped them of an educational opportunity that is given only once per individual lifetime. Meanwhile, the self-appointed social redeemers, whom West thanks for helping him along, are in reality the very people who deprived him of a chance to learn the hard, old-fashioned way, and thus helped to destroy whatever intellectual potential he may once have had.

6

Reverse McCarthyism

Fifty years ago, a demagogue named Joe McCarthy attempted to stifle the discussion of national-policy issues by labeling anyone who deviated from his conservative party line a "Communist," a "pinko" or a "red." Because McCarthy is now despised by our progressive culture, it is probably important to point out that there were indeed Communists and reds in government back then who had treason in their hearts and were working on behalf of America's enemies. But among McCarthy's targets were also Democrats and liberals, whose loyalties to America were genuine. Their real offense was failing to toe the McCarthy line. By recklessly associating those who merely disagreed with him with Communists, McCarthy was able to silence his political opposition.

Today there is a reverse McCarthyism operating in contemporary political debates, which emanates from the political left. The damning label is no longer "Communist" but "racist." Of course there are racists and bigots among us. But these stigmas are used just as the old McCarthy labels were: to threaten those who dissent from the party line. Last year, for example, Democrat Charles Rangel said of Republicans seeking to reform the Social Security system: "Don't you believe that they don't want to dismantle the Social Security system. They are afraid to come out from under their hoods and attack us directly." Rangel's colleague John Lewis

October 25, 1999, http://archive.frontpagemag.com/Printable.aspx?ArtId=24337.

was even less subtle, describing Republicans who wanted welfare reform as "Nazis." Meanwhile the White House's chief advisor on race denounced as a "crime against humanity" an academic book—a book!—showing that economic and educational opportunities for African-Americans had increased more rapidly in the twenty years preceding affirmative action than they have in the twenty years since.[1]

The use of such inflammatory labels can have only one purpose—to intimidate would-be dissenters and silence debate. Who wants to be labeled a Nazi or a racist? Who can afford it? Years ago, Jimmy the Greek lost a $350,000 job as a network sports commentator when he made an off-the-cuff remark that some black leaders attacked as racist. He was summarily fired by the network and never worked again. The same fate was meted out to former Dodger coach Al Campanis, who after eight years was still known to break down in tears of embarrassment and pain when interviewed about the incident. Because the term "racist" has the power to wound and kill it should be used cautiously, especially by those who have the authority to make it credible—minorities themselves.

Recently, I myself was the target of such an attack in the pages of *Time* by an African-American columnist who called me a "bigot."[2] The attack was occasioned by my opposition to an NAACP lawsuit against gun manufacturers and by my suggestion that, while there are racists in America, America itself is not a racist country. That political differences were the true ground of the attacks on me was underscored by a letter to *Time* from NAACP chairman Julian Bond. Bond called me a "60s turncoat" and then added the following smear: "Horowitz may ruminate about being accused of being a closet racist. He need not worry—he's outed himself." In fact, it is Julian Bond and the NAACP leadership who

---

[1] The book was Stephan and Abigail Thernstrom's *America in Black and White*, Simon & Schuster, 1997.
[2] See above, Part II, *Time's Attack*.

are the political turncoats—and racists. It is they who have embraced the same system of race preferences the NAACP opposed back in the 1960s when it was the policy of segregationists in the South. I still believe in the color-blind values of the civil rights movement I supported then. It is Julian Bond and the NAACP leadership who now take the position of George Wallace and Bull Connor, that government should adopt different attitudes towards people on the basis of their skin color. It is the NAACP that now defends the racial boxes in the U.S. census that try to pigeonhole Americans into discrete racial categories. It is conservatives like me who want the federal government to drop all racial categories and recognize that we are a diverse American family of "Cablinasians" and other racial mixtures.[3]

This, I believe, is the reason leftists like Julian Bond reach so readily for the race card in an attempt to silence those of us who disagree with them. They fear the exposure of their hypocrisy and lack of principle, unless we are discredited. The question is whether the rest of the country—black, brown, yellow and white—will continue to go along with them, defending the unsavory past; or whether the American people are ready to march forward, towards a less divisive and more diverse American future.

---

[3] Cablinasian is a Tiger Woods coinage to describe his own mixed racial identity.

7

Throw Away the Key

Y ou could be forgiven for thinking that I'd hired Jesse Jackson to launch his recent campaign as a promotion for my book *Hating Whitey and Other Progressive Causes.*[1] My book is about the moral degeneration of the civil rights movement and its conversion into a hustle designed to keep racism alive. Jackson's campaign was to support the "Decatur 6," a group of lowlife thugs who participated in an orgy of violence at a high-school football game in Decatur, Ill. Their antics, which were apparently a rumble between members of the Gangster Disciples and the Vice Lords, spread panic through the stands and endangered the safety of innocent bystanders, including women and children. When they were expelled by the Decatur school board, Jackson leapt into the fray, referring to them as "our children," while accusing the school board of racism and of barring those children from educational opportunity. Jackson got himself arrested at a November 16 protest organized to demand their return to the school they had terrorized.

Like many other school boards, Decatur's had adopted a policy of zero tolerance for violence in the wake of the Columbine shootings and similar incidents. Discipline—it should go without saying,

Monday, November 22, 1999, http://frontpagemag.com/2010/david-horowitz/david-horowitz%e2%80%99s-archives-throw-away-the-key/print/.; http://www.salon.com/1999/11/22/decatur/.
[1]https://secure.donationreport.com/productlist.html?key=
   DBERMFBVMXYH.

but evidently can't anymore—is an absolutely crucial component of a healthy educational environment. Youngsters who go to school in fear, regardless of race, are not going to be able to focus on their studies. Youngsters who disrespect authority are not going to learn at all. There is no sector of the population that needs to hear and heed this message more than young, inner-city African-American males. One in three among them is a convicted felon. Homicide is their number one cause of death, while the killers are mainly other young African-American males. Restoring social and individual discipline in the inner city by having a zero tolerance for violence is one the most crucial tasks this nation can perform if it wants to increase the opportunities and life expectancies of its most disadvantaged inhabitants.

Yet here is Jesse Jackson in Decatur, breaking the law and getting arrested in support of criminal rioters—attempting to turn gangsters into civil rights heroes. What a message! Jesse Jackson has betrayed the civil rights movement. He has squandered the moral legacy of the movement and turned it into a ritual of blaming whitey for every failure in the African-American community. "The march on Selma had to do with access to voting, equal protection under the law," Jackson admonished the press in Decatur. "The march on Washington: access to public accommodation, equal protection under the law. In Decatur: access to quality education for all children, equal protection under the law."

Like the Orwellian slogan, "Slavery is freedom," this is double-speak. Quality education and equal protection under the law are what the members of the Decatur school board are ably defending. To sustain these principles, it is absolutely imperative that Jesse Jackson remain in a Decatur jail until he has served his time for breaking the law, which in his case is officially and appropriately called "contributing to the delinquency of a minor."

What has happened to the civil rights movement? It has been clear for several decades that civil rights leaders like Jesse Jackson have run out of legitimate causes. From Tawana Brawley to O.J. Simpson, from lawsuits against gun manufacturers (because too many blacks are killing each other), to racial preferences (because some black families do not provide adequate educational support for their children), the civil rights movement has become first a caricature and then an outright betrayal of its former self.

Under the new dispensation, Al Sharpton—anti-Semite, free-lance racist, convicted liar—is now a "civil rights leader," and not just by self-appointment. He is accepted as a legitimate African-American spokesman by Democratic presidential candidates Bradley and Gore, and by First Lady and senatorial aspirant Hillary Clinton. But Sharpton has merely trod the path that Jesse Jackson and others have carved out for him. Jackson and NAACP chief Kweisi Mfume embraced the race-hater Louis Farrakhan even before Sharpton.

What a contrast this turpitude makes to the moral standard set by Martin Luther King. During his lifetime, King would not appear on a public platform beside Malcolm X because of the latter's virulent racism. King was not alone in ostracizing the Nation of Islam leader. NAACP head Roy Wilkins and Urban League President Whitney Young also refused to be associated with the racial demagogue. The purpose of this ostracism was to draw a clear moral line between what the civil rights movement stood for and what it stood against. The civil rights movement had to be as opposed to black racists like Elijah Muhammad and Malcolm X as to racists who were white. It was a matter of principle. In those days, no civil rights leader made excuses for bad behavior by blacks. No civil rights leader invoked "400 years of slavery" to exculpate criminals, or claimed that blacks themselves couldn't be racist, or that juvenile predators were racial victims. In those days, civil rights leaders set down a single standard for all—regardless of race, color or creed.

Their moral stance transformed a nation. Malcolm X himself became a convert. He renounced racism in the last year of his life and King agreed to be photographed with him. This photo has been presented as though their conflict had never taken place. It is part of the movement to erase the distinction that King made. As a result, Malcolm X has been raised to canonic status as a patron saint of the civil rights movement, which he mercilessly attacked until the last year of his life.

This blurring of distinctions between King and Malcolm is a template of the moral disaster that has befallen the civil rights movement under the leadership of epigones like Jackson and Sharpton. Perhaps the most depressing aspect of this dereliction is the absence of prominent dissenting voices within the African-American community (with a handful of marginalized black conservatives excepted). Not since the death of Rep. Barbara Jordan has there been an African-American figure on the left who has had the courage to call this wayward movement to account. In a memorable but un-remembered keynote at the 1984 Democratic Convention she declared:

> We are one, we Americans, we are one. And we reject any intruder who seeks to divide us on the basis of race and color. We must not allow ideas like political correctness to divide us and cause us to reverse hard-won achievements in human rights and civil rights. We reject both white racism and black racism. Our strength in this country is rooted in our diversity—our history bears witness to that fact. *E pluribus unum,* from many one. It was a good idea when the country was founded, and it's a good idea today!

To be sure, there are still plenty of racial incidents that require vigilant public attention. But they are perpetrated by people of all colors and all ethnicities, a fact which may not be readily apparent to those who depend on a media that will only have whitey as the villain. A month ago, for example, even as the trial of Matthew Shepard's allegedly homophobic killer was concluding, two homosexuals—one black, the other white—raped and murdered an adolescent white youngster. There was little or no news coverage of this incident, no national handwringing over a politically incorrect hate crime.

What we need, as Barbara Jordan so eloquently declared, is a single standard for all Americans in judging what is just and what is unjust. If discipline works for white youngsters, it should work for black youngsters as well, Jesse Jackson and his supporters notwithstanding. If it is wrong to hate "people of color" and to scapegoat them for every social problem, it is equally wrong to hate white people and scapegoat them for every problem.

Jesse Jackson is now the leader of the un-civil rights movement. It is the members of the Decatur school board who are the true civil rights heroes. If they can only stand their ground, they will perhaps have produced a turning point in the battle over the nation's current hypocrisy on race. In particular, they will have struck a formidable blow for access to educational quality and to equal protection under the law.

8

Racial Shakedowns

A national football league coach has a mediocre season and is released by the team. Jesse Jackson fires off a letter of protest. In Michigan, a thirteen-year-old murderer faces sentencing as an adult. Al Sharpton flies into the state and holds a press conference accusing racists in the criminal justice system of trying to take "our children." Hollywood launches a new season in which black characters rarely make the cut on the television shows on the big four networks. The NAACP threatens boycotts and two networks agree to racial quotas. The largest "civil rights" demonstration in nearly a decade is organized in South Carolina to protest the flying of a rebel flag.

These recent events have two features in common. First: from the perspective of the civil rights movement they claim as their legacy, they are charades. Second: their only shared purpose is to keep alive the idea that whites are racists and are responsible for the problems of African-Americans. The reality is quite different. The civil rights struggle was won 30 years ago. What passes for civil rights these days is a political shakedown and a racial hustle.

Sixty-five percent of the multi-millionaires on the Green Bay Packers, the football team that fired coach Ray Rhodes, are black. Rhodes had presided over the first season in seven years that the Packers did not make the playoffs. Even Rhodes says he was embarrassed by Jesse Jackson's charge. Al Sharpton notwithstanding, the

November 22, 1999, http://archive.frontpagemag.com/readArticle.aspx?
ARTID=24360.

fact that homicide is a prime killer of young black males is integrally connected to the number of homicides committed *by* young black males. A black person is six times as likely to be the victim of a homicide as a white person, while 94 percent of those who kill blacks are also black. Treating youthful black murderers as adults is not about taking black children away; it's about taking black life seriously. Sharpton has no interest in black children in the inner city, or in anyone except himself.

Is the Confederate flag a symbol of regnant racism? Are the gubernatorial mansions and the legislatures of states whose flags incorporate the Stars and Bars bastions of Confederate diehards who want to keep blacks down? Elements of the Stars and Bars are incorporated into the flags that fly over many state capitols. Among them is Arkansas, which flew the dreaded symbol during the entire twelve years that Bill Clinton was governor. Yet he still enjoys 90 percent support among African-Americans, despite his willingness to fly the rebel symbol when he was governor. The flag means a lot less, evidently, than the current civil rights crowd wants everyone to believe. The national holiday on which the rally against the Confederate flag was held—Martin Luther King Day—is the only day that Americans set aside to honor an individual. Period.

These commotions are not about racism. They are about playing the race card, and a new kind of extortion.

As for Hollywood, the entertainment industry honored the black actress Hattie McDaniel with an Academy Award in 1939, and fifty years ago produced a series of memorable films promoting racial equality. With such films as *Pinky, Home of the Brave, Sergeant Rutledge, The Defiant Ones* and *Guess Who's Coming to Dinner*, Hollywood was a pioneer of the civil rights cause. Twenty years ago, network TV created *Roots*, the most watched television program in history—an eleven-hour epic that portrayed whites as uniformly evil and blacks as long-suffering saints. Yet the NAACP would have Americans believe that liberal Hollywood is a hotbed of racism and practices systematic discrimination against African-Americans.

Not too long ago, I made an appearance on Jesse Jackson's *Both Sides Now* CNN show with *ER* actor Eriq LaSalle. The two black men complained that African-Americans are "locked out" of Hollywood and only get demeaning roles. It was hard not to laugh. LaSalle plays a doctor on *ER* and had just signed a three-year, $27-million contract. Yet, under NAACP threat, NBC and ABC signed quota agreements for black hires because they had a reasonable fear of the damage the NAACP and its followers would do to their business. Now Jackson has set up a shakedown shop in Silicon Valley, home to probably the most racially diversified industry in America. Jackson is demanding that technology firms go out of their way to help promote African-Americans. If they do not, they risk being branded racists. The civil rights movement has become an extortion operation.

Why are the media relatively silent about this malignant charade? The answer seems obvious. Democrats and leftists dominate the media. The race card is the ace-in-the-hole for Democratic and leftist politicians who need 90 percent black support to hold onto their power. That is why Bill Bradley and Hillary Clinton have rushed to kiss the ring of Sharpton, the anti-Semite, convicted liar and racist demagogue. No intelligent person really believes the charges of racism that are being flung about so frivolously in these cases. On the other hand, few are willing to take the risk to say so.

If the race card means power to Democrat politicians, it is cash money to race hustlers like Jackson and Sharpton. Budweiser is currently running commercials featuring black racial stereotypes. Ordinarily, this would be a Jackson two-fer, as Jackson has attacked Anheuser-Busch in the past for a lack of minority ownership among its distributors. But today Jesse Jackson's lips are sealed. Possible reason: Two of Jackson's sons were recently given the No. 1 Budweiser distributorship in Chicago, worth $33 million in annual revenues. And they got it, against all competitors, for almost no cash down. Was this favor to the Jackson sons a form of protection money? You think? Under the leadership of Sharpton and Jackson, the civil rights scam has become a cancer on our body politic. The only cure is to adopt a single standard for all Americans and—to use a phrase of the Sixties—tell it like it is.

9

Racial Killings &
Gun Control

A six-year-old African-American shoots and kills a six-year-old white girl in Michigan. The six-year-old shooter had been suspended earlier for stabbing another child with a pencil. Police discover that he lives in a crack house with his criminal uncle with outstanding warrants for his arrest. The boy's father is in jail. His mother is a drug addict. The Democrat in the White House responds to the tragedy by summoning leaders of Congress to the White House to pass a new law, requiring trigger locks on guns.

If ever there was a case revealing the moral bankruptcy of liberalism (moral idiocy is probably more likely), this might be it. Of course, Clinton and the Democrats are calling for trigger locks on guns because they are planning to make gun control a major Democratic issue in this year's political campaigns. Not a single liberal has publicly dissented from the idea that gun control is the lesson to be drawn from this tragedy, let alone questioned the Democrats' use of it for political ends.

Why would a family of criminals, like the one actually responsible for the murder of Kayla Rolland, obey a trigger-lock law if it were to be passed? The inhabitants of this crack house do not observe laws. They break laws. Child abuse is against the law. The six-year-old murderer in this case was abused by his mother, his criminal father, his criminal uncle, and every criminal adult that

March 3, 2000, http://archive.frontpagemag.com/Printable.aspx?ArtId= 24363; http://www.salon.com/2000/03/06/killing_2/.

entered that crack house. All these crimes are already against the law. Calling for a law to require such parents to put trigger locks on the stolen guns lying around is itself a pathology.

Democrats' use of the interracial killing of a six-year-old to attack lawful gun owners is an exercise in denial—allowing liberals once again to close their eyes to the serious moral problems in the inner city that create these tragedies, and to avoid holding those responsible accountable for their crimes. We don't want to blame the "victims," do we?

These are the important questions in the Michigan killing: 1) Why were authorities unable to rescue the six-year-old murderer from his abusive environment, particularly since he had already shown himself to be a severely disturbed child? 2) Why were the felons in the crack house able to have guns at all, including a shotgun that was stolen? 3) Why did it take the press days to reveal that the shooter was black and his victim white?

This last question is not idle. Days later in Wilkinsburg, Pennsylvania, a black racist named Ronald Taylor went on a rampage that took the lives of three innocent white people, because they were white. It took the FBI three days to charge the killer with a "hate crime." What took so long? Why did the media, which normally jump on "hate crimes," have to wait for the FBI to make this designation? Why is the White House silent about this racial outrage? Why has no black leader denounced it? Where are Al Sharpton, Jesse Jackson and their racially sensitive friends, presidential candidates Bradley and Gore?

The answer is obvious. They're too busy calling for a new gun law to add to the 20,000 already on the books, which the Justice Department refuses to enforce. They're too busy making political hay out of a Confederate flag, which may be offensive to some but hasn't killed anyone so far. Sharpton is too busy persuading black Americans that a New York jury, whose foreman was black, administered "no justice" in the trial of four police officers acquitted of all counts of criminal misconduct in the case of Amadou Diallo, a black Haitian immigrant. If any individual in America could be reasonably held responsible for the distrust and hatred of whites manifested in Ronald Taylor's rampage, it would be Al Sharpton. But it will be a long time before any "liberal" in the media or the Justice Department makes that point. Or drops the double standard that holds black criminals immune from judgment.

Instead, Justice Department officials are meeting with delegations of black leaders and deliberating whether they should invoke the civil rights laws to re-try the acquitted New York policemen. Why is the Justice Department even looking at this case? Is there a shred of evidence that the acquitted policemen were racists? Is there the slightest indication that a jury, which included four African-Americans, was prejudiced? How insulting it is to those four jurors that the Justice Department should even consider this case. What the Justice Department is saying to those four African-American jurors is that they are too stupid, too brainwashed, or too weak to insist on equal protection for a black defendant. Think about that for a moment. This, my friends, is the only really rampant racism in America.

That said, the decision of the FBI to declare the killing in Wilkinsburg a racially motivated crime is admirable. The decision of the press to report the race of the six-year-old killer in Michigan, however belated, is also a step in the right direction. The honesty of the jury in the Amadou Diallo case is praiseworthy.

Perhaps the tide has begun to turn. The next step would be for Jesse Jackson to step forward and publicly denounce the racism of blacks like Ronald Taylor. Perhaps a day will come when academic leftists no longer teach that "blacks can't be racist." Perhaps Harvard will announce a policy dissociating itself from evil doctrines like this that are taught in its classrooms. But don't hold your breath. This battle is a long way from over.

The Lead Investigator
Strikes Back

When I wrote a column about the killing of six-year-old Kayla Rolland and the exploitation of her death by President Clinton and members of the gun-control lobby, the last person I expected to send me an irate e-mail was Arthur Busch, the lead investigator in the case.[1] Least of all did I expect to get a sanctimonious lecture about race-baiting by "so-called experts ... far removed from the reality of life in America." But that is exactly what happened:

> David Horowitz ... is slowly sinking into the muck. He has begun to see almost everything through the prism of race. I led the investigation of the shooting of the six-year-old first grader in Mt. Morris, Michigan. Never once during this investigation did the issue of race ever get raised. Nor for that matter is it any factor whatsoever in this case.
>
> Our community is in pain over this tragedy. If anything it has brought the races together to mourn and to seek answers together. The type of irresponsible race baiting that Mr. Horowitz suggests in his article and in his so-called seminal question of the sordid tale of the death of this little girl is completely beyond the bounds of decency.
>
> By the way, this was his question: "Why did it take the press days to reveal that the shooter was black and his victim white?" I

March 13, 2000, http://archive.frontpagemag.com/Printable.aspx?ArtId=24364; http://www.salon.com/2000/03/13/kayla/.
[1] "Racial Killings & Gun Control," David Horowitz, Front Page Magazine, March 3, 2000, http://archive.frontpagemag.com/readArticle.aspx?ARTID=24363.

say who in the hell cares? Mr. Horowitz proves to me that pundits and so-called experts like him are far removed from the reality of life in America. He is like an orchestra with two instruments: a computer and a lot of racial animosity.

Arthur A. Busch
Genesee County Prosecutor
200 Courthouse
Flint, Michigan 48502

Here is my reply:

Dear Mr. County Prosecutor,
I'm flattered but also not a little concerned that you would take time out from your busy schedule protecting the citizens of Genesee County to wag your finger at me over alleged racial offenses in my piece. If you had time to read what I wrote more carefully, you would see that the part of it that is about Kayla Rolland is not about race but the "moral idiocy of liberalism." Therefore, I am also indebted to you for providing an exemplary instance of this problem.

In point of fact, I never once suggested in my column that the killing of Kayla Rolland was racially motivated. I hope you don't conduct all your prosecutions as irresponsibly as you have this one of me. And let me ask you this. If you never once during your investigation raised the issue of race, how do you know it was never a factor?

I have another question: How come you and your office haven't filed charges against the mother, father, and uncle of the little perpetrator of this tragic deed? Aren't there any laws in Michigan about child abuse? What about the social workers who knew this child was living with criminals in a crack house? Why aren't they under investigation? Since the killer had already stabbed another first grader, why is your office not investigating the school authorities and other public agencies who were obviously derelict in protecting Kayla Rolland, not to mention her little killer?

May I offer a hypothesis? Could it be that the liberalism that guides our municipal agencies has lost a certain moral sense of what is right and wrong, so that it has come to protect offenders like this, bending the old rules to keep what we used to call "delinquents" mainstreamed with their potential victims? *Sixty Minutes* recently featured a current case in which a District Attorney in Alabama is attempting to have a disturbed and malicious youngster (white) removed from the public-school system as a threat to other students. The D.A. is being strenuously opposed by liberal advocates of the "disabled," because the mental dysfunction that makes him a threat to others is, under current civil rights law, legally a "disability" that protects him from "persecution" by oppressors like the District Attorney.

Perhaps something like that happened all along the way in the case you have so superficially investigated to protect the killer and to expose Kayla Rolland's memory to attack. But of course that is no concern of yours. You are too busy protecting the whole mess (including your dereliction of duty) from politically incorrect busybodies like me.

One reason I asked the question as to why the press was so color-blind in this case was that I couldn't imagine a parallel situation where a little black girl in a class with an overwhelming majority of white students had been shot by a white youngster and the press would have no interest in that fact. Particularly since the killer had committed a violent act against another student previously. By the way, did you or any of your investigators bother to inquire about the race of the previous victim?

My second reason for introducing the issue of race is the way in which the dysfunctionality of the perpetrator's family was allowed to disappear from all radar screens as the tragedy was transformed by President Clinton and others into a poster case for the new trigger-lock gun law. You will remember that I asked how a family of outlaws, with stolen guns in their crack house dwelling, was going to be impressed by a new law about triggers. It seemed like a reasonable question to me. Just as it seems reasonable to me to wonder whether law enforcement's willingness to allow a bunch of criminals to have their way with two small children (the shooter and his eight-year-old brother) had anything at all to do with the fact that they were black. The same question could be put to the social workers. Social workers, as is well known, are often guided by a left-wing worldview that causes them to treat dysfunctional people who happen to be "of color" as victims of oppression who need to be protected rather than, well, as dysfunctional people who may be threats to themselves and everyone else.

Even though I did not once suggest that the killing of Kayla Rolland was racially motivated, do you really think that had the colors been reversed you and your investigators would have no interest in the question itself? Particularly if Al Sharpton had arrived on the scene to put the question to you? Perhaps that is because the existence of white racism is a cliché, while the existence of black racism is a taboo.

I suggest you take some time to consider these facts and these questions, and then think about putting your own house of law in order before you go lecturing the rest of us about denial and moral issues that are probably over your head.

Yours sincerely,
David Horowitz

Deafening Silence

Y ou probably don't remember the name Ronald Taylor, and you probably think you have never heard of John Kroll or Joseph Healy or Emil Sanielevici. Why should you? The last three gentlemen were the white victims of black racist Ronald Taylor in Wilkinsburg, Pennsylvania, just a couple of weeks ago. The story made the front pages for about a day. And then just as suddenly it fell off the nation's radar screen. However, I will bet you can identify Matthew Shepard or James Byrd or Buford Furrow or, for that matter, Tawana Brawley. These respectively were the victims, perpetrator and phony victim of politically correct crimes in which all the actors assumed roles that confirmed the prejudices of our liberal elites.

Taylor, a resident of publicly subsidized housing, recently became incensed at maintenance workers trying to fix the door to his apartment. "You're all white trash, racist pigs," he exploded. "You're dead." He then went on a rampage that killed Kroll, Healy and Sanielevici, and critically wounded two others. When the FBI searched his apartment they found anti-Semitic, anti-Asian, anti-Italian and anti-white hate literature.

Taylor's crime did not confirm the nation's most protected racial prejudices, and that is why his criminal acts have been pushed so quickly out of sight. We get no *Time* and *Newsweek*

March 15, 2000, http://archive.frontpagemag.com/Printable.aspx?ArtId= 24366.

cover stories about Taylor, no network features about black racism, no White House press conferences to berate the nation, no Capitol Hill resolutions authored by Democratic representatives like Barney Frank and Maxine Waters to condemn the outrage, and no calls for hate-crime legislation that specifically includes endangered white males.

To these indicators, let me add a personal note. As author of a best-selling biography on the Kennedys, I am familiar enough to the media so that every time a Kennedy kills himself (or someone else) I get calls from a dozen shows at the networks, the cable channels and even the *BBC* to come on as an expert commentator. But even though I have a current book in stores called *Hating Whitey & Other Progressive Causes*, which is high up on Amazon's best-seller list, I have yet to receive a single interview request to talk about this hate-whitey crime.[1]

Even more striking perhaps than the media blackouts are the racial comments from the few black spokespeople who have actually acknowledged that the crime had such a dimension. The Rev. Thelma C. Mitchell, pastor at the Wilkinsburg Baptist Church, told her congregation in a "healing" service: "You cannot run from violence in the United States because the United States was founded on violence. Why are we suddenly shocked, brothers and sisters? The whole concept of racism and prejudice and targeting people, this is not a new game. Although I in no way agree with the methods he used, I suspect Mr. Taylor really did reflect a growing frustration in this community because too many African-American young men cannot find a meaningful job." In other words, the white devil made him do it.

Far from being an extreme example, this kind of formulation functions as a mainstream excuse in the black community for the racial outrages committed by its members. Dr. Alvin Poussaint, a Harvard professor and one of the media's most quoted experts on

---

[1] https://secure.donationreport.com/productlist.html?key=
DBERMFBVMXYH.

the psychology of racism, is a case in point. Poussaint managed to identify Taylor's act as a case of "extreme racism." But in an interview with *The Washington Times* on March 3, Poussaint also speculated that the shooter may have gained a "generalized hatred toward all whites" from his personal experiences. *The Times* reported: "He [Poussaint] wondered whether the suspect was 'abused' by a white authority figure, such as a boss or a police officer. 'Or was he stopped for racial profiling,' he asked." In other words, the white devil made him do it.

According to Ronald Hampton, executive director of the National Black Police Association in Washington D.C., only the white devil can be racist. Questioned about the killings, Hampton told *The Times:* "It's impossible for blacks to practice racism on whites. Racism is the sum total of prejudice and power ... and blacks don't have power in our society." Tell that to Taylor's three dead victims.

An entire industry devoted to promoting anti-white racism has flourished for decades at elite institutions like Princeton and Harvard. In its view, blacks can only be victims and whites only oppressors. This is an academic version of the Johnnie Cochran School of Racial Litigation: indict America as racist, and let the culprit go free. Among some segments of the black community, "anti-white feelings ... are not unusual," Poussaint conceded to *The Washington Times.* "Blacks who have such feelings against whites may feel justified, because during slavery and segregation, a collection of whites kept them down."

Now imagine if white professors talked in similar tones about the racists who dragged James Byrd to his death: "When asked about the lynching of Byrd, Dr. Poussaint of Harvard acknowledged that it was a case of 'extreme racism' but wondered whether the suspects had been previously 'abused' by a black authority figure such as a boss or a police officer." What if this hypothetical Poussaint noted that blacks commit nearly half the violent crimes in the United States—many of them involving whites as victims—but speculated that whites who have feelings of hatred against blacks "may feel justified"? What would we think of Dr. Poussaint if he had said that?

The tragic deaths in Wilkinsburg have sparked at least one response from within the black left that gives cause for some hope. In a column appearing in *Salon,* Earl Ofari Hutchinson has struck exactly the right note to restore moral balance in the black community.[2] Noting the "deafening silence by blacks" about this racial outrage, Hutchinson wrote: "Blacks must mourn these murders as passionately as they do those of black victims of white attacks and just as passionately call for the harshest punishment of the killer(s)." Amen to that.

---

[2] "Why Are Black Leaders Silent on Black Hate Crimes?," Earl Ofari Hutchinson, *Salon,* March 6, 2000, http://www.salon.com/2000/03/06/hate_6/.

No Reason to Glorify
the Left's Legacy of Violence

The capture of Jamil Abdullah Al-Amin, a.k.a. H. Rap Brown, in Lowndes County, Alabama, marks the close of two eras in the history of American race relations. Both may be said to have begun in the place where U.S. law enforcement officials last week apprehended Al-Amin and ended a massive manhunt for the killer of sheriff's deputy Richard Kinchen, who had been gunned down in a vicious ambush almost a week earlier, in Atlanta.

Al-Amin had fled to the rural community where he had begun his political career in the early Sixties as a member of Stokely Carmichael's Student Non-Violent Coordinating Committee. In 1964, he and Carmichael were key activists in the Lowndes County Freedom Organization, a nonviolent Christian group that tried to put black candidates on the ballot under new civil rights laws, which that very year had put an end to the era of segregation.

The emblem of the Lowndes County Freedom Organization was a black panther. Odd for a Christian electoral effort, the panther symbol was soon to inspire a group of urban gang members in Oakland, California, led by Huey Newton. Newton called his group the Black Panther Party, a violent, radical paramilitary organization that quickly became the favorite vanguard of the New Left. Tom Hayden even christened the Panthers "America's

March 26, 2000, http://archive.frontpagemag.com/Printable.aspx?ArtId= 24367.

Vietcong," reflecting the political fantasies of Sixties radicals who considered themselves at war with America.

In 1968, at Newton's invitation, leaders of the Student Non-Violent Coordinating Committee were inducted into the Panthers. H. Rap Brown, whose path-breaking use of violent rhetoric had given him national notoriety, briefly became the Panthers' "Minister of Justice." The alliance was Newton's attempt to unite his political gang with the organization whose symbol he had appropriated. By then Carmichael and Brown had become national figures, Young Turks in the civil rights movement who were dissatisfied with the extraordinary victories the movement had peacefully achieved. Carmichael and Brown turned their backs on nonviolence and integration, derided the leadership of the Rev. Martin Luther King, Jr., and preached instead a gospel of "black power" and armed revolution. "Violence," Brown declared in the only statement for which he is known, "is as American as cherry pie." Cheered on by the mostly white radical New Left, Brown and Carmichael reviled King as an "Uncle Tom" and set themselves on a course of confrontation and violence and—above all—rejection of the American system into which King sought inclusion for black Americans.

The negative impact of the radical black left, which Newton, Brown, and Carmichael inspired over the years, can hardly be overestimated. It spawned a generation of violent rage and separatism and a legacy of black racism, which tarnished the legacy of the civil rights movement and is still with us today. Calling himself "Servant of the People," Newton extorted Oakland's inner-city community, conducting shakedown operations of local "after-hours" clubs and other illegal activities. His death came at the hands of a crack dealer he had burned.

As soon as the Sixties were over, Carmichael left the country to live as a courtier of the dictator Sékou Touré, whose brutal rule caused 250,000 Guinean citizens to flee their West African homeland. Carmichael changed his name to "Kwame Ture," thus honoring two dictators, Touré and Kwame Nkrumah. After more than a decade in exile, he returned to America to become a follower of Louis Farrakhan and a spewer of anti-American bile and racial hate.

H. Rap Brown spent the first five years of the Seventies in jail. His violent rages, dressed up as "political protest," had landed him a prison term for attempted armed robbery. (Lesser charges for inciting a riot were not prosecuted.) He emerged from confinement to become a religious Muslim, an Imam of his own mosque, and leader of his own personal cult among drug addicts and the homeless in Atlanta's West End.

Many will shrink from the cold look that these lives deserve. They will talk of the "idealism" that was once present and is now lost. Thus, in an article for *Netnoir*,[1] a black webzine, Earl Ofari Hutchinson wrote: "[Brown's] capture will almost certainly trigger another round of media reflection on how he, the Panthers, and other 1960s black radicals drowned the genuine idealism and passion for social change of thousands of blacks in an ocean of selfishness, greed, opportunism, and nihilistic violence. Some of this will be true, but what it misses is the sacrifice and struggle of thousands of men and women against injustice. And for a time that certainly included Brown."

My own view is somewhat different. I don't think there is any chance that either the media or the American public will forget or cease to honor the idealism of the old civil rights movement. What they will take from Al-Amin's criminal trajectory is a lesson about the radicalism that derailed the movement and rationalized hate. The violent conclusion of Brown's political career will be correctly taken as symbolic of the bankruptcy of the revolutionary left in the context of America's remarkably open and opportunity-rich society.

The hapless victim of Al-Amin's alleged crime was an officer of the law who led an exemplary life and who was black. The chief of

---

[1] http://www.aboutus.org/NetNoir.com.

the Atlanta Police Department, which led the hunt for the killer, is black and female. Atlanta, once the heart of the slaveholding Confederacy, is today the center of the liberated New South, itself a tribute to the triumphant moral crusade of King, the leader who preached nonviolence and integration, and whom Brown, Carmichael, and Newton temporarily displaced and tried in vain to discredit and destroy. It is King's legacy that has triumphed. The rule of law is now a rule that not only includes black Americans as King dreamed, but is enforced by black Americans as well.

What Hillary Clinton Won't Say

This year Democrats are demonstrating a talent for political fiction exceeding even the writers of *The West Wing.* Casting Al Gore as a campaign-finance reformer is one example. Posing as champions of fiscal discipline is another. Of course, Democratic spin artists benefit from the support of a shamelessly partisan journalistic fraternity that helps make their fictions credible. But to really appreciate the Democrats' literary license one has to go to the Big Apple, where Hillary Clinton and her race-baiting collaborators, the Reverends Al Sharpton and Jesse Jackson, have contrived a political melodrama to provide the emotional backdrop for the lynching of a socially liberal mayor. For seven years Rudy Giuliani has crusaded to increase the safety and well being of New Yorkers, and especially of inner city minorities. But in the past few months the Sharptonite Democrats have managed to cast Giuliani as a latter-day Bull Connor—a Yankee redneck deploying a thin blue line of racist thugs against defenseless communities of color.

The most recent episode in this ugly charade was kicked off by the left's predictable reaction to the accidental (and statistically rare) shooting of Patrick Dorismond, an unarmed man of Haitian descent. A week earlier, the physically imposing Dorismond had beaten his ex-girlfriend so badly she had called the police. According to witnesses, Dorismond—who had been previously arrested

April 3, 2000, http://archive.frontpagemag.com/Printable.aspx?ArtId= 24368; http://www.salon.com/2000/04/03/democrats_23/.

for drug buys—attacked an undercover squad of New York police officers as they were attempting to conduct a sting operation against drug dealers in a high-crime Manhattan neighborhood. Dorismond was shot by a Hispanic officer named Anthony Vasquez, who reacted out of fear for the life of a fellow officer under attack. Unfortunately, Dorismond died from his wounds.

A dead man can be useful to a lynch mob. The image of a young life lost enabled agitators to work the Haitian community into a frenzy of grief, paranoia, and revenge. At a protest meeting, Harlem religious leader, political powerbroker and all-seasons incendiary, the Reverend Calvin Butts, ranted, "White man go to hell!"—even though all the cops involved in the incident were Hispanic. Sharpton incited people to shut down the city to gain "Justice for Patrick" and helped to turn his funeral into an anti-police riot. Jesse Jackson descended on New York to call the shooting a murder and to compare it to the racist killings of nonviolent civil rights workers in the 1960s. Recently, Jackson has seemed to be on a perverse mission to discredit every last memory of that movement.

The press, of course, exhibited no concern that Jackson was condemning the accused officer in advance of the evidence. Jackson was accompanied by his new friend, lifelong thug and twice-convicted triple-murderer Rubin Carter. Carter is, inevitably, the subject of a recent Hollywood film falsely exonerating him and maliciously defaming a white police officer who, it preposterously alleges, pursued Carter from childhood just because he was black.

Arranging the scenery on the Big Apple stage were Hillary and Bill, America's dysfunctional couple. While lending her support to the lynchers, Hillary was careful to defer to Jackson in prosecuting the accused. She did not repeat her mistake in the recent case of Amadou Diallo, whose shooting death she had labeled "murder" before a jury could deliver its verdict exonerating the officers of any criminal intention or act. Not that the verdict had caused Mrs. Clinton the slightest qualm of conscience or produced the hint of a second thought. Not a word of disapproval has escaped her lips about Sharpton's outrageous crusade for a federal indictment of the acquitted officers over the same incident.

In this and other cases, Sharpton has played the role of a racist Javert. For ten years, he publicly harassed the innocent Steven Pagones with the malicious false accusations of Tawana Brawley. Now Democrats have added to Sharpton's fires by calling on the Attorney General to investigate the New York Police Department. If he proceeds to do so, it will dramatize the Democrats' insinuation that Republican mayors and Hispanic policemen are homicidal racists engaged in a conspiracy to kill innocent blacks during an election year.

Is there a liberal left in America that cares any longer about the facts? I'm not referring to the facts in the Dorismond case because nobody, except those who were present or who have read the sealed eyewitness accounts, knows what they are. Honesty would require all others to admit that they are expressing an ideological bias or proceeding from instinct based on prior experience. So let's look at that experience. In 1993, the last year that African-American David Dinkins was mayor of New York, there were 212 intentional police shootings of civilians, many of them African-Americans. This compares to only 73 shootings by the Giuliani police force in the past year. In 1991, during Dinkins's reign, there were 41 fatalities resulting from police shootings. In 1999, under Giuliani, there were only 11. Yet at no time during Dinkins's reign did the socially conscious demand that the Justice Department step in to end the epidemic of "police brutality" or the incompetence of the mayor's administration. There has been no mention of this hypocrisy in the press. Might this be because Dinkins is a Democrat, a leftist, and black?

We have all been exposed to the fiction the liberal lynch mob and its media allies have concocted about the callousness of the Giuliani police toward minorities in New York. Here's the reality. Last year there were only 417 shots fired by the Giuliani police in a city of eight million, which before his election had had one of the highest crime rates in the world. In Dinkins's last year, police fired 965 shots at the public—more than twice that number.

Here's an even more striking statistic. Under the Dinkins administration, during which Sharpton led no funeral riots against police (although he did incite one against Hasidic Jews), there were 2,350 murders in New York. Under Giuliani, the figure has dropped to 635. That means 1,700 people in New York, likely more than half of them Hispanic and black, are alive today because of the compassion, concern and competence of the Giuliani police department. And the lives of hundreds of thousands of people of all races in New York are safer, better, and richer because of the vigilance and concern of the Giuliani administration, which is under such vicious and groundless attack by Hillary Clinton and the Democrats.

This is ultimately the most damning evidence of the hypocritical racism of the civil rights left, and of its blood lust for the men and women who risk their lives defending the people's safety. If the Jesse Jacksons and the Hillary Clintons cared as much about the lives of inner-city blacks as they do about their own political power and privileges, they would long ago have been singing the praises of Giuliani. Homicide is the number-one killer of young black males in urban America, and Giuliani has reduced the homicides of African-American males in New York by 75 percent. But Jackson, Hillary Clinton and their pals are not Giuliani fans. They are his sworn enemies and detractors. The bottom line is that they don't care. For the sake of their political futures, they are far readier to defend murderers like Rubin Carter than to support those who risk their lives to apprehend his ilk.

In one of those odd synchronicities of events, Jackson's friend and one-time comrade Jamil Abdullah Al-Amin, better known by his 1960s radical trademark name H. Rap Brown, assaulted and killed a black police officer, Ricky Kinchen, and wounded another officer in Atlanta on the very day that Patrick Dorismond was shot in New York. Unlike the officers in the Dorismond case, there can be little doubt that Brown killed in cold blood. Brown was identified as the killer by the black officer he wounded. Neither officer knew his political identity. The murder weapon was found at the site of his capture. The officers were victims of an unprovoked and vicious attack with a high-powered assault weapon against which their protective vests proved useless. They didn't have a chance.

Yet, the other night Geraldo Rivera was on television entertaining former Black Panther lawyer Gerald Lefcourt and former Panther chairman Bobby Seale, soliciting their opinions of the event. Since both men have been lying about the Panthers' criminal activities for 30 years, it was no surprise to hear them once again rehearse their stale tales of "Cointelpro" conspiracies against black leaders in order to insinuate that there just might have been a police vendetta to hunt down Rap Brown. It occurred to me, watching this sordid and sickeningly familiar performance, that in recent decades many lives have been lost (both white and black) and many more will continue to be lost as a result of the anti-police paranoia whose flames are fanned by demagogues like Jackson, Seale, Sharpton, and Hillary Clinton. It occurred to me further that it would be a good moment for this country if, just once, the press would step out of its partisan lockstep to call them to account.

PART IV

Reparations for Slavery

Ten Reasons Why
Reparations Are a Bad Idea

It began as a fringe proposition favored by the politically extreme. But the idea that taxpayers should pay reparations to black Americans for the damages of slavery and segregation is no longer a fixation of the political margin. It is fast becoming the next big "civil rights" thing. Rep. John Conyers, D-Mich., has already introduced legislation to set up a commission that would examine the impact of slavery as a foreordained prelude to a legislated payback. (Conyers will become chairman of the Judiciary Committee should the Democrats win back the House.[1]) A coalition of African-Americans is claiming a debt of $4.1 trillion. A coalition of African nations is claiming a debt of $777 trillion against an assortment of governments including the United States.

Distinguished black intellectuals like Henry Louis Gates have given the idea their imprimatur; while Randall Robinson, who led the successful boycott movement against South Africa a decade ago, has written a strident anti-white, anti-American manifesto called *The Debt: What America Owes to Blacks*, which has become a bible of the reparations cause.

Nor is it just in the realm of ideas that the payback demand is gaining ground. Last week, the Chicago City Council voted 46–1

Originally titled, "10 Reasons Why Reparations Are a Bad Idea for Blacks and Racist Too," May 30, 2000. This was my first statement of a position on this subject, and it appeared without objection from the editors in the leftwing magazine Salon.com. http://www.salon.com/2000/05/30/reparations; http://archive.frontpagemag.com/Printable.aspx?ArtId=24372.
[1] Which they did in 2006.

in favor of a reparations resolution. The lopsided nature of the vote persuaded Mayor Richard Daley to apologize for slavery (in Chicago?), thus joining what has become a familiar and unseemly ritual of contrition for the Clinton-era left. The primary sponsor of the resolution, Alderwoman Dorothy Tillman, has announced she is going to organize a "national convention" to push the issue of reparations in the coming year.

So what is wrong with the idea? In truth, just about everything. Examined closely, the claim for reparations is factually tendentious, morally incoherent and racially incendiary. Logically, it has about as much substance as the suggestion that O.J. Simpson should have been acquitted because of past racism by the criminal courts. Its impact on race relations and on the self-isolation of the African-American community is likely to be even worse.

If the reparations idea continues to gain traction, its most obvious effect will be to intensify ethnic antagonisms and generate new levels of racial resentment. It will further alienate African-Americans from their American roots and further isolate them from all of America's other communities who are themselves blameless in the grievance of slavery, who cannot be held culpable for racial segregation and who, in fact, have made significant contributions to ending discrimination and redressing any lingering injustice.

1. Assuming there is actually a debt, it is not at all clear who owes it. Tillman articulated the argument for the existence of the debt this way: "America owes blacks a debt because when we built this country on free labor ... wealth was handed down to the white community." Robinson reaches back in time even further: "Well before the birth of our country, Europe and the eventual United States perpetrated a heinous wrong against the peoples of Africa and benefited from the wrong through the continuing exploitation of Africa's human and material resources." To sustain this claim, Robinson devotes entire sections of his book to the alleged depredations of whites against blacks hundreds and even thousands of

years before the "eventual United States"—i.e., the government that is expected to pay the reparations—was even created. It is necessary to insert the qualifier "alleged" because, like so many who wave the bloody shirt, Robinson makes little effort to establish causal responsibilities, but invokes any suffering of blacks to which whites were proximate as evidence that whites were to blame.

Slavery itself is the most obvious example. It was not whites but black Africans who first enslaved their brothers and sisters. They were abetted by dark-skinned Arabs (since Robinson and his allies force us into this unpleasant mode of racial discourse) who organized the slave trade. Are reparations going to be assessed against the descendants of Africans and Arabs for their role in slavery? There were also 3,000 black slaveholders in the antebellum United States. Are reparations to be paid by their descendants, too?

2. The idea that only whites benefited from slavery is factually wrong and attitudinally racist. By accusing the U.S. government of crimes against black people in advance of its existence, Robinson reveals the ugly anti-white racism beneath the surface of many arguments for reparations, especially his. According to this line of reasoning, only white Americans are implicated in slavery, just as only whites are the presumed targets of the reparations payback. Both presumptions are wrong.

If slave labor created wealth for all Americans, then obviously it created wealth for black Americans as well, including the descendants of slaves. Free blacks in the antebellum United States surely benefited from the free labor of slaves, along with whites. Are they to be exempted from payment of the debt just because they are black?

But if the "free labor" argument of the reparations claimants is correct, even the descendants of slaves have benefited from slavery. The GNP of black America (as black separatists constantly remind their followers) is so large that it makes the African-

American community the 10th most prosperous "nation" in the world. To translate this into individual realities, American blacks on average enjoy per capita incomes in the range of 20 to 50 times those of blacks living in any of the African nations from which their forbears were kidnapped.

What about this benefit of slavery? Are the reparations proponents going to make black descendants of slaves pay themselves for benefiting from the fruits of their ancestors' servitude?

3. In terms of lineal responsibility for slavery, only a tiny minority of Americans ever owned slaves. This is true even for those who lived in the antebellum South, where only one white in five was a slaveholder. Why should the descendants of non-slaveholding whites owe a debt? What about the descendants of the 350,000 Union soldiers who died in the war that freed the slaves? They gave their lives. What possible morality would ask their descendants to pay again?

4. Most Americans living today (whites and others) are the descendants of post-Civil War immigrants, who have no lineal connection to slavery at all. The two great waves of American immigration occurred after 1880 and after 1960. Is there an argument worth considering that would, for example, make Jews (who were cowering in the ghettos of Europe at the time) or Mexicans and Cubans (who were suffering under the heel of Spain) responsible for this crime? What reason could there be that Vietnamese boat people, Russian refuseniks, Iranian refugees, Armenian victims of the Turks, or Greek, Polish, Hungarian and Korean victims of communism should pay reparations to American blacks? There is no reason, and no proponent of reparations has even bothered to come up with one.

5. The historical precedents generally invoked to justify the reparations claim—that Jews and Japanese Americans received reparations from Germany and the United States, respectively—are

spurious. The circumstances involved bear no resemblance to the situation of American blacks, and are not really precedents at all. The Jews and Japanese Americans who received reparations were individuals who actually suffered the hurt.

Jews do not receive reparations from Germany simply because they are Jews. Those who do were corralled into concentration camps and lost immediate family members or personal property. Nor have all Japanese Americans received payments, but only those whom the government interned in camps and who had their property confiscated. The reparations claims being advanced by black leaders seem to imply that the only qualification required for reparations is the color of one's skin. Robinson's book is pointedly subtitled "What America Owes to Blacks." If this is not racism, what is?

6. Behind the reparations campaign lies the unfounded claim that all blacks in America suffer economically from the consequences of slavery and discrimination. It would seem a hard case to prove over a 150-year (or even 50-year) span, and the only evidence really offered by the claimants is the existence of contemporary "income disparities" and "inequalities" between the races. No actual connection (as far as they're concerned) need be made. On the other hand, African-American success stories that contradict the conclusion are abruptly dismissed.

Thus, to take the most obvious case, Oprah Winfrey may have been a sharecropper's daughter in the most segregated of all Southern states, but—victim of slavery and segregation—she was still able to become one of the 400 richest individuals in America on the strength of her appeal to white consumers. This extraordinary achievement, which refutes the reparations argument, is echoed in millions of other, more modest success stories, including those of all the prominent promoters of the reparations claim, even the unhappy Robinson. No wonder the only counter to these obvious facts is that all successes must be exceptions to the (politically correct) rule.

But the reality is that this black middle class—composed exclusively of descendants of slaves—is also a very prosperous middle class that is now larger in absolute terms than the black underclass, which is really the only segment of the black population that can be made to fit the case. Is this black middle-class majority—numbering millions of individuals—really just a collective exception of unusual people? Or does its existence not suggest that the failures of the black underclass are failures of individual character, hardly (if at all) impacted by the lingering aftereffects of racial discrimination, let alone a slave system that ceased to exist well over a century ago?

West Indian blacks in America are also descended from slaves, but their average incomes are equivalent to the average incomes of whites (and nearly 25 percent higher than the average incomes of American-born blacks). How is it that slavery adversely affected one large group of descendants but not the other? And how can government be expected to decide an issue that is so subjective—yet so critical—to the case? The fact is that nobody has demonstrated any clearly defined causal connection between slavery or discrimination and the "disparities" that are alleged to require restitution.

And how, by the way, are blue-collar whites and ethnics expected to understand their reparations payments to these African-American doctors, lawyers, executives and military officers who make up the black middle class?

7. The renewed sense of grievance—which is what the claim for reparations will inevitably create—is neither a constructive nor a helpful message for black leaders to be sending to their communities. Virtually every group that has sought refuge in America has grievances to remember. For millions of recent immigrants, the suffering is only years behind them, and can be as serious as ethnic cleansing or genocide.

How are these people going to take the payment claims from African-Americans whose comparable suffering lies in the distant past? Won't they see this demand as just another claim for special treatment, for a rather extravagant new handout that is only necessary because some blacks can't seem to locate the ladder of opportunity within reach of others, many of whom are even less privileged than they are? Why can a penniless Mexican, who is here illegally and doesn't even speak English, find work in America's inner cities while blacks cannot? Can 19th-century slavery or even the segregation of 50 years ago really explain this?

To focus the social passions of African-Americans on what some Americans did to their ancestors 50 or 150 years ago is to burden this community with a crippling sense of victimhood. It is also to create a new source of conflict with other communities.

A young black intellectual wrote the following comments about reparations: "I think the reparations issue will be healthy. It will show all Americans (white, Hispanic, Asian) how much blacks contributed to helping build this country." Actually, as Robinson's book makes clear, what it will accomplish is just the opposite. It will provide black leaders with a platform from which to complain about all the negative aspects of black life—to emphasize inner-city pathologies and failures, and to blame whites, Hispanics and Asians for causing them.

How is this going to impress other communities? It's really just a prescription for sowing more racial resentment and creating even greater antagonism.

8. This raises a point that has previously remained off the radar screen, but will surely be part of the debate to come: What about the "reparations" to blacks that have already been paid? Since the passage of the Civil Rights Acts and the advent of the Great Society in 1965, trillions of dollars in transfer payments have been made to African-Americans in the form of welfare benefits and racial preferences (in contracts, job placements and educational admissions)—all under the rationale of redressing historical racial grievances.

In fact, reparations advocates already have an answer to this argument, and it is a revealing one. Here is how Robinson refers to this massive generosity and contrition on the part of the white political majority in America during the past 35 years: "It was only in 1965 ... that the United States enacted the Voting Rights Act. Virtually simultaneously, however, it began to walk away from the social wreckage that centuries of white hegemony had wrought." Take that, white, Hispanic and Asian America! If a multi-trillion-dollar restitution and wholesale rewriting of American law and fundamental American principle in order to accommodate racial preferences and redress injustice are nothing, then what will fill the claimants' bill?

9. And this raises another question that black leaders might do well to reflect on: What about the debt blacks owe to America—to white Americans—for liberating them from slavery? This may not seem like a serious question to some, but that only reveals their ignorance of the history of slavery and its fate. Slavery existed for thousands of years before the Atlantic slave trade was born, in virtually all societies. But in the 1,000 years of its existence, there never was an anti-slavery movement until white Englishmen and Americans created one. If not for the anti-slavery attitudes and military power of white Englishmen and Americans, the slave trade would not have ended. If not for the sacrifices of white soldiers and a white American president who gave his life to sign the Emancipation Proclamation, blacks in America would have remained slaves indefinitely.

If not for the dedication of Americans of all ethnicities and colors to a society based on the principle that all men are created equal, blacks in America would not enjoy the highest standard of living of blacks anywhere in the world, and indeed one of the highest standards of living of any people in the world. They would not enjoy the greatest freedoms and the most thoroughly protected individual rights. Where is the gratitude of black America and its leaders for those gifts?

10. The final and summary reason for rejecting any reparations claim is recognition of the enormous privileges black Americans enjoy as Americans, and therefore of their own stake in America's history, slavery and all.

Blacks were here before the Mayflower. Who is more American than the descendants of African slaves? For the African-American community to isolate itself even further from America would be to embark on a course whose consequences are troublesome to contemplate. Yet the black community has had a long-running flirtation with separatists and nationalists in its ranks who must be called what they are: racists who want African-Americans to have no part of America's multiethnic social contract. This separatist strain in black America's consciousness has now been joined with the anti-Americanism of the political left to form the animating force behind the reparations movement.

In this regard, Robinson—himself a political leftist—is a movement archetype. Anti-white sentiments and anti-American feelings stand out on every page of *The Debt*, including a chapter he devotes to praising Fidel Castro, one of the world's longest-surviving and most sadistic dictators. A rhapsody for Fidel Castro's Marxist police state would seem a bizarre irrelevance to a book on reparations for American blacks—except that, for Robinson, Castro is a quintessential victim of American "oppression." Robinson despises America that much. "Many blacks—most perhaps," he asserts in his discussion of Castro, "don't like America." Is Robinson saying they prefer Castro's gulag?

This unthinking, virulent anti-Americanism is the crux of the problem the reparations movement poses for black Americans, and for all Americans. The reparations idea is about not liking America. It is about an irrational hatred of America. It is about holding America responsible for every negative facet of black existence, as though America were God and God had failed. Above all, it is about denying the gift America has given to all of its citizens through the inspired genius of its founding.

In Robinson's view, Thomas Jefferson, author of the proclamation that "all men are created equal," was merely "a slave owner, a racist and—if one accepts that consent cannot be given if it cannot be denied—a rapist." The fact that Americans still honor the author of the Declaration of Independence makes his personal sins into archetypes that define America, according to Robinson: "Does not the continued un-remarked American deification of Jefferson tell us all how profoundly contemptuous of black sensibilities American society persists in being? How deeply, stubbornly, poisonously racist our society to this day remains?"

This hatred for America, specifically for white America, blinds Robinson—and those who think like him—to a truth far more important than Jefferson's dalliance with Sally Hemings, which may or may not have been unwilling. (Contrary to Robinson, consent obviously can be given even when it cannot be denied.) For it is the words Jefferson wrote, and that white Americans died for, which accomplished what no black African did. They set Robinson's ancestors free.

For all their country's faults, African-Americans have an enormous stake in America and above all in the heritage that men like Jefferson helped to shape. This heritage—enshrined in America's founding and the institutions and ideas to which it gave rise—is what is really under attack in the reparations movement. This assault on America, conducted by racial separatists and the political left, is an attack not only on white Americans but on all Americans—African-Americans especially.

America's black citizens are the richest and most privileged black people alive—a bounty that is a direct result of the heritage that is under attack. The American idea needs the support of its African-American citizens. But African-Americans also need the support of the American idea.

Dredging up a new reason to assault this idea is not in the interest of African-Americans. What would serve the African-American community better would be to reject the political left as represented by people like Randall Robinson, Jesse Jackson and every black leader who endorses this claim. What African-Americans need is to embrace America as their home and to defend its good: the principles and institutions that have set them—and all of us—free.

2

Reparations Are Still a Bad Idea

"Does Oprah need reparations?" is the straw-man question with which Earl Ofari Hutchinson begins his reply to my article "10 Reasons Why Reparations for Blacks is a Bad Idea for Blacks, and Racist Too." He had seized on a *Salon* tag line the editors had used to promote my article, not anything I actually wrote in the article. I had brought up Oprah Winfrey in my text to highlight a problem with one of the central claims of the reparations camp—that blacks alive today still suffer significant damage from a system of slavery that was ended 135 years ago, and from the regime of segregation that was brought to a close 35 years ago; that other Americans should pay them compensation for these injuries; and that Americans should pay them more compensation than the trillions of dollars they have already provided in the form of welfare and other transfer payments and in special privileges afforded by the racial-preference arrangements called affirmative action. I mentioned Oprah, who was raised in the segregated South and earned her way to becoming the richest woman in America, only to point to the tip of an iceberg: the existence of millions of very successful, middle-class African-Americans, which refutes the idea that the deprivations of the black underclass are irreparably caused by historical forces like slavery and segregation.

Hutchinson's failure to deal with the argument I actually put forward regarding Oprah pretty much sums up the rest of his

June 5, 2000, http://archive.frontpagemag.com/Printable.aspx?ArtId=24373; http://www.salon.com/2000/06/12/hutchinson_4/.

"reply" as well. Hutchinson contends that my first argument against reparations is that only "a handful of Southern planters were responsible for and profited from slavery." Actually, I didn't make this claim. Instead, I argued that if America's wealth is built on the free and exploited labor of black slaves, as reparations proponents claim, then those blacks who are alive today (and are thus the proposed beneficiaries of reparations) are also the beneficiaries of slavery and slave labor. Identifying slave owners as a small cohort in the population served to demonstrate that the vast majority of living non-black Americans are not the descendants of slave owners and are really in the same boat morally as the descendants of slaves; both are innocent of the crime of slavery and of having benefited from the fruits of slavery.

Hutchinson's statement that whites and non-whites who came after slavery (and therefore had no role in it) did not experience "racial terror and legal segregation" is not even a half-truth. Discrimination—and job discrimination in particular—against Jews, Poles, Irish, Asians and Hispanics, to cite a few minorities, certainly caused significant economic hardship to these groups and put significant obstacles in their path. Hutchinson's dismissal of their suffering is just one example of the narcissism and self-pity that reparations proponents promote.

Legal segregation, as commentators like Hutchinson tend to ignore, was confined to the South. To make a case that legal segregation has led to a permanent handicap of blacks alive today, one would have to conduct a sociological study to show a significantly greater economic deficit among blacks and the descendants of blacks who were actually subjected to legal segregation. Nobody appears to have done this. Nor is there a body of sociological study or comparable evidence provided by reparations proponents to support any of their claims.

Instead, there is rhetorical bombast like this: "Through the decades of slavery and Jim Crow segregation, African-Americans were transformed into the poster group for racial dysfunctionality that Horowitz giddily reminds the world of." Of course, this is simply false. The 80 percent out-of-wedlock birthrate in the inner city—to take one important example—is a *post*-Sixties phenomenon that has no link to slavery or segregation, but rather to progressive welfare schemes. Black families were 90 percent intact in the 1940s, and as late as 1965 were 75 percent intact. I raised the fact that slavery is so far in the past to point out that those who claim that it still has effects on present generations have a heavy burden of proof, which none of them—Hutchinson included—has even attempted to provide.

Hutchinson then imputes to me the claim that "blacks are living better than ever." I never made the claim. Some blacks—the majority—are indeed living better than ever. But others—inner-city blacks in particular—are worse off. Those who are living better demonstrate that history, even a history of suffering, is not necessarily an obstacle to success. The worse off are suffering the effects of bad social policies, drugs and other urban ills that have nothing to do with slavery or segregation. I also pointed out that very poor Mexicans and Vietnamese come to America and, despite immense language barriers and ethnic prejudice, do better than inner-city blacks. Hutchinson does not even take note of this argument.

Instead, he invokes a poll by the National Conference for Community and Justice which finds that "blacks are still overwhelmingly the victims of racial discrimination." What is this supposed to mean? Who was polled? What evidence was provided that most blacks are discriminated against? If most blacks are discriminated against, and most carry with them the legacy of slavery and discrimination, how is it that some black communities are economically thriving while others are not? Even after reading what I have written about this, Hutchinson seems unable to recognize the argument he thinks he is refuting. As a result, his counter-claims are intellectually sloppy and irrelevant.

For example: according to Hutchinson, the result of "the hideous legacy of slavery" is that blacks make up more than half of the 2 million prisoners in American prisons. Come again? When young black males form gangs in the inner city and shoot other young black males, are we to understand that slavery made them do it? Why didn't they do it in the Twenties, when the KKK had twenty million members? Why did they choose the era following the triumph of the civil rights movement—the Seventies and Eighties—to launch these homicidal assaults? "[Blacks] receive stiffer sentences than whites for possession of drugs." But slavery had nothing to do with the harsh sentences for crack cocaine. They were put in place because black leaders went to Congress in the Eighties and demanded harsher sentences for crack cocaine, which was associated with the violence that was tearing apart their communities. In Hutchinson's hands, "slavery" is no longer part of a rational argument; it is a magical incantation invoked to explain every ill and pathology suffered by inner-city blacks. That's pretty much what I said about the logic of reparations' proponents in my article.

The way Hutchinson reads my article, I said, "Reparations will make everyone hate blacks more." What I said was that the reparations claim will be racially divisive and will self-isolate blacks even more than they already are. I specifically singled out the separatist currents in the black community and said that this grievance-mongering, coupled with the attack it entails on the entire American heritage of blacks, will have a destructive effect on the black community itself.

As a rebuttal to his straw man, Hutchinson observes that most Americans agree slavery was morally wrong. To this I would add the obvious fact that most Americans would agree discrimination was and is morally wrong. But this just shows how completely he misunderstands the issue at hand. The fact that everyone agrees slavery was wrong is very different from the effort to make everyone responsible for slavery, which is exactly what the reparations claim does. How much more resentment do black leaders want to create?

Hutchinson takes issue with a claim I am supposed to have made: "There's no precedent for paying blacks for their suffering."

What I actually said was that the precedents invoked by reparations claimants are inapt because they involved immediate sufferers on one side, and the people or agencies who caused their suffering on the other. The victims of the Tuskegee experiment were actually surviving victims of the Tuskegee experiment. Since Earl Ofari Hutchinson has not been a slave, he is not an obvious "victim" of slavery in any actionable sense. Since he has provided no evidence that he has suffered actual damages from slavery, e.g., that he would be earning more money now if his great grandparents—or is it his great-great-grandparents?—had not been slaves, why should I or Lola Martínez or Nguyen Van Troi pay him reparations? This is the actual argument I made, and Hutchinson hasn't answered.

Because the past is about the dead, its injustices cannot be redressed. The attempt to do so is likely to cause problems for the living that are not easy to calculate and that extend into the future. Regarding German reparations to Israel for the Holocaust, to which Hutchinson refers, the relationship between Germany and Israel is very different from the relationship between the African-American descendants of slaves and America. The German government—a government elected democratically and overwhelmingly supported by the German people—set out to exterminate the Jews. Israel is a country that was created to provide a refuge for the survivors of this holocaust that no other country would. Therefore, a collective guilt is certainly attributable to the German government and its people; particularly since in 1952, when the reparations were agreed upon, the members of that government had all been adults during the years in which the extermination had been carried out.

America, by contrast, did not create slavery, nor did it create the slavery that engulfed American blacks. Moreover, America designed itself as a nation dedicated to the propositions that men are equal and should be free. Over the course of fourscore and ten years (the lifetime of an individual) America did in fact fulfill this promise. As of 1807 America had outlawed the slave trade, in which it had been a participant, and helped to destroy the slave trade internationally. In a civil war that cost the non-slave states of the North 350,000 young men, African-Americans were freed. They were freed in America before they were freed in Africa. The present government of the United States is lineally descended from the free states of the North, not the slave South. So the analogy is inappropriate in this case.

Unfortunately, Hutchinson has chosen mainly to ignore what I wrote in my article and to invent a series of other arguments to "refute." In addition to the above, he has ignored the entire corpus of arguments I put forward as to why the reparations claim is 1) bad for blacks and 2) racist too. Was this an oversight? A failure of comprehension? I wouldn't know. But his obtuseness does not bode well for the course of this debate.

3

Racial McCarthyism
on College Campuses

A ctivities planned for Black History Month this year featured a series of conferences, rallies and "awareness days" on college campuses across the country. The events were organized to promote the idea that the American government should pay reparations to African-Americans as restitution for slavery and the unpaid wealth it produced. A quick perusal of the speakers and agendas at these supposedly educational events showed that only one point of view on the reparations issue would be represented.

To rectify a situation, which seemed to me both a violation of the spirit of historical inquiry and of the responsibility of educational institutions to present more than one side of a controversial issue, I attempted to place an ad on the subject in several college newspapers. I composed the ad from the article on reparations I had written for *Salon* magazine and titled it: "10 Reasons Why Reparations for Slavery Is a Bad Idea—and Racist Too." The current reparations demand is racist, I argued, because payment is being demanded on the basis of skin color. This ignores the fact that there were thousands of blacks who were slave owners themselves, or freemen, and that the ancestors of most non-blacks had either been opposed to slavery, or non-slaveholders, or had immigrated to America after slavery was abolished. I also observed that African-Americans alive today have benefited from slavery too,

March 15, 2001; this op-ed column was solicited by the *Los Angeles Times*, but then rejected. http://archive.frontpagemag.com/Printable. aspx?ArtId=19932.

since the average black citizen now in America is between 20 to 50 times richer than the average black in the West African nations from which the slaves were taken.

The response to my ad has been revealing.[1] Only four college newspapers have printed the ad and managed to do so without incident or apology. Eighteen have rejected the ad, including the college papers at Harvard, Columbia, Minnesota and Virginia. Two that rejected my ad for political reasons—Penn State and Notre Dame—had no problem a few years ago printing an ad that denied the fact of the Holocaust .[2]

When the University of Wisconsin's *Badger-Herald* printed my ad, its editorial offices were stormed by 150 angry protesters. Campus police instructed the editors to take refuge in their dorms and lock the doors to ensure their safety. The Wisconsin *Cardinal,* a larger campus paper, then printed a counter-ad, which did not address the points in mine but merely smeared the *Badger* and its editors as "racists" for printing it. When the campus papers at UC Berkeley and UC Davis printed the ad, their editorial offices were visited by delegations of angry protesters. The following day, the editors performed public acts of contrition for "inadvertently" becoming a "vehicle for bigotry" and for printing "discriminatory statements." At both UC and Wisconsin, copies of the papers that had printed the ads were stolen and trashed by student mobs.

These incidents dramatize a disturbing situation on American campuses in which the political left is fully in control of the campus public square and is able to censor views it finds objectionable. The bullying tactics of these activists include moral and physical intimidation, wild accusations of racism and bigotry, and indiscriminate use of guilt by association. Unfortunately, university officials across the country have adopted a tolerant, hear-and-see-no-evil attitude towards these outrages, a posture that clearly

---

[1] An account of the campaign can be found in David Horowitz, *Uncivil Wars: The Controversy Over Reparations for Slavery,* Encounter 2001.
[2] Ibid.

encourages them. The assistant chancellor at the University of California, Berkeley, actually accused me of bringing an unwanted difference of opinion to his campus. In a letter dated March 12, he wrote: "No demand for 'dialogue' existed prior to your effort to provoke it." In fact, professors on his own campus were conducting "reparations awareness" sessions with their students before I conceived the ad.

The current political harassment on our college campuses has reached intolerable proportions. Universities should not view themselves as political institutions or be captive to a political faction. Diverse views should be encouraged on controversial issues. The only remedy for the political correctness that now prevails is public outcry. If my reparations ad has provided a catalyst for this kind of educational reform, it will have been well worth the trouble and the attacks.

4

The Underhanded Journalism
of Jonathan Alter

In the course of an ill-conceived personal attack on me, *Newsweek* senior editor Jonathan Alter derides the idea that "McCarthyism" characterizes the campaign against my "Reparations" ad on college campuses.[1] Most editorialists and writers in the liberal press have been supportive of my right to place the ad, and have defended the legitimacy—whether they agree with it or not—of the case I have made. "McCarthyism" is an accepted term for, among other things, the deployment of gross exaggeration to defame a person you disagree with. Thus Alter describes me as a thinker of "the extreme right" when, in fact, I am a mainstream conservative—moderate on issues like abortion, a libertarian on issues of media expression, a defender of gays, a staunch advocate of civil rights for blacks and other minorities, and of government support for those left behind.

Another accepted meaning of the term is the defamation of others through "guilt by association." Alter says the ad I wrote "reminds me of those tiresome rants supporting a NAAWP (National Association for the Advancement of White People)." Alter doesn't even attempt to produce a citation from my text that would support this slander. The reason is that he can't.

March 29, 2001, http://archive.frontpagemag.com/Printable.aspx?ArtId= 22645.
[1] "Where PC Meets Free Speech," Jonathan Alter, *Newsweek*, April 2, 2001, Vol. 137, Issue 14, p. 53, http://connection.ebscohost.com/c/ articles/4276349/where-pc-meets-free-speech.

My ad is a commonplace argument that expresses the views of 70 percent of the American people, according to current polls. Almost all of its ideas were previously articulated in print by such distinguished African-American writers as Thomas Sowell, Walter Williams and libertarian columnist Larry Elder. Adrian Walker, an African-American columnist for the *Boston Globe*, who is no conservative, and who does not agree with every argument I have made, has defended both my right to place the ad and also to be free from undeserved charges of "racism." To insinuate against all evidence that I am a white racist, as Alter does, is reprehensible. It is also a clear case of racial McCarthyism.

Finally, "McCarthyism" is the imputation of self-incriminating agendas without evidence to substantiate the charge, or in defiance of such evidence (e.g., McCarthy's attack on the patriotism of General George C. Marshall). Alter concludes his column by claiming that "the not-so-subtle subtext [of the Horowitz reparations ad] was that we've given 'them' enough, and so should give up on addressing the continuing problems of race and poverty in America." There is nothing in my ad or my political life that would give the slightest warrant for this conclusion.

I am presently the head of an organization that works with 57 inner-city charities in Los Angeles to benefit disadvantaged children who are mainly black and Hispanic; I am the architect of legislation proposed last year by Congressman James Rogan that would provide $100 billion in government scholarships for 12 million mainly black and Hispanic children in failing government schools; and I am an outspoken and well-known crusader inside the Republican Party to turn its attention to the festering problems of America's largely minority inner cities.

The subtext of my ad is a critique of the bankrupt civil rights leadership, which thinks it is more important to launch an inflammatory and divisive claim for "reparations" over a crime committed more than 100 years ago, than it is to unite all of America's communities in an effort to address the problems that currently afflict poor Americans generally and African-Americans in particular. That a senior editor at *Newsweek* is unable to understand or appreciate these facts speaks volumes about the parlous state of our racial politics today.

5

No Decency, No Shame

My Andy Warhol moment has come just as I would have wanted it: while going on offense, baiting the left. The ad I wrote and attempted to place in more than 50 college newspapers challenged a racial orthodoxy that is suffocating the promise of American pluralism and setting ethnic communities against each other. It is sinking African-Americans in a sea of negativism and hostile posturing that threatens to isolate them and sabotage attempts to elevate those who have been left behind. Denouncing as "racist," "not legitimate" and "anti-civil rights" an American president who has brought more diversity to Washington than any of his predecessors and has vowed to "leave no child behind" is just one emblem of the moral and political bankruptcy of the current civil rights leadership. Claiming "reparations for slavery" 136 years after the fact is another.

As a result of the ad I placed in an attempt to draw attention to this problem, I have been predictably attacked as a racial provocateur and a racist as well. Those smears are the reason no one else has made a similar attempt before me. The smears and attacks are also the reason, ironically, that so much attention is now being paid to this issue. More than twice as many editors have refused my ad as have agreed to publish it (the actual score right now is 34–14 against) even though I was offering to pay for the space to run it. Only eight college papers have been able to print the ad

April 3, 2001, http://archive.frontpagemag.com/Printable.aspx?ArtId= 22531; http://www.salon.com/2001/04/02/reparations_6/.

without incident. Six editors who published it have been visited by howling mobs, and three of those have decided to apologize for doing so. At Wisconsin, Brown and Duke, editors have courageously stood up to mobs bent on intimidating them. The net result has been to bring the issue of intellectual freedom on American college campuses before millions of Americans who otherwise would have been unaware that it was a problem. I couldn't be more pleased by the attention these issues are getting. And I know from my emails and from the widespread support I have gotten in the press that other Americans who cherish their freedoms are pleased as well.

What is going on here? When I stepped onto the stage in the Life Sciences Building at the University of California, Berkeley, accompanied by thirty armed campus police, I was reminded of the old Richard Pryor album where he appears cowering, half-naked and surrounded by hooded Klansmen who are about to lynch him. The cover line is, "Is it something I said?"

Actually, it *was* something I said. Any understanding of what has happened must begin by focusing on that fact. How is it that the expression of ideas—let alone ideas shared by a majority of Americans (a *Fox News* poll now indicates that 81 percent of the public are opposed to reparations) should require 30 armed police on a university campus to protect it?[1] The answer is that we live in a time of racial McCarthyism. Fifty years ago, witch-hunters warned that there were "reds under the beds." Now it is something like "racists in the heads"—a closet bigot behind every white face. Actually there *were* reds under the beds in the McCarthy era, a lot more of them (as recently opened Soviet archives show) than many had previously thought. And of course, there are racists still among us. The problem of "McCarthyism" was the abuse of a reality that prompted people's legitimate fears.

---

[1] "The Politics of Racial Reparations," Charles P. Henry, *Journal of Black Studies*, November 2003, pp. 131-152, jbs.sagepub.com/cgi/reprint/34/2/131.pdf.

McCarthy and his allies exploited those fears to achieve political agendas unrelated to matters of national security. McCarthy exaggerated the facts, made false accusations and used sinister innuendos in order to assault his political opponents in the Democratic Party, and to stifle opposition from all quarters. Nobody wanted to be accused—however falsely—of being a Communist, of coddling Communists, or of being associated with Communists. This is exactly what is happening on matters of race on our college campuses and in the political arena today.

My reparations ad was a straightforward argument that blacks alive today are two, three and four generations removed from slavery. Hence, their claim would not conform to existing reparations formulas as applied to victims of the Holocaust, interned Japanese Americans, or survivors of the Rosewood race riot. The claim, I argued, would pit the black community against all other ethnic communities, and would focus blacks on their victim status and on negative thoughts about their lives in America. It is possible, by way of contrast, to look at African-Americans as a people who started literally from nothing—stripped of their language, culture and family roots—but who a century later, thanks to their own efforts and the opportunities that America afforded them, have become the 10th-richest nation in the world. Normally, such an attitude would be called "empowering." In the dispute over my ad, however, it has been called "racist."

In apologizing for publishing my ad, the editor of the campus paper at UC Berkeley explained that the ad was a "vehicle for bigotry." This is a weasel phrase typical of McCarthyism. What is a "vehicle for bigotry"? Does it mean that someone might misread it and use it for bigotry? Does it mean that facts or arguments appearing in the ad may be used by bigots themselves? Or does it mean that some black person's feelings were hurt by the ad, which on sensitivity-trained campuses is interpreted as tantamount to bigotry?

Actually, in these times the definition of racism itself has become problematic. At the University of Wisconsin, the *Badger-*

Herald published the ad on February 28. Five days later, the rival student paper, *The Daily Cardinal*, published an ad it provided for free to the Multicultural Students Coalition. This ad did not reply to my ten points—and in fact there has not been a single reply to those points so far. Instead, the *Cardinal* ad attacked the *Badger-Herald* as a "Racist Propaganda Machine" for publishing my ad. The editorial offices of the *Badger-Herald* were then besieged by a mob of 100 students demanding the resignation of editor Julie Bosman and apologies (for racism) from its staff. These are tactics that have a long and regrettable history with the fascist and communist mobs of the 1930s, sent to break up the peaceful meetings of their social democratic rivals. This is the politics of smear and intimidation designed to silence opposition and stamp out free speech. Nothing could be more inimical to a university setting; yet not a single student involved in these activities has been disciplined or reprimanded by the university administration.

Tshaka Barrows is the leader of the Multicultural Students Coalition and, as it happens, the son of the university's vice president for Student Affairs. He was interviewed by *The Daily Cardinal* about the campaign:

> **Cardinal:** Does the Horowitz ad fit your definition of racism?
> **Barrows:** Exactly. Because of the reality of our society, his prejudice was allowed to be institutionalized, and [16,000] of his statements were presented to our campus. He was actively, as well as the *Herald*, exercising their racism, their power to institutionalize their racism.
> **Cardinal:** [What] is your definition of racism?
> **Barrows:** Racism is having the power to institutionalize your prejudice.[2]

In other words, my offense is publishing ideas, which Barrows doesn't like. As for racism, Barrows's definition is a standard

---

[2] http://solargeneral.com/jeffs-archive/free-speech/blacks-and-jews-battle-is-sent-at-the-university-of-wisconsin/.

concoction of tenured leftists, whose doctrine is that "only whites can be racist."

Insinuating racism—without taking the trouble to establish actual racism—is the McCarthy method. It was on display in a column Jonathan Alter wrote about me in the April 2 edition of *Newsweek*.[3] A color photograph illustrating Alter's column was placed in the middle of the page. It showed one of the student protesters at UC Berkeley carrying a sign with the words: "PROTEST DAVID HOROWITZ, RACIST IDEOLOGUE." Alter's article had made no reference to the photo. Nor did it explain that the protesters were members of the Spartacist Youth League, a Trotskyist splinter group who also denounced me as a "capitalist running dog." The image was allowed to just stand there, and indict me. In his column, Alter derisively dismissed my claim that I was under siege by "left-wing McCarthyism." Alter's defense of the campus censorship went like this: "Please. Newspapers, exercising their own freedom, routinely reject advertising they believe might offend the sensibilities of their readers." They do. But being offended by *ideas* that you disagree with is hardly a press norm.

A similar attack on my ad appeared in *The Washington Post* by liberal columnist Richard Cohen. Cohen suggested that while I was not an actual racist, and while "word for word, the ad makes sense," the ad provoked campus fascists into their attacks on free speech, so editors were justified in not running it. The reason Cohen gave was that my tone and address were "insulting" and "offensive."

"I'm not sure I can put my finger on what exactly offended me when I first read the ad. It might have been its statement that blacks as well as whites engaged in the slave trade and owned slaves. True enough, but only blacks were slaves. It might have been the what's-the-big-deal tone to the argument that almost all African-Americans live so much better than almost all Africans

---

[3] See above, Part III, *Jonathan Alter's Underhanded Journalism.*

that they ought to be downright grateful that their ancestors were kidnapped and dumped on the beach at Charleston. Or it might have been Horowitz's assertion that welfare payments constitute reparations of a sort. This is a downright insulting statement."

Of course, this is a caricature of what the ad said, and hardly compatible with his previous statement that "word for word, the ad makes sense." But even so, does it justify attacks on the editor of one of the newspapers who ran the ad as the manager of a "racist propaganda machine?" What Cohen forgets is that my ad is not a statement out of the blue on reparations. It is a specific response to the claims of reparations proponents—a response that students would not have been able to hear if I hadn't decided to buy the space to provide them with an opposing point of view.

What is truly insulting is that the proponents of reparations have addressed Americans as though white America *en masse* is responsible—and solely responsible—for slavery and its real and alleged after effects; as though no apologies have ever been made for slavery and no recognition of its horrors is on record; as though all the disadvantages of black Americans (income gaps, education gaps and criminal incarceration gaps) were attributable solely or even mainly to white racism; and as though all Americans who are not black should feel they owe a debt to all Americans who are black. Now *that* is offensive.

But it is in fact the case made by Randall Robinson and every other reparations proponent known to me. Has there been an apology for slavery or recognition by white America that slavery is evil? Of course there has. Abraham Lincoln called slavery an offense to God, said that every drop of blood from the lash would be paid by a drop of blood from the sword, and called the destruction of the South a judgment of the Lord for the sin of slavery. And this was not in an obscure speech but his Second Inaugural Address. What more in the way of recognition could be asked?

And what is so insulting, as Cohen seems to think, about the suggestion that welfare is a form of reparations for injuries done by slavery and discrimination? If the entire income gap between black Americans and other Americans is attributable to slavery and its aftermath—as Robinson and the reparations advocates maintain—then of course welfare could be considered an attempt to make up that deficit and repair that injury. Welfare payments to African-Americans represent a net transfer of wealth of trillions of dollars from other communities to theirs.[4]

Should African-Americans be grateful for slavery because they (incontrovertibly) live better in America than blacks do in Africa today? Nobody in his right mind would say so, and I certainly didn't.

What is really at issue in this campus tempest is not so much the right of an individual to publish his views. Rather, it is the right of an individual to publish reasonable views on race matters without being stigmatized as a racist and someone too indecent to consider seriously.

---

[4] "Examining the Means-Tested Welfare State: 79 Programs and $927 Billion in Annual Spending," Robert Rector, Heritage Foundation, May 3, 2012, http://www.heritage.org/research/testimony/2012/05/examining-the-means-tested-welfare-state.

6

A Protection Racket

Last spring I waged a campaign on college campuses against the idea that reparations for slavery—an institution that has been dead for 137 years—should be paid to people who have never been slaves, and paid to them on the basis of their skin color alone. Friendly critics to my left and right asked me why I would even bother to conduct a campaign against an idea that is so obviously discreditable, and which had no chance of being put into law. Why endure the smears of racial demagogues—who these days are legion—to oppose a bizarre idea that could not possibly fly?

The kind of optimism these views reflected presumes a general rationality on the subject that is as misplaced as the reparations idea itself. This is not, by the way, an irrationality of ignorant masses. In fact, the leaders of the reparations movement—and the most dangerous elements within it—are Harvard professors. Its intellectual godfather, Randall Robinson, was a Harvard law graduate, while Harvard law professor Charles Ogletree has organized a team of billion-dollar class-action attorneys to prosecute the cause.

Ogletree's posture as a civil rights advocate hasn't prevented him from signing on as political adviser to racial arsonist Al Sharpton's presidential campaign. Ogletree also lends Harvard's prestige to the campaign to save convicted cop-killer Mumia Abu-Jamal.

February 27, 2002, http://archive.frontpagemag.com/Printable.aspx? ArtId=24453; http://www.salon.com/2002/03/02/reparations_7/.

Ogletree heads an organization called the "Reparations Coordinating Committee." This is the legal "dream team" proposing to sue any large corporation that can be tied—however tenuously—to a corporate predecessor that may have profited from slavery 150–200 years ago. The team includes Johnnie Cochran, a lawyer famous for inflicting injustice on the families of the victims of his criminal clients, and Cornel West, another Sharpton adviser. The dream team receives unsolicited but valuable help from the nation's media, who are forced by current racial protocols to treat the entire scam as a legitimate enterprise. *USA Today,* whose publisher is one of the targets of the shakedown, recently ran a full-page survey of the legal efforts of Ogletree's team. The feature began with the following melodramatic presentation of the reparations claim:

> They owned, rented or insured slaves. Loaned money to plantation owners. Helped hunt down the runaways. Some of America's most respected companies have slavery in their pasts. Now, 137 years after the final shots of the Civil War, will there be a reckoning? A powerhouse team of African-American legal and academic stars is getting ready to sue companies it says profited from slavery before 1865. Initially, the group's aim is to use lawsuits and the threat of litigation to squeeze apologies and financial settlements from dozens of corporations. Ultimately, it hopes to gain momentum for a national apology and a massive reparations payout by Congress to African-Americans.[1]

The "they" in this paragraph does not refer to any real person or corporation who might actually be hauled into court. In the first place, many of the corporations targeted did not even exist before the Emancipation Proclamation and are not really the same corporations as those identified in the claims. Instead, they are only

---

[1] "Corporations Challenged by Reparations Activists," James Cox, *USA Today,* February 21, 2002, http://usatoday30.usatoday.com/money/general/2002/02/21/slave-reparations.htm.

connected to the allegedly offending corporations as a result of mergers and acquisitions. Absent a legal monopoly, no corporation is the same as its legal ancestor of more than a hundred years' vintage. The presumption behind the reparations suit is that a corporation is a fact of nature, like a mountain or a tree. But the wealth of corporations is not simply accumulated like water in a stream—or money in the bank.

Within the last six months, two of the largest corporations ever created have sunk ignominiously into oblivion, going from hundreds of billions in assets to practically zero.[2] Corporations are institutions composed of living beings and require enormous effort and sacrifice and relentless performance to keep them prospering and growing. The reparations suit will unjustly punish living officers, employees and shareholders of the targeted corporations (not to mention their customers) for acts which they had nothing to do with, and which were not even crimes when they were committed 150 years ago, since slavery was legal at the time.

To compound the injury inherent in their claims, the reparations law team has targeted corporations that have been pioneers in affirmative action and diversity programs, in huge benefactions to black institutions in general, and to schools and scholarship programs for black children in particular. The suits are a way of extorting even more money from people who have already given generously, by accusing them of crimes they didn't commit. It is a repellent and preposterous idea. But it remains a compelling one at Harvard nonetheless.

The good news is that the law will not allow the extortionists their pound of flesh. The torts are too old, the accusations too vague, the connections to real world facts too tenuous. To allow the reparations suits to succeed would set a destructive precedent and permit massive injustice to leak into the system.

---

[2] http://en.wikipedia.org/wiki/Enron_scandal; "WorldCom," Dennis Moberg and Edward Romar, Santa Clara University—Markkula Center for Applied Ethics, 2003, http://www.scu.edu/ethics/dialogue/candc/cases/worldcom.html.

The bad news is that the law doesn't matter, since it can be overwhelmed by a racially inflamed emotional tide. This was the gravamen of a statement by Owen Pell, an attorney who represents targeted companies, who told *USA Today* that the reparations movement couldn't win in court, but added: "Companies have learned you don't judge a lawsuit by its merits. You judge it by the potential public-relations damage. Corporate America is following this issue. They understand how nasty it could get if someone comes in and says you have blood on your hands."

I also understand this, personally. I was at the University of Pennsylvania recently to speak on a panel on reparations. It was the first time I had been to Penn since my reparations ad campaign last spring. The campus newspaper, *The Daily Pennsylvanian,* had refused even to print the ad. Ugly characterizations of me and the suppressed ad were thus allowed to circulate without rebuttal on the campus. After the reparations panel on which I spoke, the political science professor who opposed me came up afterwards and said, "You're actually not so bad. They told me you were a monster."

Corporations cannot afford to be viewed as monsters. When Jesse Jackson attacked Texaco a few years ago, he didn't even have to claim that the blood of slaves was on company hands in order to win reparations. Not a shred of evidence that Texaco had discriminated was ever heard or evaluated in a court of law. Yet Texaco executives shelled out nearly $200 million just to make the extortionists go away.

The reparations movement is not a legal movement. It is a protection racket, a shakedown operation whose Harvard brain trust has devised a corrupt legal strategy to whip up the political frenzy that will achieve the desired effect. The big prize is not even corporate money. As *USA Today* put it: "One certainty is that the new corporate cases are merely the undercard for the main event: The Holy Grail for the reparations movement is a national apology from Congress and a massive federal payout that could take the form of direct payments to African-Americans or trillions in new spending on education and social programs aimed at them."

The truth, of course, is that American taxpayers have already spent (and are spending) trillions of dollars on education and social programs which benefit African-Americans. Thanks to the very people they want to sue for reparations, black Americans are the richest and freest blacks on earth. Yet black Americans are the only group in America that seems unable to take yes for an answer. The reparations movement is not only insulting to the already demonstrated generosity and compassion of non-black Americans; it is dangerous and destructive to the American community as a whole, including its black members.

More than 80 percent of African-Americans now support reparations, while only 11 percent of non-blacks do. A nation divided against itself is a nation weakened in its core. A few days after the *USA Today* feature appeared, it was followed by a column headlined "Black U.S. History Makes National Unity a Tougher Sell."[3] The article, by black columnist Sean Gonsalves, was blunt about the terms of unity he would find acceptable: "Before there can be a fruitful national dialogue about reparations, there needs to be some political consensus that a debt is owed." This is a line verbatim from Randall Robinson's America-hating book, *The Debt*, the bible of the reparations movement.[4]

Ten days before al-Qaeda's attack on the World Trade Center Towers, members of the Congressional Black Caucus were in Durban, South Africa to attend the UN "Conference on Racism." Heading the delegation was John Conyers, the ranking Democrat on the House Judiciary Committee and the author of the reparations bill. The delegates were there to make common cause with Iran and other radical Islamic regimes to condemn the United States and Britain for slavery and to demand reparations. As a

---

[3] "Black U.S. History Makes National Unity a Tougher Sell," Sean Gonsalves, *USA Today*, February 21, 2002, http://groups.yahoo.com/neo/groups/openyourthirdeye/conversations/topics/7661.

[4] Randall Robinson, *The Debt: What America Owes to Blacks*, Dutton, 2000. I have taken Robinson and his book apart in my *Uncivil Wars: The Controversy Over Reparations For Slavery*, 2001.

matter of historical fact, the United States accounted for less than 2 percent of the world slave trade and—with Britain—led the world in abolishing slavery. Neither the U.S. delegates nor their Middle Eastern allies made any mention of existing black slavery in Muslim-run Sudan or demanded reparations from that country. The anti-American subtext of the exercise was underscored by NAACP chair Julian Bond, also present, who urged the UN to "highlight American racism," as though America had not been the leader of the *anti*-slavery and *anti*-racism movement, and the Arabs with whom Bond linked symbolic arms had not been the primary originators and practitioners of the global slave trade.

In the wake of September 11, Charles Ogletree's pal Al Sharpton told a "State of the Black World" conference in Atlanta, "We don't owe America anything; America owes us."[5] This is as terse a summation of the reparations point of view as we are likely to get. If the reparations movement and its hostile attitude towards America are not roundly rebuffed, civil discord will only be the beginning of our problems.

---

[5] "Black Leaders Rally on Racial Rhetoric at Conference," Steve Miller, *The Washington Times*, November 20, 2001, http://www.washington-times.com/news/2001/nov/30/20011130-031531-7204r/.

7

Reparations Buffoons
on the Washington Mall

In 1943, A. Phillip Randolph organized a civil rights march on Washington to demand full citizenship for black Americans. At the time, the descendants of slaves were disenfranchised and legally segregated in the South and discriminated against everywhere else. Twenty years later, Martin Luther King Jr. led a triumphant reprise of Randolph's protest and delivered what has become, second only to the Gettysburg Address, the most famous speech in American history. Within two years of King's march, Congress passed laws with eighty and ninety percent majorities of both political parties guaranteeing full citizenship rights and political equality to blacks. King himself won a place in the pantheon of American heroes, displacing Washington and Lincoln to become the only American honored with a national holiday in his name — a powerful symbol of the guilt Americans felt for the crimes of slavery and segregation, and a living reminder of the lengths to which Americans have gone and are prepared to go to right the wrongs of their country's racial past.

But since King's day of glory, the Washington mall has become the platform for a series of increasingly embarrassing displays of racial histrionics and anti-American bathos in the name of civil rights. In 1991, America's most prominent black racist, and the spiritual head of a crackpot religious cult, led an improbable "Million Man March" to the hallowed site. On the mall where King

August 19, 2002, http://archive.frontpagemag.com/Printable.aspx?ArtId= 23179.

had given his "I Have a Dream" speech, Louis Farrakhan delivered a disquisition on the numerology of the integer "19" and denounced "white supremacy," which he identified as the most pressing problem in America and the world. This was a throwback to the era of racial charlatans like Marcus Garvey and Farrakhan's own mentor, the improbable prophet, Wallace Fard.

Two years ago, the Reverend Al Sharpton claimed the same podium for what he called his "Redeem the Dream" march, an appalling effusion of race-baiting diatribes. Malik Zulu Shabazz, the "Minister of Defense" of the New Black Panthers, called for a race war. Farrakhan was absent but sent his "Queen" to represent him at the event. Participants included members of the congressional black caucus and HUD Secretary Andrew Cuomo, along with sometime felon and current boxing promoter Don King, who provided the only levity of the day.

This year witnessed a full-blown return to the buffoonery of those occasions in the "Millions for Reparations March." One speaker referred to the event as a revival of the Sixties, chanting "Black Power! Black Power! Black Power!" But the presiding spirit of the day was not Stokely Carmichael or Martin Luther King. It was Marcus Garvey, famous for launching a "Back to Africa" movement and then bilking those who bought tickets on his Black Star Line in the hope of going "home." The afternoon included many paeans to Garvey, whose 115th birthday it was, along with a genuine Garvey impersonator in Admiral Nelson hat and ostrich plumes. The only rival to this marvel was a white-robed gentleman calling himself the "Prince of Israel," who began by garbling a Hebrew prayer and then delivered a sermon on the evils of the Constitution and the racism of the American Way.

Malik Zulu Shabazz came for a return appearance—tarted up in Salvation Army drag, which is apparently the uniform of the New Black Panther Party—to deliver the following message: "The President wants to talk about a terrorist named bin Laden. I don't want to talk about bin Laden. I want to talk about a terrorist called Christopher Columbus. I want to talk about a terrorist called

George Washington. I want to talk about a terrorist called Rudy Giuliani. The real terrorists have always been the United Snakes of America."

New York City Councilman Charles Barron followed with a confession that he was so angry, he wanted to go up to a white person—"any white person"—and "slap them," while explaining, "it's a black thing." Barron was determined to show that he had more than mild mayhem on his mind as he repeatedly injected the word "fire" into his sentences and warned, "If they don't pay us reparations now, we're talking about scorched earth."

The theme of the march was, "We are owed," and the afternoon provided many imaginative variations on this idea. One black rapper chanted, "Show me the money, or I'll show you my Glock," while another sang, "Reparations, reparations ... I want my house on the hill and my Coupe de Ville." When the theme of the speakers wasn't demands or threats, it was an almost religious invocation of identity, and not the American one at that. A professor named Camille Yarbrough, draped in a pink dashiki, summed up these sentiments in a bongo-accompanied anthem with the refrain, "We are the people of Africa, we are the family of Africa."

While the platform mainly belonged to the fringe, Congressman John Conyers also spoke, taking time to gratefully acknowledge the presence of "Minister Farrakhan," and to demand "Reparations now!" Conyers is the author of the House reparations bill HR 40, which is the legal charter of the movement. If the Democrats win the House in November, Conyers will be the chair of the House Judiciary Committee, with the power to bring his reparations bill to the congressional floor. [The Democrats did not win.]

In the end, the best thing that can be said of the "Millions for Reparations" March is that it was a complete flop. At several points in the day, organizers of the march came to the microphone to urge the crowd to move to the center of the mall so that its pitiful numbers would look larger. The AP reported there were "hundreds" in attendance. Event "coordinator" Viola Plummer could not stifle her despair: "When I look out, it is an empty field," she said, then put on a brave front to call for a reparations demonstration at the UN in September 2003.

This march displayed the authentic roots of the reparations cause—the fringes of the kooky left. This is a fact of which even Conyers took note, while asserting that it was also a movement whose time had now come. For the real firepower behind reparations comes not from Sixties leftovers and the politically disturbed, but from the black civil rights establishment and the African-American elites it represents. The spiritual godfathers of the current reparations claim are Harvard luminaries Randall Robinson and Charles Ogletree, the law professor whose writings and legal suits have energized the movement and made it a serious one. Ogletree's lawsuits will be unveiled in September, and that will be a moment to assess where it might end up.

On the other hand, Ogletree's Harvard contingent shares two common and essential themes with the rag-tag army of misfits who gathered on the Capitol lawn on August 17 and claimed Martin Luther King's day as their own. The first of these is the anti-American animus that inspires both movements. This is evident in Ogletree's article, "The Case for Reparations," which appeared in a special section provided by America's largest newspaper, *USA Today*, on the weekend of the march.[1] Ogletree's case opens with the following fallacious and misleading claims:

> Beginning in the early 1600s, millions of Africans were brought to this country against their will, auctioned off like cattle, kept in bondage and forced to perform hard labor under the most wicked of institutions. As many as 25 million lives were lost. This atrocity was compounded by the US government's resistance to issue even a formal apology in the 139 years since slavery was abolished.

---

[1] "The Case for Reparations," Charles Ogletree, *USA Weekend*, Aug. 18, 2002.

The United States—"this country"—was not even in existence until 150 years after the first slaves arrived in 1619—something Ogletree is well aware of and, like every other reparations spokesman, chooses to ignore. The figure "246 years of slavery"—used by everyone in the movement—refers to the years from the arrival of the first slave ship in Jamestown, in 1619, to the end of the Civil War and the general emancipation of the slaves in 1865. But for more than 150 of those years there was no United States. A correct figure for the existence of slavery in "this country" would be more like 89 years. This is not a small issue for Ogletree's argument, since his intention is to make the "government" liable and not individual tax-paying Americans (although this is obviously an impossible distinction). If the government of the United States did not exist until 1776 or 1787, how can it be sued for what happened before?

This elision is itself a statement that goes to the anti-American heart of the reparations movement. For Ogletree and his supporters, the American Revolution was an insignificant event; the Declaration of Independence merely hypocritical; the 89 years of struggle to abolish slavery by Americans who were not slaves, really nothing at all. The 600,000 lives and enormous national treasure the nation lost in a civil war to free the slaves were actually not lost in a war to end slavery, and therefore should not be part of any reckoning in payment of the "debt."

One could continue with the litany of acts undertaken by Americans and their government over the next hundred years, which have had ramifications for minorities and oppressed people everywhere; including the civil rights battles to end segregation and discrimination, the trillions of dollars devoted to economic programs, and affirmative action projects designed to uplift the poor generally and blacks in particular. These are all dismissed by reparations enthusiasts as nothing.

Ogletree's claim that there has never been an official American apology for slavery implies that white Americans never noticed that an injustice had been done. Forget Thomas Jefferson's foreboding—

"I tremble for my country when I reflect that God is just"—a sentiment carved in stone on the Jefferson Memorial. Recall only Lincoln's Second Inaugural, hailed generally as the greatest speech in the English language, in which he said that slavery was an offense to God, that the Civil War was God's retribution on America for slavery, and that every drop of blood shed by the lash would be repaid by a drop of blood shed by the sword. Robinson's and Ogletree's studied disdain for these expressions of the nation's soul reflect the seething hatred for the American heritage and achievement which is just beneath the surface of the reparations movement. This sentiment is as contemptible as it is dangerous— especially at a time when the nation is under attack.

The second theme common to all reparations proponents is the idea encapsulated in the slogan of the Washington *opéra bouffe,* which is: "We Are Owed." Everything wrong with the civil rights movement for the last twenty years is summed up in this whine. Beginning with Tawana Brawley and working inexorably towards Rodney King, the principal causes of civil rights campaigns in the last two decades have been disparate sentences for drug crimes, perceived injustice in the treatment of criminals by local police, and unsubstantiated claims about the disparate impacts of social policies among racial groups ("institutional racism").

Reparations for slavery and its alleged legacies is just the latest unsubstantiated claim: "The legacy of slavery is seen today in well-documented racial disparities in access to education, health care, housing, employment and insurance, and in the form of racial profiling, the high rate of single parent homes and the disproportionate number of black inmates."[2]

This argument is spun entirely out of a thin air called "disparities." It is true that 70 percent of black children are born out of wedlock, for example, and this does constitute a "racial disparity," since the figure for whites is about 30 percent. But in 1965, nearly

---

[2] Ibid.

70 percent of all black children had two parents, and that was 100 years after slavery's end. In other words, while this may be a racial disparity, it would take an entirely different argument to establish that it is connected to slavery, segregation or discrimination. Lack of a father in the home, however, is a powerful indicator of poverty and crime. The racial disparity in the commission of crimes is inseparable from "the disproportionate number of black inmates," although no civil rights advocate like Ogletree takes note of this. Ogletree's racial indictment of America is a house of cards built with a stacked deck.

Rodney King—the most celebrated civil rights "victim" of the last quarter century—was a convicted felon resisting arrest. The President of the United States and the U.S. Justice Department took up King's grievance despite his record, despite his race (more probably because of it), and despite the exoneration of the officers involved in the incident by a jury of their peers. The police were tried a second time—a procedure directly against the American legal grain—and Rodney King emerged triumphant. He had received his "justice."

Since then, Rodney King has squandered the three million dollars in reparations he was awarded. He has shown himself through multiple subsequent arrests to be a habitual criminal and a willfully unproductive member of society. What did his reparations do for him, and what does his subsequent history tell us about the incident itself? Was he beaten because he was black or—as the officers contended—because he was a felon resisting arrest and they were angry because of the 100-mile-an-hour, life-endangering chase he had led them on? Was his treatment a legacy of slavery, or a by-product of the mean environment in which battles with urban predators take place? These are the crucial questions that neither Ogletree nor any other reparations advocate is prepared to answer.

When Martin Luther King gave his speech in Washington, *he* was disenfranchised; *he* could not eat at lunch counters reserved for whites or sit in buses when whites were standing; *he* could not use facilities other than those designated "for colored only." What exactly are Charles Ogletree and Randall Robinson, two well-heeled Harvard princes and counselors to presidents, denied by America? What are they owed by the ordinary Americans who must pay the taxes for reparations and whose ancestors, in their vast majority, had nothing to do with slavery or gave their lives to end it? And who dedicated themselves to fighting segregation and discrimination?

Thanks in part to the efforts of the majority of Americans who were not slaves and who are not black, blacks in America today are the richest and freest blacks on God's green earth—richer and freer than black citizens of any black nation in the world. Seventy-five percent of black Americans live above the poverty line and 50 percent are solidly in the middle class. In other words, the greatest ambition of the civil rights movement has been achieved. The doors of opportunity have been opened, and the rules have been made as neutral as they humanly can be to ensure that the competition is fair.

Is there a level playing field? There is no level playing field for anyone. Short of a totalitarian state that controls the families that individuals are born into, there can be none. A free society is inevitably a society of great inequalities, because individuals themselves are greatly unequal. This is a fact that is obvious—or should be—to everyone who is willing to think about it.

America did not create black slavery, but ended it. The Civil War was won. America has outlawed segregation and discrimination. The civil rights cause was victorious. It is time for everyone including Randall Robinson and Charles Ogletree to get used to it, and to move on to more productive causes.

PART V

Progressive Racism

Death of the
Civil Rights Movement

The good news is that Al Sharpton's "Redeem the Dream" march to end racial profiling was only a modest affair. Its numbers didn't approach the Million Man March, and the roster of speakers was notable for its gaps. The bad news is that it was an event at all. For this was a march that showed just how far down the scale of rationality we as a nation have slid on race in this fourth decade of the civil rights movement.

Sharpton's event was held on August 26 at the Lincoln Memorial as a reprise of Martin Luther King's 1963 march, and was co-hosted by Martin Luther King III, just to make the connection. Its stated purpose was to commemorate the victory over government-enforced segregation in the South. But its main, contradictory agenda was to claim that government racism was as big a problem as ever. One could hardly imagine a more embarrassing caricature of King's triumph than this carnival of sham grievances and double standards (white racists bad, black racists ok).

Unlike Martin Luther King's great march, which deliberately excluded the Nation of Islam, Sharpton's platform embraced Farrakhan and other black promoters of racial hate. Speaker after speaker celebrated a totalitarian unity of the race—the NAACP and Farrakhan, the National Council of Negro Women and the "New Black Panthers." There was even an "I Have A Black Dream" speech (in exactly those words), delivered by Malik Zulu

September 5, 2000, http://archive.frontpagemag.com/Printable.aspx?ArtId=24392; http://www.salon.com/2000/09/05/profiling/.

Shabazz, the "Minister of Justice" of the new Panther Party whose national chairman is the raving anti-white, anti-Jew, anti-Catholic, anti-gay Khalid Muhammad. Zulu Shabazz's "black dream" was that "for every casket and funeral in our community there should be a casket and funeral in the enemy's community." Not only was there no reaction to thinly veiled incitements to race war; the message itself was not so different from the thematic slogan of the march— "No justice, no peace." This now standard "civil rights" chant is a transparent threat of civil mayhem. Sharpton has made it his mantra; it flashes on his website, right above the photo of his booster, former senator and presidential aspirant, Bill Bradley.[1]

Today this *is* the "civil rights" movement. The racial arsonists from the Nation of Islam, the Old and New Black Panthers, and Sharpton's National Action Network were joined at the microphone by the president of the NAACP, Kweisi Mfume, the president of the ACLU, Laura Murphy, the national president of Blacks in Government (who told the crowd "privatization is nothing but a plan to eliminate a race from government"), the head of the Urban League, Hugh Price (who was clearly uncomfortable and spoke for less than two minutes), Representative John Conyers, the ranking Democrat on the House Judiciary Committee, and Andrew Cuomo, Secretary of Housing and Urban Development. And of course there was Johnnie Cochran, who told the assembled: "Go and serve on a jury. Somebody who looks like you is on trial and needs you to serve on a jury for them." Get it, whitey?

All in all, it was a disgraceful day.

Deplorable as the march was, however, it was not an insignificant event. Its principal theme, the injustice of racial profiling, has become the principal theme of the civil rights cause, extending up to the highest councils of state. On the eve of the event, Sharpton met with Attorney General Janet Reno and called for an executive

---

[1] National Action Network: http://www.discoverthenetworks.org/group-Profile.asp?grpid=7642.

order from the White House to block federal funding for cities that engage in a proven pattern of racial profiling. Al Gore has promised that, if elected, he will make sure the first civil rights act of the new century will end racial profiling.

For the Sharptonites, the question of what might actually constitute racial profiling hardly exists. "Study on this issue should be over," proclaimed Martin Luther King III to the crowd, "the facts are on the table." Well, not exactly. What the facts tell us is anything but simple. Profiling, in general, is an indispensable tool of law enforcement, and essential in utilizing its scarce resources efficiently. While the civil rights left claims that profiling of African-Americans is racist, not even Sharpton has yet accused the police of arbitrarily stopping elderly black women. The obvious reason young black males are stopped so frequently is that one in three is already a convicted felon; and although black males constitute only 6 percent of the population, they commit roughly 40 percent of the violent crimes.[2] The fact that such profiling sometimes casts unfair suspicion on non-criminal young black males is certainly regrettable. But it is not necessarily racism.

Los Angeles police chief, Bernard Parks, who is both African-American and a supporter of racial profiling properly defined, offered the following example to a reporter for *The New York Times Magazine:* "We have an issue of violent crime against jewelry salespeople.... The predominant suspects are Colombians. We don't find Mexican-Americans, or blacks or other immigrants. It's a collection of several hundred Colombians who commit this crime. If you see six in a car in front of the Jewelry Mart, and they're waiting and watching people with briefcases, should we play the percentages and follow them? It's common sense."[3] Jesse Jackson, in a rare moment of candor, conceded the same truth: "There is nothing more painful to me at this stage in my life," he

---

[2] *Uniform Crime Report for the United States,* FBI, 1997.

[3] "The Color of Suspicion," Jeffrey Goldberg, *The New York Times,* June 20, 1999, http://www.nytimes.com/1999/06/20/magazine/the-color-of-suspicion.html?pagewanted=all&src=pm.

said in 1993, "than to walk down the street and hear footsteps and start to think about robbery and then look around and see somebody white and feel relieved."[4]

It's common sense, then, for police to include race along with other factors in creating a profile of possible perpetrators. It makes everyone—and especially law abiding citizens of high crime areas who are often disproportionately black—a lot safer. The courts have already ruled sensibly in these matters. "Large groups of our citizens should not be regarded by law enforcement officers as presumptively criminal based upon their race. [However], facts are not to be ignored simply because they are unpleasant."[5] In short, the court ruled that the Constitution does not prohibit police from routinely taking race into account, as long as race is only one of several factors considered and it is not done for the purposes of harassment.

But common sense is the last guide of high-minded "progressives." On June 4, the ACLU ran a full-page accusatory ad about racial profiling on the inside cover of *The New York Times Sunday Magazine*. The ad, which cost approximately $80,000, featured headshots of Martin Luther King and psychotic killer Charles Manson. Its headline read: "THE MAN ON THE LEFT [Martin Luther King] Is 75 Times More Likely to Be Stopped by the Police While Driving Than THE MAN ON THE RIGHT [Charles Manson]." The reason: "police stop drivers based on their skin color rather than for the way they are driving."[6] In a special ACLU

---

[4] "Jesse Jackson's Message Is Too Advanced for Most," Mike Royko, *The Baltimore Sun*, December 3, 1993, http://articles.baltimoresun.com/1993-12-03/news/1993337169_1_jesse-jackson-killers-fear.

[5] U.S. v. Weaver, Docket No. 89-2887, United States Court of Appeals, Eighth Circuit, Submitted June 12, 1990, Decided June 5, 1992, *Leagle,* August 11, 1992, http://www.leagle.com/decision/19921357966F2d391_11271.

[6] Print ad created in 1999 by the DeVito/Verdi advertising agency for the American Civil Liberties Union. It ran in the *The New York Times Sunday Magazine, The New Yorker* and many other liberal mainstream outlets. http://www.rickrivas.com/lessons/gdes35/gdes35_lesson_03_images/racism.jpg.

report, "Driving While Black," the same false claim is made: "no person of color is safe from this treatment [racial profiling and traffic stops] anywhere, regardless of their obedience to the law, their age, the type of car they drive, or their station in life."[7] No evidence is adduced in the report or in the ad to show that elderly black women are the routine targets of police stops, or to explain why black police officers would go along with such a practice.

But the "explanatory" text of the ACLU ad reveals just how far an organization of "civil liberties" lawyers is prepared to go in manipulating falsehoods (every claim the ad makes is a lie) to hoodwink Americans into believing that racism is rampant among police departments and on the nation's highways. The only evidence actually offered by the ad for its claim about the nation's law enforcement is this: "For example, in Florida, 80 percent of those stopped and searched were black and Hispanic while they constituted only 5 percent of all drivers." That is, in fact, *all* the ACLU has to offer to justify its racially inflammatory ad, which is written so as to implicate not just Florida but law enforcement agencies in America. (Is it possible that *The New York Times* would have printed such malicious propaganda if its implicit message were that black or Hispanic police officers were racist?)

In fact, the ACLU ad is 100 percent wrong, even about the driving statistic. According to the Florida Department of Highway Safety and Motor Vehicles, 11 percent of Florida's drivers are Hispanic or black, or twice as many as the ad claims. Even that is not quite accurate because Florida authorities count Mexicans and Cubans as "white." But the really important error—assuming it is only an error—is to overlook the fact that 85 percent of the convicted drug dealers in Florida—likely targets of road stops in a state where drugs are a major trade—are Hispanic or black.[8] While

---

[7] "Driving While Black," David A. Harris, American Civil Liberties Union, June 7, 1999, https://www.aclu.org/racial-justice/driving-while-black-racial-profiling-our-nations-highways.
[8] Florida Department of Corrections, 1997–1998 Annual Report, http://www.dc.state.fl.us/pub/annual/9798/.

black males constitute only 6 percent of Florida's population they commit 50 percent of the serious crimes. Sad statistics like these—call them the crime census—*ought* to be the factual and defensible basis of the state's law enforcement policies. In other words, the state ought to be focusing its prevention efforts on the individuals who commit crimes and the communities most likely to be their victims.

Unhappily, it is not. To avoid legal harassment from groups like the ACLU, Florida's Highway Patrol has taken steps to keep its law enforcement policies politically correct and, therefore, as much as possible within the racial and ethnic parameters of the population census rather than the criminal census. According to its own statistics, in June of this year, 17 percent of traffic stops were of Hispanics and 19 percent of the stops were of blacks.[9] Of course, the ACLU can't be bothered with yet another question: How many traffic stops conducted by Florida officers were made by officers who were Hispanic or black themselves? Since 20 percent of the Florida Highway Patrol is black or Hispanic, the answer would seem to be crucial to any attempt to demonstrate racial prejudice on the basis of statistics. But in the Orwellian world of the American left, such questions do not even exist.

This lack of concern for fact was dramatized by a tragic incident that took place in a Dearborn shopping mall, two months before the "Redeem the Dream" march. A young black girl was arrested for stealing a $4 bracelet from the department store Lord & Taylor. Her stepfather, angered by the arrest, assaulted a security guard. During a scuffle with the five guards who rushed to the scene, the father was choked to death. Al Sharpton then appeared with 9,000 protesters in tow, chanting "No Justice, No Peace." The protestors sliced up Lord & Taylor credit cards to demonstrate their outrage against the capitalist racists whom they held responsible for the "hate crime." Michigan Representative John

---

[9]"Sworn Minorities Employed," Florida Highway Patrol, October 30, 2001, http://www.flhsmv.gov/fhp/html/min_emp.html.

Conyers—possibly the next chair of the House Judiciary Committee—demanded Justice Department intervention, declaring: "It's
not just a matter of driving while black. It's a matter of shopping
while black, living while black." The only problem was that four
of the five security guards were also black, including Dennis
Richardson, the guard eventually charged with manslaughter.[10]

When facts like these make no difference, it is a sure sign that
we are in the presence of ideologues who are disconnected from
reality. In the months leading up to the march, the nation's consciousness was bombarded by a media-powered propaganda campaign about alleged racial injustice. The core of the effort was a
series of partisan "studies," issuing from America's politicized
universities and leftwing think tanks, timed to influence the presidential election. "Racial Disparities Seen as Pervasive in Juvenile
Justice," *The New York Times* headlined a story about one of
these studies in its April 26 edition.[11] "Justice is Not Color Blind,
Studies Find," a May issue of the *Los Angeles Times* agreed. The
sub-header informed *Times* readers, "Researchers Say Blacks,
Browns Receive Tougher Treatment From Legal System."[12] *The
Washington Post* reported additional racism in society's efforts to
assert discipline: "Study Finds Racial Disparity in 'Zero Tolerance'
Enforcement."[13] A June edition of the *Los Angeles Times* reported:
"Study By Human Rights Watch Finds African-Americans Make

---

[10]"Reno Is Asked to Investigate Death of Black Man at Mall," Nichole M.
Christian, *The New York Times*, July 7, 2000, http://www.nytimes.com/
2000/07/07/us/reno-is-asked-to-investigate-death-of-black-man-at-mall.
html.

[11]"Racial Disparities Seen As Pervasive In Juvenile Justice," Fox Butter-
field, *The New York Times*, April 26, 2000, http://www.nytimes.com/
2000/04/26/us/racial-disparities-seen-as-pervasive-in-juvenile-
justice.html.

[12]"Justice Is Not Color Blind, Studies Find," Erin Texeira, *Los Angeles
Times*, May 22, 2000, http://articles.latimes.com/2000/may/22/local/
me-32797.

[13]"Study Finds Racial Disparity in 'Zero Tolerance' Enforcement," *The
Washington Post*, republished in *Los Angeles Times*, http://articles.
latimes.com/2000/jul/05/local/me-47936.

Up 62% Of Imprisoned Narcotic Offenders, Despite Accounting for 13% of U.S. Population."[14]

A common feature of each of these reports rendered every one of them specious. This was the absence of any statistics regarding the actual crimes committed. It is true, for example, that more cocaine customers—and thus "offenders"—are white, but more blacks are in jail for cocaine offenses. But unless the nature of these offenses is described, any claims about punishments being disparate are meaningless. It was liberal lawmakers (supported by the Congressional Black Caucus) who formed the consensus that removed the penalties and lifted the pressures on drug *consumption*, while increasing those on violent and organized drug *traffic*. The reason was that liberals deemed consumers harmful only to themselves, while the traffickers were harmful to others. Right or wrong, it was a distinction with a difference. Conservatives went along. But now it has become apparent that the violent career criminals who conduct the drug business are mainly black and brown. That is a problem, but it is not a problem created by racist laws and police.

Professional drug dealers are often also involved in criminal gangs, which terrorize whole communities—another reason why black and brown criminals fill the nation's jails. There are an estimated 31,000 gangs in the United States that have a combined membership approaching one million. Eighty percent of these gang members are Hispanic and black. Seventy percent of the violent juvenile defendants in criminal courts are black males; 60 percent of the juvenile murder defendants in criminal court are black males; 72 percent of the rape defendants, 78 percent of the robbery defendants, 61 percent of the assault defendants and 65 percent of defendants charged with other types of violent crime are also black

---

[14]"Blacks Unfairly Targeted in Fight on Drugs, Report Says," Jesse Katz, *Los Angeles Times*, June 8, 2000, http://articles.latimes.com/2000/jun/08/news/mn-38784.

males.[15] These facts amply account for the disparity in prison statistics.

The false images cooked up by the left, and so casually promoted by the working press, have tragic consequences for the very communities they purport to defend. Only 79 percent of juveniles convicted of violent crimes are actually sent to prison. The reason for this is decorously explained in the already cited government report: "Under the 'disproportionate minority confinement' requirement in the Juvenile Justice and Delinquency Prevention Act, states must determine whether the proportion of minorities in confinement exceeds their proportion in the population. If such over-representation is found, states must demonstrate efforts to reduce it...." And the "racist" state governments do so these days by releasing convicted violent criminals back to the streets, where they will be free to commit even more mayhem.

Back in the fantasy world of the racial demagogues, however, "the disparity in treatment is staggering" in the current juvenile justice system. Proponents of the racial profiling myth have even come up with a theory that blames the justice system itself for criminality among black youth. In a recent op-ed column, "The Juvenile Injustice System Disgraces the Rule of Law," Jesse Jackson wrote: "The disparity begins before the kids get into trouble. Too many of these children are raised against the odds.... Their mothers work, but they have no day care or Head Start. They go to school hungry.... Zero tolerance puts some on the street. Racial profiling targets those who are on the street. And the system of juvenile injustice kicks in, making it harder for them to complete their education, to get jobs, to become decent husbands and fathers. Juvenile injustice tags youngsters for life...."[16]

---

[15]*Juvenile Offenders and Victims: 1999 National Report,* Office of Juvenile Justice and Delinquency Prevention, https://www.ncjrs.gov/html/ojjdp/nationalreport99/toc.html.

[16]"The Juvenile Injustice System Disgraces The Rule of Law," Jesse Jackson, *Los Angeles Times,* April 28, 2000.

If only life were so simple. To begin with, 70 percent of inner-city black youngsters are born out of wedlock, which is one disgraceful disparity impacting these issues that Jackson chooses to overlook. It is well settled that statistics for fathers absent from the home correlate closely with those for youth violence and criminality. In the second place, mothers of youthful criminals in the inner city probably do not work; isn't that the point of William Julius Wilson's celebrated explanation for the very existence of the underclass, *When Work Disappears: The World of the New Urban Poor?* In fact, a high percentage of the mothers of youthful criminals are probably abusive parents and on drugs. Moreover, far from being immediately "tagged," delinquent youth are generally arrested twenty or thirty times for crimes they commit before they are ever sent to juvenile hall. One could go on *ad infinitum* in attempting to impose reality checks on racial mythologies, but what's the point when you are dealing with ideologues whose enemy is "the white power structure," rather than the criminal element that actually preys on the law abiding members of minority communities?

The idea that black youth are the targets of a racist system that is indifferent to their fate is a monstrous libel against the professionals in the criminal justice system, white, black and brown, who work against impossible odds to keep these youngsters on the right side of the law. Of 1.5 million cases of juvenile delinquency and crime processed in 1994, for example, only 55 percent resulted in legal action. Of these, only 1.4 percent—the very hardest cases—were handled in criminal court.[17] These statistics reflect the scarcity of resources for law enforcement and the enormously tolerant view of the system itself, which in metropolitan areas, where these crimes are concentrated, is largely administered by "progressives" and liberals who share many of Jackson's political prejudices if not his delusional views.

---

[17]*Juvenile Offenders and Victims,* op. cit.

Large metropolitan law enforcement agencies are now multi-ethnic and multi-gendered rather than simply white and male. The much-despised Los Angeles Police Department, to take a prime example, is a 53 percent minority force. But in the rhetoric of ideologues like Sharpton and Jackson, "white supremacy" is always the demon that oppresses. (Otherwise, *cui bono?*) Neither man has stopped short of inventing racist crimes by whites in order to sustain their lucrative hatreds. The Tawana Brawley incident is well known. More recently, however, Jesse Jackson launched his own campaign of intemperate racial accusation, in an effort to transform a tragic suicide in Mississippi into a white "hate crime."

On June 16, a 17-year-old black teenager named Raynard Johnson was found hanging from a tree in his front yard in Mississippi. According to the coroner's report, he had no marks on his body, no broken bones, no wounds, no bruises, and "he was not beaten up." His death was ruled a suicide. There are 3,700 such youth suicides every year in America. In the words of Surgeon General David Satcher, "more teenagers and young adults [die] from suicide than cancer, heart disease, AIDS, birth defects, stroke and lung disease combined." But, like many parents, Raynard Johnson's could not accept their tragedy. In their denial, they claimed their son had been "lynched." The evidence they offered for their suspicion was that they didn't recognize the belt he had used to hang himself; they thought they heard dogs barking before he died; and they felt that because their son was an honor student who seemed happy, he would not have taken his own life. Most ominously, he had been dating a white girl.

This was enough for Jesse Jackson, who hopped a plane to Mississippi to announce that "some man or men did this evil." He led a thousand marchers who chanted, "Stop the lynching now; stop killing our children."[18] Sharpton naturally joined in. Attorney

---

[18]"The Racism-Industry Lynch Mob," Michael Fumento, *National Review*, July 21, 2000, http://old.nationalreview.com/comment/commentprint072100c.html.

General Reno met with Jackson and the Johnson family. The FBI entered the case, followed by the NAACP, the Southern Poverty Law Center and other righteous protestors eager to pour oil on the flames of racial paranoia. But when the investigation was concluded, it was clear that there had been no lynching. Investigators discovered that Raynard's white girlfriend had recently broken up with him, a plausible catalyst of his depression.

Still, all wasn't lost for the Jackson vigilantes. Chances are that millions of Americans have forgotten the actual circumstances of Raynard Jackson's death and remember only the lynching charges. Author Michael Fumento did a Lexis search that turned up 170 media mentions with the terms "Raynard Johnson" and "lynch," a large proportion covering the agitations of Jackson himself.[19] The function of these efforts, after all, is not to seek justice but to keep alive the myths that allow this kind of racial hucksterism—and the racism it spawns—to flourish.

Any person not in the grip of the progressives' racial *animus* can plainly see that racist profiling does not in fact characterize the institutions of the American polity. But it does define the agenda of the political left. What is the "civil rights" cause, as articulated by the left, *but* race profiling after all? It is the civil rights left that demands racial boxes in the U.S. census. It is the civil rights left that defends racial preferences in admissions policies and government job contracts. It is the civil rights left that requires political positions and judicial appointments to conform to a quota system based on skin color. It is the civil rights left that agitates for a race-conscious (as opposed to a color-blind) system of government and laws, reversing the entire meaning of the civil rights struggles of the 1960s, which were fought specifically to outlaw such systems in the segregated South. And it is the conservative opponents of race profiling, led by University of California regent Ward Connerly, who have spearheaded the campaign to end

---

[19]Ibid.

current legal discrimination by government bodies and restore a single standard based on individual merit and achievement, not ethnicity and skin color.

Racial profiling in the name of racial justice has its own catalogue of victims both black and white. Every inner-city youngster killed by a black criminal who has been released from jail because of the "disproportionate minority confinement" requirement is a victim of Jesse Jackson and the progressive race profilers. Every law enforcement officer (black and white) unjustly targeted for suspicion is a victim of left-wing racism. And every false seed of doubt sown in minority communities about the fairness of law enforcement bears a bitter fruit in increased power for the predators who terrorize those communities and fill the lives of their inhabitants with fear.

Just two months before Jesse Jackson descended on Mississippi to accuse unnamed and unknown whites of lynching Raynard Jackson, an eight-year-old white boy named Kevin Shifflett was attacked by a black racist in Alexandria, Virginia, a suburb of the nation's capital. The racist attacker was a 29-year-old parole violator, previously incarcerated for a hammer attack on an unarmed white male whom he did not know, and whom he referred to only as "whitey." This time, the attacker used a knife to slash the throat of eight-year-old Kevin. According to an eyewitness, the attacker shouted a racial epithet at the third-grader as he went in for the kill. Later, police found a note in the suspect's hotel room: "Kill them raceess [sic] white kidd's [sic]. . . ."

For three months, the Virginia authorities concealed the racial identity of the suspect, as well as the fact that it might have been a racial attack. Eventually, *The Washington Post* did run a couple of stories describing how police had withheld the facts and how they had found the note in the suspect's room. But the rest of the media ignored the case. Could it possibly be that the authorities (and the press) were silent for three months because the killer was black and his eight-year-old victim was white? That is indeed the kind of racial profiling which Jesse Jackson, Al Sharpton, the

NAACP, the ACLU and other members of their vanguard have imposed on our moral discourse.

If Kevin had been black and his attacker white, consider the national media coverage that would have attended this case. Moral edicts and blanket charges would have been hurled from the Capitol rotunda at an anguished national audience; a presidential press conference would have devoted itself to extravagant *mea culpas* while denouncing the outrage. As it is, there is not one person in ten thousand reading this who until now even knew that this event took place. Before Americans give further credence to the racial arsonists of the civil rights left, they may want to ponder the facts above and the awful implications of the silence that still engulfs an eight-year old Virginian who happened to be white, and who was brutally slaughtered for the color of his skin.

Sadly, there is no longer a civil rights movement in this country. Ironically, grotesquely, in its place there is only a self-righteous, fact-denying lynch mob looking for white victims and law enforcement officials to make the targets of their wrath.

2

Washington's Disgraceful Report to the UN

The Report on U.S. Racism filed with the UN by the Clinton State and Justice Departments shows how deeply entrenched the anti-American left is at the highest levels of government. One of the signatories to the report, Bill Lann Lee, has previously distinguished himself as an opponent of anti-discrimination law in California. As an NAACP lawyer, Lee designed a consent decree with the Los Angeles police and fire departments that would have circumvented California's anti-discrimination Proposition 209. The decree was signed 10 days before the election, when it was clear the vast majority of California voters would support Prop 209. Lee argued that a proposition clearly stating that the government should not make laws that discriminate on the basis of race and gender was "unconstitutional." Lee's undemocratic and racist consent decree was thwarted by lawyers for the Individual Rights Foundation (a program of the Center for the Study of Popular Culture), who succeeded in getting an injunction against it.

Why is the United States officially embarrassing itself before the UN, a body that includes states like the Sudan, which practices slavery, and Rwanda, which practices genocide? Or Zimbabwe, which is carrying on an officially sanctioned race war against its white citizens? The U.S. report ignores these realities to complain about American "racism." It refers to the alleged racism of American

September 26, 2000, http://archive.frontpagemag.com/Printable.aspx?ArtId=19852.

society as "subtle" and "elusive," the typical cant of the radical left.[1] American racism is subtle and elusive because in fact it is virtually non-existent. There are racists among us to be sure, as there will always be. And they can even hold titles like Deputy Attorney General for Civil Rights. But American society is not racist, and the extraordinary progress of African-Americans in the last forty years is as clear an indication of that fact as one could ask for.

The report itself is a compendium of the false accusations of the anti-American left, including the alleged injustice to the parole-violating felon Rodney King, who resisted arrest and was subdued according to the book, as his only legitimate trial showed. (See both the *American Lawyer* article by Roger Parloff and *Official Negligence*, the investigative book by Lou Cannon.[2]) The report also includes the recent incident caused by the Adams Mark Hotel delinquents who trashed a hotel on a school break holiday and happened to be black. Also included are the "startlingly high incarceration" rates, which in fact reflect startlingly high black crime rates (a fact the report fails to mention). Most laughable are the alleged "rollbacks in affirmative action" and "erosion in voting rights"—the latter because racist districting in favor of blacks has been declared unconstitutional, and the former because apartheid-style race preferences have been similarly rejected by voters in California and Washington.

This report is reminiscent of the petition to the UN organized by the American Communist Party in the Stalin era, called "We Charge Genocide," which was designed to avert the public's eyes from the slaughter of innocents in the Worker's Paradise. The same progressives, with the same "idealistic" agendas, are behind this fiasco.

---

[1] "The Convention on the Elimination of All Forms of Racial Discrimination," Department of State, September 2000, http://www.state.gov/www/global/human_rights/cerd_report/cerd_toc.html.

[2] "Maybe The Jury Was Right," Roger Parloff, *The American Lawyer*, July/August 1992, http://www.soc.umn.edu/~samaha/cases/parloff_jury_right.htm; Lou Cannon, *Official Negligence : How Rodney King and the Riots Changed Los Angeles and the LAPD*, Times Books/Random House, 1998.

3

Racial Witch-Hunt

On December 14, as the holiday season was getting into full swing, five young men and women, all professionals with bright careers ahead of them, were accosted at gunpoint in a townhouse belonging to one of them, sexually tortured and then shot in the head. The sadistic criminals who perpetrated this atrocity were brothers. Only one young woman survived. Naked and bleeding from her head wound, she staggered a mile through the snow to safety. In a poignant footnote to the tragedy, she discovered, when one of the criminals stole a diamond ring from a drawer in the apartment where her companions were killed, that her now-dead boyfriend had intended to propose to her.

Despite the story's horror, despite its drama, despite its "human interest" dimension, not a single national news outlet reported the case. The reason: the monsters who committed this horror were black, the victims white. Just as there can be no black racism, according to Spike Lee and other sages of our progressive culture, so there can be no black hate crimes. Had the victims and perpetrators been of the same race, the fact that this crime was so horrific and that it occurred during the holiday season would have made it national news. That it wasn't reported in the national press is a measure of how fiercely the political culture protects the myth of racial oppression: if a racist monster is African-American, he mustn't exist.

January 22, 2001, http://archive.frontpagemag.com/Printable.aspx?ArtId=24413; http://www.salon.com/2001/01/22/inquisition/.

The same culture of politically-correct, anti-white attitudes works locally as well. The official position over the killings in the editorial rooms of the *Wichita Eagle* and the local district attorney's office was that the December 14 hate crime was not a hate crime at all. Why? Because the victims had been robbed and the motive therefore was not racism but robbery. Hogwash. Matthew Shepard—the poster boy for hate crimes—was robbed.

Neither the crime nor the silence surrounding it is an isolated instance. Last February, 6-year-old Jake Robel was dragged five miles to his death in Missouri because a black carjacker was deaf to a white child's screams for help. The nation was not informed. Last April, eight-year-old Kevin Shifflett had his throat slit by a black racist in broad daylight, in a suburb of the nation's capital. No one reported Kevin's murder as a hate crime, and the crime itself was smothered in a politically-correct news blackout. These crimes of recent vintage remain invisible. But a two-year-old hate crime, familiar to every citizen through endless repetition in the news media, congressional keenings and presidential pronouncements—because it was committed against a black man—became a central feature of the Democrats' campaign against presidential candidate George Bush, whom they found guilty of association with the incident because it took place in Texas.

Why should these facts surprise anyone, when everyone knows that in America it is politically correct to hate white people? Hatred of whites is a well-developed intellectual doctrine at our nation's most prestigious universities and law schools. Whole faculties are devoted to it. Hatred of whites is widely taught in our nation's schools, where white people are portrayed as history's racists and oppressors. It is inscribed in our nation's laws, which provide racial privileges and racial protections for those whose skin color is any shade but white. Meanwhile, the Democratic Party campaigns to ensure that hate crimes are identified exclusively with straight white males. Its surrogate in this campaign is the nation's leading so-called civil rights organization, the NAACP, which ran a multi-million dollar TV effort during the presidential race, insinuating that George W. Bush hates black people and is in league with a lynch mob because he did not think extending a hate crimes law to include special protections for gays was a prudent idea. No Democrat has condemned this racial McCarthyism.

With calculated cynicism, the Democratic Party has whipped up racial paranoia in the African-American community by lending credibility to the lunatic charge that there was systematic disenfranchisement of black voters in Florida during the presidential election, committed by racists who remain unnamed but are obviously Republican. The U.S. Civil Rights Commission has even staged a show trial to demonstrate the un-demonstrable. Witness after witness appeared before the commission to claim racial intimidation, and then were forced to admit under questioning that they had actually been able to vote. Not a shred of evidence exists that there was a conspiracy to deprive African-Americans in Florida of the right to vote. Yet the NAACP has filed lawsuits making just that accusation. And millions of black people have been persuaded by racial demagogues and their liberal abettors that such a conspiracy exists—that the election was "stolen" from them in order that Republicans could appoint racists to government.

The witch-hunting mentality that has taken possession of the Democratic Party is on full display in a notorious Internet column written by Clinton strategist and Gore advisor Paul Begala:

> Yes ... tens of millions of good people in Middle America voted Republican. But if you look closely at that [electoral] map [showing counties that voted Republican in red] you see a more complex picture. You see the state where James Byrd was lynch-dragged behind a pickup truck until his body came apart—it's red. You see the state where Matthew Shepard was crucified on a split-rail fence for the crime of being gay—it's red. You see the state where right-wing extremists blew up a federal office building and murdered scores of federal employees—it's red. The state where an army private who was thought to be gay was

bludgeoned to death with a baseball bat, and the state where neo-Nazi skin-heads murdered two African-Americans because of their skin color, and the state where Bob Jones University spews its anti-Catholic bigotry: they're all red too.

One could respond to Begala in Begala fashion: "The state where left-wing extremist, Muslim terrorists blew up the World Trade Center—that's blue. The county where a race riot over a jury verdict destroyed 2,000 Korean businesses and caused the deaths of 58 people—that's blue. The states where Colin Ferguson and Ronald Taylor killed 8 whites and Asians because leftwing race baiters convinced them they were victims of a racial conspiracy—are blue. The counties, nationwide, where the vast majority of murderers, rapists and child molesters live and operate—those are blue, too."

But far more important is how Begala's outburst reveals the casual way in which a mainstream progressive strategist can smear an entire political party—routinely identified by his political comrades as a "white party"—as a den of racial killers. Not since the heyday of Senator Joe McCarthy has there been a demonization of whole categories of Americans or a national witch-hunt on a scale like this.

Now a focus of this witch-hunt is the nomination process for the new president's cabinet. What used to be the *pro forma* confirmation ritual of an incoming administration has been turned into an orgy of character assassination. Consider the spectacle. George Bush has nominated the most diverse cabinet in American history. He has appointed African-Americans to the highest positions on record. He has appointed a Chinese-American and an Arab-American to cabinet positions for the first time. He has appointed Hispanic-Americans and African-Americans and a Japanese-American, and of course women. Yet his nominations are the targets of a Democrat campaign to portray his nominees as racists, homophobes and even, in one frenzied historical leap, *Torquemadas.*

All this has had a predictable effect on a reliably uninformed public. Does a national icon of the popular culture, Ricky Martin, have the temerity to accept an invitation to sing at the new president's inauguration? In other times, this would have been seen as a high honor—in this case, an honor to the entire Puerto Rican community to have one of its sons assume such a nationally visible role. But in the atmosphere the left has poisoned, Ricky Martin must be prepared to have his life and career torn apart to accept the invitation. On hearing of his decision to attend, Martin's childhood friend and professional partner, the man who produces and writes his songs, told the nation's press that the singing gig was "a betrayal of everything that every Puerto Rican should stand for." "This is a president," according to Robi Rosa, "who would have people in his Cabinet who would obstruct the exercise of civil rights, human rights, consumer rights, the right to choose, the right to be free of gun violence and the right to a clean environment."[1] All Democratic talking points; all lies. In the atmosphere of hysteria whipped up by left-wing McCarthyites, one news channel even billed a program on the nominee for Attorney General this way: "Bush calls him a man of integrity; critics call him frightening." Begalism *über Alles*.

What are the specific charges the Democrats have brought against Bush's nominee for Attorney General? John Ashcroft is accused of the crime of opposing racial preferences (along with 70 percent of Americans, who share that view). According to the witch-hunters, this makes him a closet racist. He is accused of opposing a failed program—forced busing as a means of integration—which has been rejected even in liberal Democrat cities like Los Angeles and Boston, and among blacks. For this he is accused of "racism." He is accused of sympathies for the Confederacy because he didn't condemn the Confederate flag and thought the

---

[1] "Arts And Entertainment Reports From The Times, News Services And The Nation's Press," Elaine Dutka, *Los Angeles Times*, January 13, 2001, http://articles.latimes.com/2001/jan/13/entertainment/ca-11754.

Confederate cause may have embraced other issues besides slavery, although normally the left argues that it was about anything *but* slavery. In fact, a Democratic senator, Fritz Hollings, raised the Confederate flag over South Carolina's capitol and Bill Clinton signed official proclamations commemorating the Confederacy while governor of Arkansas—with no such backlash effects. Ashcroft is accused of opposing one black judicial nomination out of a total 26 such nominations because Ronnie White, the black judge in question, overturned the death penalty of a cold-blooded killer who had murdered the wife of a sheriff in front of her children at a Christmas Party, arousing the passionate interest of Missouri sheriffs. For this—and this alone—a man with two decades of unimpeachable public service, a supporter of integration, a proponent of Martin Luther King's vision of equal rights under the law, is pilloried as a "racist."

The time has come to pose to Democrats and the left the same question the liberal hero of America's most famous witch-hunt finally put to Senator McCarthy himself: Have you no decency, sir? Have you no shame?

4

Progressive Crime Wave

Just before the July 4th holiday, a story appeared in the pages of one big city newspaper about a series of violent crimes in its impoverished African-American neighborhoods. The story has already made the rounds of conservative media outlets but, like other reports from the real world that might disturb progressives' sense of their own virtue, it will not travel much beyond the city in question.

The city is Cincinnati, the scene in April of a black race riot whose targets were Cincinnati police and the white population, triggered by the shooting death of a local criminal. The lawless indignation of this event rallied self-appointed champions of "social justice" from coast to coast, as it always does. It was not referred to as a "black race riot" by any mainstream media institutions, of course. Although white citizens of Cincinnati were dragged from their vehicles and beaten for their skin color, there was scant concern for the "hate crime" aspects of the outrage. It was treated, instead, as a black "protest" against "racial profiling" and "police brutality"—charges legally untested and factually unsupported but nevertheless accepted by progressive elites who would not know what to think otherwise.

In response to Cincinnati's riot and perceived injustices, all the forces of progressive self-righteousness descended on the city. The usual race hustlers ranted about rights; local politicians folded

July 10, 2001, http://archive.frontpagemag.com/Printable.aspx?ArtId= 24434; http://www.salon.com/2001/07/09/cincinnati_3/.

under the moral assault and indicted the police instead of the criminals; even the Ashcroft Justice Department joined in. (How could one expect a man who had been nearly lynched in the nation's media for having "pro-slavery" prejudices acquit himself otherwise?) In a tediously familiar scenario, the Cincinnati events became another charade of American injustice towards blacks. But when all the shouting was done, and the civil rights agitators had gone home, the reality of the war that lawless inhabitants had waged against defenders of the civil peace remained. The results of that war were the subject of a post-riot story in the *Cincinnati Enquirer*, which the national media predictably ignored:[1]

"41 Shootings in 10 Weeks—
All But One of 59 Victims Were Black"
In the weeks after the April riots, gunfire crackled at an alarming rate through Over-the-Rhine, West End, Avondale, Bond Hill and other predominantly African-American neighborhoods . . . neighborhoods that paid a toll in broken glass and looted buildings during the riots . . .

To put the statistics in perspective, understand that last year— before the race riot and the liberal assault on Cincinnati police— there were less than 10 shootings in the same 10 weeks in these same neighborhoods, where the most vulnerable of Cincinnati's citizens live. A successful riot against police will do wonders to lift the spirits of criminal predators. That is why this year, as the *Enquirer* reports, "black-on-black shootings noticeably spiked after April 7,"[2] the date the anti-law enforcement riot began. Like the young criminal whose flight from police and consequent death was the incident that precipitated the riot, all of the 22 suspects arrested for these shootings were black males.

---

[1]"41 Shootings In 10 Weeks—All But One of 59 Victims Were Black," Susan Vela, *Cincinnati Enquirer*, July 2, 2001, http://enquirer.com/editions/2001/07/02/loc_41_shootings_in_10.html.
[2]"Stories of 15 Black Men Killed by Police Since 1995," Dan Klepal and Cindi Andrews, *Cincinnati Enquirer*, April 15, 2001, http://www.enquirer.com/editions/2001/04/15/loc_stories_of.html.

Now consider the other side of the story. Consider the perspective of the law enforcement community in Cincinnati. This community was in the habit of reading Miranda rights to every predator it arrested, however calculating and vile his criminal misdeeds. But now it saw itself treated as a vigilante squad of racists, presumed guilty in front of the entire nation before evidence of any crime had even been presented. This community now witnessed a swifter indictment lodged against one of its own than against many of the felons it had pursued. Overnight, and without probable cause, it became the target of a national lynch mob seeking "justice" from a policeman for the crime of performing his protective duty. This community could not fail to notice that, in advance of any trial or presentation of the facts, it had been put in the criminal dock and had no defenders in the national press or even among city officials, who were presumably pledged to uphold the law and support the public good.

The reaction of law enforcement is not really difficult to imagine. But no speculation is necessary. A recent newsletter to members of the Cincinnati Fraternal Order of Police contains this warning from its president: "If you want to make 20 traffic stops a shift and chase every dope dealer you see, you go right ahead. Just remember that if something goes wrong, or you make the slightest mistake in that split second, it could result in having your worst nightmare come true for you and your family, and City Hall will sell you out."[3]

Allow me a certain bluntness in interpolating these facts. In Cincinnati, the crusade for social justice conducted by self-righteous race hustlers, myopic idealists and political whores has produced a police force predictably (and sensibly) reluctant to continue enforcing the law at its own unappreciated expense. This has

---

[3] "Police Frustration Brings Slowdown—Arrests Plummet from 2000; Officers Seek Jobs in Suburbs," Sheila McLaughlin and Jane Prendergast, *Cincinnati Enquirer*, June 30, 2001, http://www.enquirer.com/editions/2001/06/30/loc_police_frustration.html.

produced an equally predictable crime wave whose mounting roster of victims is—also inevitably—black.

Days before the *Cincinnati Enquirer* ran its story, a related feature appeared in *The Seattle Times,* in which another protested police shooting had recently taken place.[4]

Wary of Racism Complaints, Police Look the Other Way
The cops on the street have different names for it: de-policing, selective disengagement, tactical detachment. They even joke about it, calling themselves "tourists in blue."

The report describes the new police posture as "passive law enforcement," and explains that this is a practice that takes place when officers become reluctant to make preventive "stops," cease to aggressively pursue criminals—specifically when the criminals are black—and only respond to 911 calls: "Many officers, wary of being labeled racists or racial profilers, say they hold back or bypass opportunities to make traffic stops or arrests of black suspects."

And why should they do otherwise, when there's a national campaign to make them the criminals for pursuing such methods? "Racial profiling"—as interpreted by a civil rights mafia and a desperate-for-the-black-vote Democratic Party—means that more blacks are stopped by police than are represented in the population as a whole. But blacks commit more than 40 percent of the violent crimes in the nation. In other words, the only way to avoid racial profiling as defined by the left is to cut crime prevention by 28 percent, or some roughly similar figure.

Racial profiling may exist. But like other police abuses, it will be committed by individual officers, black as well as white. There is no evidence that racial profiling is a systemic practice in any police department in the country. Not a single reported study takes into account the race of officers making the alleged racial

---

[4]"Wary of Racism Complaints, Police Look the Other Way in Black Neighborhoods," Alex Tizon and Reid Forgrave, *The Seattle Times,* June 26, 2001, http://community.seattletimes.nwsource.com/archive/?date=20010626&slug=police26m.

stops, to mention just one problem of current profiling statistics. Without such an inquiry, how could one possibly ascertain whether stops are actually racially motivated?

Racial profiling as a systematic persecution of black males is a myth, and a dangerous one.[5] Yet, in the atmosphere of racial hysteria that has been whipped up by the Democratic Party and the civil rights left, it would take a brave politician to withstand the pressure for racial-profiling laws and stand up for the safety of citizens who are poor and mainly minorities, and who inhabit the high-crime areas of our inner cities.

In the Seattle story, a black policeman describes the problem of racial profiling as "a phantom." He explains the obvious fact that police deployments are made in response to the incidence of crimes. An inexorable sequence follows: The greater the incidence of crimes, the greater the concentration of police, the more contacts with the public, the greater potential for conflict—the potential, that is, for unscrupulous criminals and their willing political allies to manufacture a racial incident and an urban riot.

The young man whose death provided a pretext for the events in Cincinnati had fourteen warrants for his arrest and was fleeing 12 officers with drawn guns at the time of his demise. It was reasonable for any responsible law enforcement official to suspect that he was more dangerous than in retrospect he turned out to be. Hence the conflict. In a similar incident in New York City, which became a much bigger national story, Amadou Diallo was accosted in the dead of night in a high-crime area by police responding to a call for help and in pursuit of a vicious rapist.[6] Another conflict. But it was the inflammatory intervention of demagogic arsonists like Al Sharpton and Jesse Jackson, and the credulous cast of

---

[5] Heather MacDonald, *Are Cops Racist? How the War Against the Police Harms Black Americans*, Ivan R. Dee, 2002.

[6] "Officers in Bronx Fire 41 Shots, And an Unarmed Man Is Killed," Michael Cooper, *The New York Times*, February 5, 1999, http://www.nytimes.com/1999/02/05/nyregion/officers-in-bronx-fire-41-shots-and-an-unarmed-man-is-killed.html?pagewanted=all&src=pm.

progressives who followed in their wake, that turned this and a second incident into a racial melodrama which left a trail of civic damage in its wake.

Through aggressive policing in the previous seven years, the Giuliani administration had made New York City safer for the African-Americans who inhabit its high crime areas than any previous administration on record. Giuliani's methods reduced the number of police shootings of New Yorkers by nearly 80 percent, and reduced the criminal homicide rate by two-thirds. Yet the racial demagogues were able to exploit an egregious abuse of police authority in another case—that of Abner Louima (for which the guilty were quickly prosecuted)—and parlay it into a public lynching of Giuliani and the New York police force. By the time liberals were through tarring the mayor as a genocidal racist, opinion polls showed him losing 98.8 percent of the black vote in New York. This was a result the devil himself could not surpass. The practical consequence of this racial witch-hunt: recruitment of police in New York City has itself become a major law enforcement problem. Who is going to suffer as a result?[7]

The war against alleged racial profiling, which is being zealously prosecuted by every self-worshipping progressive in America, is really a war against poor blacks and other inner city minorities who are the main targets of violent crime. It is feebly opposed by Republicans, who are themselves under racial attack from the left and who, like the police, cannot see any benefit in resisting the trend. Why be burned as a racist when you can go along and get along, and maybe sneak through? Which leaves the most vulnerable and voiceless members of the American community with few to defend them against the predators who roam their mean and dangerous inner-city streets.

---

[7] "NYC Officer Arrested in Alleged Sexual Attack on Suspect," Maria Hinojosa, CNN, August 14, 1997, http://www.cnn.com/US/9708/14/police.torture/; "The Prince of New York," Fred Siegel, *The Weekly Standard*, August 21, 2000, http://www2.sunysuffolk.edu/formans/GiulianiSiegalReview.htm.

5

Chris Matthews:
White and Blind

Sometimes the easiest truths to understand are the hardest to
actually learn. "Thinking doesn't make it so," is one. "Just
because it *feels* good doesn't mean it *is* good," is another.
The failure to learn this distinction is actually the cause of liberalism, and it lies at the heart of the liberal confusion about race.

The liberal view begins with adopting a morally correct tone,
which is actually quite easy. All it involves is taking a correct
stand against evils like racism. The liberal view then goes on to
something like this: "Even though it's hard to find an actual racist
standing in a schoolhouse door anymore, and even though white
people won't admit it, there's still a lot of racism in American society, and it's an obstacle to the progress of black citizens." There's a
corollary to this moral posture: The more racism you think there
is, and the bigger the obstacle you think it presents, the more liberal you are. And the better you feel about yourself. You are the
sensitive one. You are the one who can imagine yourself shoulder
to shoulder with the civil rights soldiers of the past, who faced
down police hoses in Alabama and lynch mobs in Mississippi.
Detecting racism, even where it may not exist, heightens the
sense of one's own virtue and links one to the heroes of the past.

But just because it feels good doesn't make it good. Serving
one's appetite for self-love can be a profound disservice to the people one thinks one is helping. Suppose an athletic team with a

July 23, 2001, http://archive.frontpagemag.com/Printable.aspx?ArtId=
24437.

roster of black stars is having a poor season. Suppose the coach were to explain his players' poor performance by blaming the racism of the referees instead of his players' performance. For all the internal satisfaction he might get, in the real world he would be crippling his team by denying it the only opportunity it has to improve its game, which is by holding itself accountable. In the real world, the role played by racial prejudice in holding African-Americans back has steadily diminished. Every survey of public attitudes on race shows that there has been a dramatic decline of such attitudes among white Americans over the last sixty years. Paralleling these findings, there has been an equally dramatic advance in the status of black citizens over the same duration. To take one key figure: In 1940, only 10 percent of blacks were middle-class.[1] The figure is now 49 percent.[2] If that isn't progress, what is?

But the liberal myopia regarding race persists. A good example is offered in a recent column by Chris Matthews, otherwise a seasoned political commentator. Matthews's column is called "White Blindness," by which he means the blindness to black oppression resulting from persistent racism.[3] His observations were inspired by a recent poll that showed a majority of white Americans believe that blacks have "about the same opportunities in life [as] whites have," and that there is not a lot of discrimination against blacks remaining. Quipped Matthews, "I accept the accuracy of the survey.... It's the white people I don't believe."

As Matthews sees it, white people lie to themselves and to pollsters about race because "many whites do not want to admit racial discrimination for fear it will be used to justify affirmative action." Liberals, being more moral than other whites, support affirmative action with the following logic: By holding blacks

---

[1] Defined as having twice the income of the poverty level.

[2] Abigail and Stephan Thernstrom, *America in Black and White*, Simon & Schuster, 1997, pp. 18, 81, 533.

[3] "White Blindness," Chris Matthews, *Jewish World Review*, July 16, 2001, http://www.jewishworldreview.com/cols/matthews071601.asp.

back, racism gives unfair privileges to whites. Justice requires that some privilege be redistributed to blacks to "level the playing field." Since whites are adversely affected by affirmative action—they lose a race privilege—the unenlightened will oppose it. But they don't want to appear racist, so they will deny that racism exists (or that it is a significant obstacle to black aspirations). Hence "white blindness."

The problem with this argument is that the principal opposition to affirmative action comes from two sources that have nothing to do with racism. The first is a belief that any kind of racial preference is an offense to the American idea that individuals should be judged on their merits. The second is the pragmatic conclusion that affirmative action policies work badly in the real world, not only for whites but for blacks and other minorities as well.

The 50th question on the same poll that Matthews cites (but fails to quote) is this:

> In order to give minorities more opportunity, do you believe race or ethnicity should be a factor when deciding who is hired, promoted, or admitted to college, or that hiring, promotions, and college admissions should be based strictly on merit and qualifications other than race or ethnicity?

Ninety-four percent of the whites interviewed answered this question negatively, which would seem to confirm Matthews' point. But eighty-six percent of blacks also answered the question negatively, along with eighty-eight percent of Hispanics.

Matthews thinks it's obvious that opportunities for blacks are dramatically less available than opportunities for whites. "Can a white American, with Harlem, Watts or any of this country's huge racial ghettos in mind, defend his or her claim that blacks have the same 'opportunities'?" he asks. It's an odd but typically liberal idea that all blacks live in Harlem or Watts, or some "huge racial ghetto." It makes putting scare-quotes around the word "opportunities" an easier task for sure. But the reality is that 78 percent of blacks have incomes above the poverty line, and don't live in inner cities or "ghettos." This wasn't always the case. In 1940, 87 percent of blacks were poor.[4] Job and housing discrimination had big impacts then. But now things are obviously different. How come the remaining 22 percent of blacks are still living in poverty? Can their failure really be blamed on white racism? Are whites forcing some blacks to live in inner cities, while allowing the vast majority to escape?

Part of the problem is the now habitual use of the word "ghetto." Blacks in America don't live in "ghettos" in the original meaning of that term. When Jews were forced to live in ghettos in Europe, they were actually forced to do so. They couldn't leave. The word "ghetto," like many other terms—"Holocaust" and "Diaspora" are two—have been appropriated from the annals of Jewish suffering by black activists for obvious reasons. But for the same reasons these words carry with them many false implications.

The Middle Passage, for example, which brought black slaves to America and which Toni Morrison and others refer to as a "Black Holocaust" was actually not a calculated genocide, as was Hitler's extermination of the Jews. The slave traders were businessmen who had money invested in their grim cargos, and did not buy slaves in Africa to kill them on the way to the plantations across the ocean. The term "Diaspora" refers to the forced dispersal of the Jews from Israel and their existence for two millennia as a pariah group, without a homeland of its own. The population of black Africa was not dispersed by an external power. Black Africans sold their brothers and sisters into slavery, while retaining continuous sovereignty in their own lands. The slaves who were sent into exile lost their connection so thoroughly in the process that there is no significant movement among American blacks to return to a "homeland." American blacks are not living in a Diaspora as permanent aliens. They are home.

Each of these terms heightens the perception of victimization beyond the circumstances. That is their purpose, but thinking

---

[4] Abigail and Stephan Thernstrom, *America in Black and White,* Simon & Schuster, 1997, p. 18.

doesn't make it so. Matthews and other liberals don't accept this analysis. As Matthews tells it, blacks are "consigned" to certain neighborhoods. He is too smart to state this false claim baldly, so he asks it as a series of rhetorical questions. "What does consign blacks to" various inner cities? "Because they are not wanted in nicer neighborhoods, and would rather not have their families put up with the hassle? Because real estate agents steer black buyers away from the better openings? Or because the black home buyer simply doesn't have the money to buy better homes? Whatever answer you choose involves a denial of equal opportunity."

The idea that blacks can't buy nice middle-class homes is demonstrably false, given the existence of such a large black middle class. Even the smaller truths in Matthews' statements hide the much bigger ones that confound his claims. Recently, black civil rights organizations raised a hue and cry about a small symbol, the Confederate flag. Does Chris Matthews seriously believe that the reason the same organizations are not protesting rampant racial exclusion in real estate is to avoid a *hassle?* If this kind of exclusion were systematically keeping middle class blacks from living where they wanted to, doesn't it seem likely that Jesse Jackson would have long ago alighted in the neighborhood at the head of a concerted campaign to integrate it? And to prosecute all those nasty realtors working (as it happens illegally) to keep the neighborhood pure?

A more interesting question Matthews might want to ask is whether there are in fact large numbers of middle class blacks who want to live in predominantly white neighborhoods in the first place. Does he think that the persistence of "historically black" colleges is the result of white colleges keeping blacks out? Perhaps Matthews missed the recent article by a black reporter in *The Washington Post* who announced she was proudly relocating in "Chocolate City" and didn't want any "Vanilla" there.[5] In fact,

---

[5] "Keeping Whitey Out," Jonah Goldberg, *National Review Online,* June 18, 2001, http://old.nationalreview.com/goldberg/goldbergprint061801. html.

recent studies show that black segregation in housing is largely a product of self-selection.

I had reason to think about liberals' perception problems the other day in a different context. As it happens, the day was July 4th and I was looking out over miles of ocean beaches stretching from the Pacific Palisades to Malibu, crowded with holiday bathers. What caught my attention was the fact that there was not a black person in sight. I thought to myself that a liberal would immediately call this segregation, and explain it as a product of "institutional racism." Black people—or so the story might go—can't afford to live in Malibu or the Palisades or even in the white suburbs near them. South Central is quite far away. Even if black people were inclined to make the trip, they probably wouldn't want the hassle of spending time on the beach with whites who don't want them. In whatever the case, the explanation for the absence of blacks would be white racism.

The problem with this analysis is that about three-quarters of the people who were in fact enjoying the surf and sand were Hispanics from East L.A, which is much farther from the coast than the black inner cities of Compton and Watts—and just as impoverished. Moreover, there are a lot more black actors and music moguls living in Malibu and the Palisades than there are Mexicans. The problem with the liberal viewpoint is that it fails to take into account people's cultural choices, *their free will.*

"Ever watch an NBA game," asks Matthews, "and notice that the players are black but that nearly 100 percent of seats within a hundred feet of the court are filled with whites? Ever go anywhere and not see the whites in the better seats, the better houses, the better jobs?" For Matthews, these questions answer themselves and add up to the case that discrimination is responsible for denying blacks the opportunities that would get them those better seats and houses. It all reminds Matthews of a Groucho Marx line: "Are you going to believe me or your lying eyes?"

Well, it all depends on whose eyes are doing the lying. The fanciest house in my neighborhood is owned by Laurence Fishburne, the black star of *Searching for Bobby Fisher, Othello, The Matrix* and other films. Somewhere out there, the growing black middle class is living well, even if Chris Matthews is a stranger to their neighborhoods. Just to pick a non-entertainment, non-sports field of endeavor that will be familiar enough to provide an example: the black middle class, too, has some pretty respectable jobs with six-figure salaries, like running Atlanta, Washington, DC, Detroit, Baltimore and other major American cities.

As for the NBA, if Matthews had looked at the other seats in the house, he wouldn't have found many blacks there, either. But if he had looked, say, at the front-row seats for a Mike Tyson fight in Las Vegas, he would have seen Jesse Jackson, Don King, the late Tupac Shakur, the record mogul Suge Knight and other Armani-suited fans of a darker hue. What accounts for the difference at NBA games? Beats me, but then I couldn't tell you why there are almost no black hockey players, let alone black hockey fans, let alone season box holders. Nor could I tell you why, if you were hiking in the Sierras or any national park—where the fees are nominal—a black person would be harder to find than a unicorn. Disneyland, which is very expensive, is crowded with working class Mexicans, but there are almost no blacks to be seen. Cultural choices are mysterious. But they *are* choices. And one thing is certain: it's not money or opportunity that's keeping blacks from occupying the high-dollar seats at NBA games.

Unfortunately, the feel-good racial fantasies of liberals like Matthews result in a blindness whose destructive consequences are real. Last April, a black criminal resisting arrest in Cincinnati was shot and killed by police. Some individuals in the black community started a riot. They attacked police first and then whites generally, blaming racism for what had happened. Irresponsible black leaders and racial muggers from the NAACP descended on the scene. Instead of defending the law and calling for an orderly inquiry, they fanned the flames of racial grievance and blamed "racist" law enforcement. White politicians, striving to earn their "liberal" credentials (*racist police? of course we're against them*) piled on. The result was reported in *The New York Times* on July 17: "Since the protests, there [have] been 59 shooting incidents in the city with 77 gunshot victims compared with 9 shooting and 11 victims in the comparable 3-month period last year." Seventy-six of the 77 gunshot victims were black.

Under attack—and lacking any political support—Cincinnati police officers did the sensible thing. They took themselves out of the line of fire. "There has also been a decline of nearly 55 percent in traffic stops," noted the *Times* reporter, explaining that traffic stops are "a tactic that the [police] union chief defend[s] as crucial to policing but that blacks often decry as harassment rooted in racial profiling." What could be clearer? When racial muggers and feel-good liberals join forces in hunting down racists who may not exist, the result is a lot more misery for blacks.

Or take Matthews's own Rosetta stone, affirmative action. Some years ago, the liberals in the state education establishment in Michigan put in place aggressive affirmative action programs to overcome the "institutional racism" they imagined was keeping blacks out of Michigan universities. Of course, Michigan universities already couldn't discriminate against blacks if they wanted to. It was against the law. The purpose of the new affirmative action programs was to rig the entrance requirements at these institutions so that black students who were not adequately prepared could get in anyway. That would bring about "diversity." Liberals could feel good. So even though the students were not prepared, the liberals recruited them aggressively anyway to give them those front row seats that were just out of reach. When black enrollment lists swelled, liberals looked at these plums and said "My, what good boys (and, of course, girls) we are."

But *The Detroit News* recently spoiled the fun by showing what was wrong with the picture. *The News* conducted an investigation of the program results at seven Michigan universities, which revealed that, among black students who were freshman in 1994, only 40 percent got their diplomas after six years. Sixty percent had failed or dropped out. "We're throwing them out after taking their money and they're getting nothing out of it," summed up a history professor at Ferris State University who had helped start one of the programs designed to keep minority students in college. "We're mugging [the majority] of them, taking their money, taking their dignity. I feel like I am participating in a vast criminal conspiracy."[6]

The professor was probably a liberal. But the way I look at it, he's a liberal who's been mugged by the facts and is probably a conservative now.

---

[6] "Blacks Can't Hack College Egalitarians Baffled," Janet Vandenabeele and Jodi Upton, *The Detroit News*, July 15, 2001, http://www.solargeneral.com/jeffs-archive/black-failure/blacks-cant-hack-college-egalitarians-baffled/.

6

Racism at
The Washington Post

An article by veteran Sixties radical Courtland Milloy, an African-American columnist for *The Washington Post*, is titled "Colin Powell: Bush Man or Black Man."[1] It is a good example of the racism now fashionable at *The Post*. Milloy suggests that Secretary of State Colin Powell is somehow not "black," since he refuses to support the UN World Conference Against Racism. What could be wrong with a conference that promises to focus on Zionism as evil and promote reparations claims against white governments, and only white governments? Several racial genocides are currently being conducted in Africa by black governments, including Robert Mugabe's tyrannical regime in Zimbabwe, which will be ignored by the UN conference; the attack on Zionism is itself a genocidal assault but none of the participants would realize that.[2]

The reparations claim being advanced by black African states is self-evidently racist (except to the ideologically blind) because it is only directed against white governments. The island of Cuba imported more slaves than all of North America, but is not on the list of UN concerns. Nor are any of the African regimes whose

July 31, 2001, http://archive.frontpagemag.com/Printable.aspx?ArtId= 21208.

[1] "Colin Powell: Bush Man or Black Man?," Courtland Milloy, *Front Page Magazine*, July 29, 2001, http://archive.frontpagemag.com/readArticle. aspx?ARTID=21207.

[2] "Zimbabwe Prez Declares Open Season on Whites," Editor, *Front Page Magazine*, June 20, 2000, http://archive.frontpagemag.com/readArticle. aspx?ARTID=21944.

predecessors enslaved blacks for a thousand years before any European trader set foot on the continent. Nor are the Muslim countries whose forbears transported more black slaves than were transported during the entire Atlantic slave trade.

Most brazenly, there is still slavery in Africa today, which will be overlooked since 1) it is slavery conducted by non-whites and 2) the African governments involved do not have deep pockets; or rather, their pockets have already been picked by their own leaders.

The Zionism-is-racism slander embraced by Milloy is a cornerstone of the campaign to wipe out the Jewish state. Some years ago the UN gave a standing ovation to a cannibal named Idi Amin, and at the same time passed the resolution denouncing Zionism as racism. The resolution was later withdrawn under U.S. pressure; but now, with the help of the *Washington Post* columnist, there is a revival afoot. Zionism is the only liberation movement that the UN and Courtland Milloy have ever criticized for being nationalist. For fifty years, Palestinian leaders have proclaimed their hatred of Israel and the Jews, and exhibited their determination to proceed with the destruction of both. Palestinian school children are indoctrinated through their school books in the imperative of destroying Israel and the Jews. The *Intifada* is carried on as a holy war under a genocidal incitement of the Koran to "slay the infidel," particularly Jews. This is a purer and more overt doctrine of genocide than the one in *Mein Kampf,* but it will not be discussed at the UN conference.

Racist disregard for the human rights of non-whites is nothing new for Courtland Milloy. In the past, he has praised murderers because they were black; in particular the leaders of the Black Panther Party, who were ideological soulmates in his activist days. No white journalist with these repulsive values would be employed by *The Washington Post,* and no article as racist as this would be featured in its pages if the author weren't black. What a commentary on our times.

7

Blacks in Vietnam:
Another Leftist Myth

We live in an age of lies manufactured by progressives to discredit America and its promise. They do this, above all, by sowing racial and ethnic hatred—in particular by spreading destructive myths among African-Americans to make them hate their own country.

One of the most widespread of these myths is that African-Americans were sent to die in extraordinarily high proportions in the Vietnam War, relative to the rest of the population. This was ostensibly the result of American racism; it is a reason given by several blacks for why they were ready to betray their country in the current war with *jihadist* Islam and line up with Osama bin Laden and his genocidal friends.

The short answer to these myths is that the only ethnic group in the Vietnam war that died in greater numbers than their proportion in the population was whites.

Here are the facts:

- During the Vietnam War era (draft era to be precise) blacks made up 13.5 percent of America's military-age population, while only 9.7 percent of the Vietnam-era military forces were black.
- 88.4 percent of the men who actually served in Vietnam were white.

November 5, 2001, http://archive.frontpagemag.com/Printable.aspx? ArtId=21237.

- 10.6 percent of the men who actually served in Vietnam were black.
- 86.3 percent of the men who died in Vietnam were white.
- 12.5 percent of the men who died in Vietnam were black.
- 86.8 percent of the men who were killed in actual battle were white.
- 12.1 percent of the men who were killed in actual battle were black.

In sum, while blacks were 13.5 percent of the military-age population, they accounted for 12.5 percent of the deaths in Vietnam.[1]

The African-Americans who gave their lives for freedom in Vietnam should be honored by all of us. But we should all remember to honor America, which is one of the only countries in the world—black nations included—where an ethnic minority is guaranteed protection against being slaughtered for the color of its skin or its ethnic background.

---

[1] "Statistics about the Vietnam War," *The History Channel*, June 2, 2008, http://www.vhfcn.org/stat.htm; "US Casualties in Southeast Asia—January 1, 1961, through April 30, 1975," *Department of Defense*, November 11, 1986, http://www.dod.mil/pubs/foi/International_security_affairs/vietnam_and_southeast_asiaDocuments/191.pdf.

8

Freedom From Race

Ward Connerly's new "Racial Privacy Initiative" would bar government from asking citizens what their race is. These days, even the government admits it's hard to tell anyone's race. The current census allows citizens to choose from among 63 racial and ethnic categories, although there is no obvious reason for stopping at 63 and there is no constitutional basis for asking the race question at all. The constitutional rationale for the census is to count heads for the purpose of determining congressional districts. Congressional districts are not determined on the basis of race or ethnicity. Connerly has described his new campaign as an attempt to "eliminate racial profiling," and it has provoked a frenzy of opposition from the usual racial reactionaries—the NAACP, the ACLU and the entire civil rights coalition—who simply can't imagine life without racial boxes.

Peter Beinart, editor of *The New Republic,* used this twisted logic to oppose the initiative in a recent TRB column: "On the one hand, conservatives blithely endorse Connerly's initiative as the natural extension of their longstanding battle against racial preferences. On the other, since September 11, conservatives have unceremoniously junked the very principle on which all that anti-affirmative action crusading rests: color blindness. When it comes to Arabs and the war on terrorism, conservatives don't want to 'eliminate racial profiling' at all. They want the ACLU and all the

July 9, 2002, http://archive.frontpagemag.com/Printable.aspx?ArtId= 23802 .

other politically correct guilt-mongers to get out of the way and let the government start practicing it."

Actually, it's Islamists who declared war on America on September 11, not Arabs; and it is indeed the left whose cynical abandonment of its own color-blind standard created racial preferences, an obvious form of racial profiling. Having marched in the Sixties to establish the principle of color-blindness, the left switched sides in the next decade to support the principle it had successfully opposed. Its rationale for embracing the profiling principle in the guise of "affirmative action" was that it was necessary to use racism to combat racism (although it is politically incorrect to express it so bluntly). This was the gravamen of the infamous Blackmun opinion in the *Bakke* decision, which held that it may be necessary to take race into account to get beyond it. This is the most widely embraced Orwellian principle in our culture today. It allows the cynical manipulators of race on the left to smear conservatives who oppose race-consciousness and race-privilege as "racists." It allows the left to call itself a "civil rights" movement even while it embraces the very principle that made segregation possible.

Ideological sleight-of-hand is not unusual in these matters. In fact, it is normal for so-called liberals to saddle conservatives with the sins they have themselves initiated. For example, when liberals blamed conservatives for launching the politics of personal destruction during the Clinton impeachment battles, it was obvious that some of the attacks on Clinton were a belated retaliation for the personal assaults on Robert Bork and Clarence Thomas, when lynch parties of the left set out to defame two Supreme Court nominees by rifling through their personal garbage (literally) in a campaign that marked a dramatic departure from confirmation hearings in the past.

Conservatives never seem to appreciate fully that issues are never the issue where the left is concerned. For the left, the issue is power. Whatever serves their need for power is right; whatever frustrates it is wrong. When racial profiling is to their advantage, it is good. In cases where it isn't, it is bad. The left's hypocrisy knows no limit. After decades of demanding racial profiling in job placements, school admissions, scholarships, corporate boards and government agencies, the left began decrying alleged racial profiling in law enforcement procedures without a missing a beat.

In fact, the law enforcement procedures to which the left objects do not constitute racial profiling at all. They are time-honored, race-neutral practices, enforced by minority police officers themselves, and completely consistent with a color-blind society properly understood. Obviously, a color-blind society does not mean either a society where racial characteristics are invisible or where racists do not exist. A color-blind society means a society with a single standard for all races and ethnicities.

Security profiles should be designed to protect law abiding citizens from likely criminal predators. Profiles that include the ethnicity or race of potential suspects—but are not limited to those characteristics—do not constitute racial profiling in any meaningful sense of the term. The inclusion of race in a security profile is in itself as harmless as the inclusion of gender or height or any other identifying characteristic. It does not imply racism on the part of the profilers. On the other hand, rigging admissions or contract standards for selected racial groups does. The security profile is about process. The racial-preference profile is about results. The sole purpose of affirmative action preferences is to achieve a race-specific result. They are designed to target and provide specified racial groups with racial privileges. This is exactly what segregation and apartheid were about.

It is not what the security profiling supported by conservatives is about. Conservatives do not want Muslims to be arrested as terrorists if they are innocent. The profile is not constructed out of a desire to stigmatize Muslims as terrorists. It is based on already established incidences of terror in which Muslims are exclusively involved. It is intended to heighten awareness of where the danger may be coming from. To raise suspicions about groups whose members have in fact targeted innocents for harm bears no relation to ethnic or racial prejudice as long as the suspicions are not raised solely by ethnicity or race. An unintended side effect may be to raise suspicions towards members of the group who are innocent. But this is not the same as convicting them, and it is no different from the suspicions cast, for example, on men in an area where a rape may have taken place. Causing inconvenience to innocents is regrettable but it is a price people are willing to pay for safety, regardless of ethnicity or race. It is a characteristic of all preventive programs that innocents will be screened along with the guilty. But the ultimate target is the guilty, not the innocent, and the guilty may turn out to be of any ethnicity or race. In affirmative action preferences, by contrast, the target itself is racial.

The so-called "War on Terror" in which we are now engaged is a war with radical Islam. All the terrorists who have targeted us are Muslim. Not to have heightened suspicions of Muslims in these circumstances is mindless, not to say suicidal. To draw *conclusions* solely on the basis of the fact that people are Muslims would be unwarranted and prejudiced. But conservatives are not calling for the conviction of Muslims on the basis of their ethnicity.

The same observations obtain for the scrutiny of criminal suspects in the practice of crime prevention. If more than 40 percent of the violent crimes in the United States are committed by black males, who comprise only 6 percent of the population, it stands to reason that black males as a group would merit heightened scrutiny by law enforcement officials. The campaign against these law enforcement practices is form of racism itself, because it exposes law abiding African-Americans, who constitute 95 percent of the victims of black crime, to greater risk because they are black.

Ward Connerly's mission is really a mission to save America from the hypocrisies of political correctness. The price of this political correctness is higher crime rates, exacerbated racial tensions and lost opportunities. A color-blind society means a society in which government judges all Americans by a single standard and does not single out particular races for privilege or prejudice. It does not mean a society that is blind to the dangers confronting it.

The Casual Racism
of Phil Donahue

L ast Friday, MSNBC-TV talk show host Phil Donahue had a
guest whose name—if memory serves—was Alonzo Washington and whose cause was the search for missing black
children. Donahue described Washington as a local hero. The two
men sat and commiserated over the "fact" that if black children
are missing, nobody notices and nobody cares. According to the
two of them, if the missing white child Samantha Runnion had
been black, you wouldn't be recognizing her name. Alonzo Washington expressed the somber hope that one day America would be
a place where both media and citizens would care about a missing
child, "even if the child weren't white."

Even on the face of it, this solemn and sanctimonious conversation was insulting. After all, one of the most famous serial killer
cases, which made national headlines for months some years ago,
involved 27 missing black children in Atlanta. Perhaps Donahue
and his guest forgot this little episode because the killer (disappointingly) turned out to be black. During the very weeks when
Samantha was on the nation's TV screens, there was an abduction
in Los Angeles that also moved to the very top of the TV news
cycle. This was the kidnapping of two teenage girls at gunpoint
from the car they were sitting in with their boyfriends. The two
girls were Hispanic and black, and it was front-page news all over
the country. Putting the teenagers on the front pages actually

August 12, 2002, http://archive.frontpagemag.com/Printable.aspx?ArtId=
23272.

saved their lives. A statewide manhunt eventually located the kidnap vehicle and rescued them. The perpetrator was shot and (mercifully) killed. Perhaps Donahue and Washington blanked on this one too, because the perpetrator was (disappointingly) brown.

This presumption that America is racist, that whites are bigots, that white America controls the media and uses that control to diminish and oppress minorities in general and black people in particular, is a lie. Yet black racists like Mr. Washington and liberal racists like Mr. Donahue are somehow part of the mainstream conversation about race in America today.

In fact, liberalism—if you want to call it that—has become a form of political extremism. It is conspiratorial-minded, blind to the obvious, and filled with a venomous, unthinking bias against people whose skin colors include whiter shades of pale. Do black males abandon their children and commit five times the number of violent crimes that males from other ethnic groups do? White racism is responsible. Do black mobs tear up a city like Cincinnati because violent criminals are shot by police? Progressives know that the problem is really slavery, segregation and institutional racism, and cheer the rioters on.

The facts of American life roundly refute the prejudices of liberal extremism, but to little effect. America is not racist. If anything, the social establishment and the media exhibit far more concern for the fate of black Americans than they do for any other racial or ethnic group. A three-quarters-white actress declares herself black to *gain* status in Hollywood. And everybody knows she's smart to do it. The predisposition of the media is far more likely to believe the worst about whites and to bend over backwards to legitimize racial paranoia among blacks. How else could an inciter of racial hatred, convicted liar, wannabe drug dealer, paid snitch and shakedown artist like Al Sharpton become a civil rights leader and Democratic Party presidential candidate? Does an LA prosecutor indict O.J. Simpson for killing his wife because he beat and threatened her, skipped town and tried to flee the country after the crime was committed, and was tied to the crime by blood and

DNA samples? *He must have been framed by racist whites on the Los Angeles police force.* The reader is correct in recalling that the media didn't draw this conclusion; but, then again, the media treat with respect the Johnnie Cochrans who did.

On January 19 of this year, a white man named Ken Tillery was lynched by four blacks in Jasper, Texas—the very same small Texas town where James Byrd had been lynched by whites four years earlier. Byrd's lynching was on the front page of every American newspaper. The president made speeches about him. The nation hated his killers. Ken Tillery disappeared without a trace. You think Phil Donahue will make a show out of that?

An Argument With the Racial Right

E arlier this year, I ran a story on my website, *Front Page Magazine,* about the brutal robbery and execution of four white youngsters by two criminal brothers who happened to be black.[1] It was our second look at this tragic incident, which took place at Christmastime two years ago, and went unnoticed in the national media. We published a second story about the murders when the perpetrators went to trial because it crystallized for us a national hypocrisy on race. This is the hypocrisy that regards the murder of blacks by whites as an indication of a characteristically *American* racism and therefore banner news, while the far more prevalent murder of whites by blacks is routinely considered to be without racial overtones and—as in the Wichita case—not newsworthy at all.

The more recent article about the Wichita events had originally appeared on the website of American Renaissance, a white racialist group founded by Jared Taylor. Reposting it from this site seemed to require some explanation. In the commentary I wrote to accompany our feature, I described Taylor as "a man who has surrendered to the multicultural miasma that has overtaken this nation and is busily building a movement devoted to white identity

---

August 27, 2002, http://archive.frontpagemag.com/Printable.aspx?ArtId= 23072; http://www.salon.com/2002/09/03/white_nationalism/.

[1] "The Wichita Massacre," Stephen Webster, *Front Page Magazine,* July 16, 2002, http://archive.frontpagemag.com/readArticle.aspx?ARTID= 23641. This article is taken from the August 2002 issue of *American Renaissance.* See "Racial Witch-Hunt," Chapter 4 above.

and community"—agendas we "did not share."[2] I further explained: "What I mean by 'surrendering' is that Taylor has accepted the idea that the multiculturalists have won. We are all prisoners of identity politics now. If there is going to be Black History Month and Chicano Studies, then there should be White History Month and White Studies. If blacks and Mexicans are going to regard each other as brothers and the rest of us as 'Anglos,' then whites should regard each other as brothers and others as aliens as well."

Within the multicultural framework set by the dominant liberalism in our civic culture, Taylor's claim to a white place at the diversity table certainly makes sense. But there is another option, and that is getting rid of the table altogether and going back to the good old American ideal of *E pluribus unum* — out of many, one. Not just blacks and whites and Chicanos, but Americans first of all. In the current issue of American Renaissance,[3] Jared Taylor replies to my comments and raises the fundamental question of whether America is or should be a multi-ethnic, multi-racial society, or whether it was conceived and should be preserved "as a self-consciously European, majority-white Nation." Among literate conservatives, Jared Taylor is the most blunt in expressing this vision, but it is a theme of others who might be called "Euro-racialists." This may be a bastardized and somewhat incoherent coinage, but it is one that adequately describes a bastardized and somewhat incoherent perspective.

Prominent among the advocates of Euro-racialism are Peter Brimelow, who writes for the website VDARE.com, and Pat Buchanan, whose best-selling book *The Death of the West* articulates its most familiar version. If Buchanan's last electoral run is any indication, Euro-racialism is still thankfully a fringe prejudice

---

[2] "Black Racism: The Hate Crime That Dare Not Speak Its Name," David Horowitz, *Front Page Magazine*, July 16, 2002, http://archive.frontpagemag.com/readArticle.aspx?ARTID=23638.
[3] www.amren.com/interviews/2002/0715horowitz/taylor_reply.html.

among conservatives. But if it were to emerge as a majority view, it would in my opinion mean the death of the conservative movement. Since I consider the conservative movement the last bulwark in the defense of America and the West, it would ironically also fulfill the prophecy in the title of Buchanan's book.

Taylor describes me as a "neo-conservative," a label I reject, since I have no idea what pertinence it has to my positions or my work. The term originally referred to a group of former liberals who had defected from liberalism over its failure to stay the course in fighting the anti-Communist battle during the Cold War. Following the end of the Cold War, the founders of this movement, never happy with the term "neo-conservatism," abandoned it altogether, saying that it had become indistinguishable from conservatism itself. I have never identified myself as a "neo-conservative" because, belonging to a younger political generation, I did not share some of the social attitudes and prescriptions of the neo-conservative founders. Since attitude is in some sense fundamental to the conservative outlook, I have preferred to define my understanding of what it means. In my view, to be a conservative in America is to defend where possible, and restore where necessary, the framework of values and philosophical understandings enshrined in the American Founding.

My brand of conservatism is based on a belief in the fundamental truth of individualism; in the idea of rights that are derived from "Nature's God" and are therefore inalienable; in the conservative view of human nature and the philosophy of limited government that flow from them; and in the recognition that property rights are the proven foundation of all human liberties. Because America is a nation "conceived"—and not just a nation evolved—the meaning of the American Founding is and will always be a contested issue for Americans.

For me, Taylor's racialist challenge is a challenge to what it means to be an American and therefore what it means to be an American conservative. It is not an accident that the issue of the Founding is the very first to which Taylor turns in his response to my comments. Taylor contends that the national motto *E pluribus unum* refers not to many races or ethnicities but simply to the 13 colonies. This is a rhetorical argument that ignores the actual populations of the 13 colonies, which even at that time were multi-ethnic and multi-racial. In 1776, American citizens included not only ethnic Englishmen but Dutchmen, Germans, French, Scotch-Irish, Jews, free blacks and others. In an attempt to support his case, Taylor quotes John Jay to the effect that Americans were a united and connected people because they had common ancestors. But Jay is obviously mistaken because this was certainly not true in any ethnic or racial sense. Even insofar as Americans were European in origin, "European" is not an ethnicity; the history of Europe is the history of wars *between* its ethnicities and its racial groups. An acquaintance of mine, who is of Scotch-Irish descent, maintains that his forebears came to the New World expressly for the opportunity to fight the English. Whether this is an accurate memory or not, it illuminates the error made by both Jay and Taylor. America was created out of a British Empire that was virtually global in scope; and its various peoples, European and otherwise, far from being a cohesive group with a common ancestry, were often at war with each other.

The fundamental mistake of the Euro-racialists is to confuse ethnicity with culture. How is race or ethnicity integral to the American idea or the American culture? Are not Francis Fukuyama, Dinesh D'Souza and Thomas Sowell quintessential Americans despite their Japanese, Indian and African lineage? The Jews have remained a people united by culture and, to a lesser extent, language for 2,000 years; but as a people they embrace a world of ethnicities and races.

Culture is the force that is crucial to shaping the American identity, not ethnicity or race. Jay's observation that speaking a common English language is a critical element in uniting the American people and transmitting this culture is probably correct. Here, there is ground for agreement. An American identity cannot exist outside an American culture. Even though that culture can and inevitably must evolve and incorporate new elements, it cannot leave behind its European roots without losing, in some fundamental sense, its self. It is this American culture, not a racial or ethnic heritage, which we need to preserve.

Ironically, Taylor and the Euro-racialists have fallen into a trap set by the multicultural left, whose assault on America is focused on our national culture. Behind the smokescreen of "diversity" and "inclusion" (values Americans have always held), the left has injected an anti-American curriculum into America's educational system, and has attempted to alienate America's youth from their heritage. It has rewritten America's laws, subverted its Constitution, and conducted a campaign to institutionalize group rights and racial privileges to supplant individual rights and laws that are race-neutral.

This is a perfectly diabolical scheme. In the name of diversity and inclusion, the left is systematically destroying the framework of individualism and the rule of neutrality that make diversity and inclusion possible. But instead of fighting this sinister attack on the very foundations of the American system, Jared Taylor and the Euro-racialists are eager to validate it. They have even embraced the destructive narrative devised by the left to kill the American dream. Taylor's construction of American history directly parallels the maliciously distorted version of the nation's history in works of such anti-American fanatics as Noam Chomsky and Howard Zinn.

In Taylor's telling, America has become the racist nightmare of leftist fantasy. Taylor begins his historical reconstruction with Thomas Jefferson, who "thought it had been a terrible mistake to bring blacks to America, and wrote that they should be freed from slavery and then 'removed from beyond the reach of mixture.'" Taylor then describes a pantheon of notable Americans who were officers of the American Colonization Society designed to promote the same "solution"—including Andrew Jackson, Francis Scott Key and Chief Justice John Marshall. He observes that the capital of Liberia, Monrovia, is named after the chief architect of the

Constitution, James Monroe, "in gratitude for his help in sending blacks to Africa." Naturally, Taylor includes the chief icon of the left's deconstruction project, Abraham Lincoln, who "also favored colonization" and invited the first delegation of blacks to visit the White House in order to "ask them to persuade their people to leave." The purpose of Taylor's pantheon of political leaders is transparent. It is to establish that white America is racist, and racism is just the American creed.

This picture of the American mind is no less a caricature coming from Jared Taylor than when it comes from Louis Farrakhan or the "race-traitor" left. There are obviously many motives that could have prompted a 19th-century American statesman to consider "colonization" a reasonable alternative to the problem of assimilating people who had been brought to America against their will and who had suffered grievous injustice at the hands of American citizens. But even granting Jefferson's racial prejudice, to presume that this exhausts the complexity of his attitude and to set aside his historic role in shaping America's perspective on racial equality is both vulgar and absurd. It was Jefferson whose Declaration sowed the ideological seed not only of the 13th Amendment to the Constitution, which granted emancipation to slaves, but also the 14th Amendment, which guaranteed every American, black and white, equal citizenship under the law.

If Jefferson planted the seeds of this liberation, it is the American people who implemented it, through the sacrifice of hundreds of thousands of lives in a civil war. The denigrators of Lincoln hate the fact that he resolved the schizophrenia of America's birth in favor of Jefferson's idea that it was a nation conceived in liberty and dedicated to equality. Reactionaries like Taylor may want to take this country back to the social order that existed before 1776, but there are few Americans alive today who will follow them. Moreover, it is a gross historical misrepresentation to call this project "American," as Taylor and his followers do.

Taylor's recounting of the legislative past is equally selective and ahistorical. The fact that the first American naturalization bill made citizenship available only to "free white persons," or that it took more than a hundred years to expand citizenship rights to all races and ethnicities, would have the significance he asserts *only* if the weight of American history were not behind this expansion, and *only* if the premise of that expansion were not the very principles that constituted the Founding itself. The text of the Constitution does not contain the terms "black" and "white," *because* it does not recognize racial distinctions in respect to citizens and their rights.

To conclude his argument Taylor turns personal, which may be appropriate for a discussion that attempts to address both the universal and the particular: "Mr. Horowitz deplores the idea that 'we are all prisoners of identity politics,' implying that race and ethnicity are trivial matters we must work to overcome. But if that is so, why does the home page of FrontPageMag carry a perpetual appeal for contributions to 'David's Defense of Israel Campaign?' Why Israel rather than, say, Kurdistan or Tibet or Euskadi or Chechnya? Because Mr. Horowitz is Jewish. His commitment to Israel is an expression of precisely the kind of particularist identity he would deny to me and to other racially conscious whites. He passionately supports a self-consciously Jewish state but calls it 'surrendering to the multicultural miasma' when I work to return to a self-consciously white America. He supports an explicitly ethnic identity for Israel but says American must not be allowed to have one.... If he supports a Jewish Israel, he should support a white America."

There is a lot that is wrong with this picture. To be a prisoner of identity politics is not the same as regarding race and ethnicity as "trivial matters," and I don't. To portray me as a political Jew who identifies primarily with Jewish causes, or who would not rally to the defense of Israel if he were of some other ethnicity, is very wide of the mark. My political causes are public record and go back more than fifty years. In my autobiography, *Radical Son,* I have even recorded my interior thoughts about why I took on these causes. None of them was ethnically motivated. If there has been an ethnic group to which I have devoted the major portion of my political energies over the course of a lifetime, it has been African-Americans, not Jews.

As a Marxist, of course, I was a deracinated Jew—never *bar mitzvah* and a stranger in synagogues and other places of Jewish worship. As an editor of the leftwing magazine *Ramparts,* I did write a cover story called "The Passion of the Jews," and did defend the existence of Israel as a "raft state" for survivors of the Holocaust rejected everywhere else. But the article itself was an argument against Jewish particularism, while recognizing its validity in a world in which Jews had become the objects of campaigns for their extermination. At the time I wrote the article, however, I still believed in a socialist revolution that would dissolve these prejudices and forge an international community free from such atavistic crusades. This utopian delusion was killed for me shortly after I wrote the piece, in circumstances I have described elsewhere. But to recognize the fact of ethnic particularity is not equivalent to becoming a racialist or a nationalist in the narrow, tribal sense to which Jared Taylor adheres.

Even after I rejected the progressive illusion, I did not become the prisoner of an ethnic calculus in selecting conservative causes. The American creed is universal, and a conservative will defend it wherever it serves as an inspiration for others. Call this American ethno-centrism if you will, it is a lot more inclusive than the white European nation for which Jared Taylor longs. I do not fool myself for a moment into thinking that it would not matter to me as a Jew if the Arabs succeeded in their determination to destroy the state of Israel. But I also do not expect any American of any national origin to be unaffected by the infliction of great harm to his or her ancestral community. Despite this concession, ethnicity does not define the way I or most Americans, in my view, measure right and wrong, or decide how to commit our political passions.

Israel is under attack by the same enemy that has attacked the United States, and for the same reasons. It is the "Little Satan" to America's "Great Satan." Palestinian terrorists were involved in the first World Trade Center bombing and the bombing of the Khobar Towers. In defending Israel, as I have defended other countries—Afghanistan for example, when it was attacked by the Soviets—I have no ambivalence about my national identity, which is American. It is not Israeli, and most certainly not "white." If I support an ethnic Jewish state in principle, it is because if Muslim Arabs were to become a majority in Israel they would persecute, kill and expel the Jews as they have for a thousand years. No sober person can believe otherwise. But I also support an ethnic Jewish state because it is merely the granting of equality to Jews among the family of nations. Would a Frenchman feel sanguine about a German majority in France?

America is a nation that from the beginning has encompassed many ethnicities and more than one race. It was created as a "new nation" and its creators defined its identity not in categories of blood and soil, but in holding to principles that are universal. This makes America different from other nations in its essential construction. One could argue, of course, that the very fact of America's uniqueness proves the reactionaries' case—that human beings are incapable of transcending their ethnic and racial particularities to form a common national bond. But that would require arguing that the two-and-a-quarter centuries of the American experiment have failed. I am not ready to believe this, even if Jared Taylor and the Euro-racialists are. I could be mistaken. But I would rather be wrong as an ordinary American than be the president of Jared Taylor's Euro-white alternative. Moreover, I remain certain of at least two things: that America *is* such a multi-ethnic and multi-racial experiment, and that is worth fighting to defend.

11

African-American
Lynch Mob

I s anybody else as sick and tired as I am of lynch-mob racists like Jesse Jackson and Al Sharpton who don the mantle of the "civil rights" movement to indict non-blacks in advance of the facts, and incite racial rage against them? Yet that is exactly what they—and scores of black leaders—are doing to a Hispanic individual named George Zimmerman. Along with a cast of thousands, they are holding him guilty of racism before the fact, justifying a hatred as inflammatory as any once spewed by Southern crackers against blacks.

There is no evidence whatsoever that race was a defining factor in the tragic death of Trayvon Martin. Notwithstanding the absence of evidence, this unhappy incident is now the occasion for school shut-downs, mass marches and public death threats by enraged African-Americans displaying behaviors reminiscent of the lynch mobs that were once a scourge of their parents' generation in a now rejected past.

The facts surrounding the death of Trayvon Martin have not been investigated and are still uncertain. But the lynch mob has delivered its verdict: George Zimmerman is guilty of a race crime; Trayvon Martin was killed because he was black. "Trayvon is the Emmett Till of our generation," said one mob leader, referring to the 14-year-old who was murdered by white racists in 1955 for whistling at a white woman. There is no evidence for such a

March 26, 2012, http://www.frontpagemag.com/2012/david-horowitz/african-american-lynch-mob-1/.

claim. According to the lone eyewitness to come forward, it was Martin who attacked Zimmerman and was on top of him and beating him when the fatal shot was fired. The fact that Zimmerman's face was bloody when the police arrived is an apparent corroboration of this version of the event. But is this what happened? We don't know. It is a claim that needs to be tested in a court of law. Unfortunately, evidence is irrelevant to a lynch mob, and the conclusion foregone.

If the demonstrators were merely calling for an investigation into the facts, that would be proper. But the cries for retribution and the accusations of racism are not. That goes not only for the cries of the protesters but for the statement by the president as well. Not willing to be separated from his racial constituents, even when they are behaving badly, Obama has lent his prestige to the insinuation that the crime was inspired by the victim's race. Otherwise, there would be no reason to mention the fact that "If I had a son, he would look like Trayvon." Everyone who has a son should be concerned by the loss of this life. By making it racial, the president is establishing guilt without evidence, and indicting non-black America in the process.

The display of racial outrage over this case is a national disgrace. It is a throwback to the past and a shameful repudiation of the values the civil rights movement once stood for but apparently does no longer.

12

Second Thoughts
About Trayvon

Is the Zimmerman case really open-and-shut? Many conservatives seem to think so. But are they letting leftists dictate their
conclusion? Are they not guilty of the same rush to judgment
that made liberals convict Zimmerman before the facts, and
merely reacting to *that* injustice rather than to the actual elements of the case? Is it not possible that they are themselves victims of a toxic environment that polarizes all things racial? It is a
fact that many conservatives, if not most, have already concluded
that George Zimmerman is innocent of any crime in connection
with Trayvon Martin's death and should be acquitted if justice is
to be served. Indeed, this opinion was formed long before the trial
began as a reaction to the outcry of liberals that Zimmerman was
guilty—as well as white—and that the crime was murder, needing to be punished. But just because a lynch mob has formed to
condemn Zimmerman in advance of the facts does not mean that
Zimmerman is innocent of Trayvon Martin's death.

The political melodrama that surrounds and often overwhelms
judgments in this case reflects a culture war that has been roiling
this country for decades. It is a war in which the liberal ethos of
"political correctness" dictates that whites are bad and blacks are
victims. Right-thinking individuals are justified in rejecting this
poisonous standard. But in the interests of justice, the political
melodrama should also not be allowed to obscure the reality of the

July 5, 2013, http://www.frontpagemag.com/2013/david-horowitz/is-the-
zimmerman-case-really-open-and-shut/ .

289

trial: it is about the death of an unarmed 17-year-old who was not a felon, who was on a neighborhood run to get Skittles, and whose life has been extinguished. Given that the young man was unarmed, and that he inflicted very superficial injuries on his adversary during their scuffle, Zimmerman's claim that he was in fear for his life has to be taken with a grain of salt, to say the least.

What we have learned through the process of the trial thus far is that the only surviving witness, Zimmerman, is not credible. He has lied on several revealing matters; first, about not having any money to post bail when he had $150,000 in his account; second, about not being aware of the Stand Your Ground Law, when he had taken a class that discussed the law; and third, most importantly, about Trayvon jumping out of the bushes to attack him— because those bushes don't exist. So one has to ask, did he also lie about returning to his vehicle and that only then he was attacked? Or was he still following Trayvon, provoking the alleged attack?

Most disturbing to me is the interview Zimmerman gave to Sean Hannity before the trial began. Hannity asked him if he regretted anything he did that night. He said no. Hannity rephrased the question and asked him if there was anything he did that night that he would do differently. He said no. Then Hannity asked him to explain why not. He said, "It was God's plan."

I thought to myself, even if I had been jumped and beaten until I was scared for my life—as Zimmerman claims—now that I knew my victim was an unarmed 17-year-old with no criminal record, who was angry that I had followed him, wouldn't I have had *some* second thoughts about shooting him through the heart? Wouldn't I have felt I should have phoned 911 from my vehicle and left it at that? Wouldn't I have wished that I had been more careful with my firearm and aimed it away from his chest? Or not carried it at all that night? Wouldn't I have been full of remorse that I had taken a young man's life?

This led to other thoughts. Might it not be possible that the toxicity of the racial environment also affected Zimmerman, so that he saw in Trayvon a caricature from the melodrama—a black thug about to get away with a crime—and not the actual young man who was walking in front of him? Might Travyon have been a victim of the same racially poisoned atmosphere then, as Zimmerman appears to be now?

We'll never know. What really happened that night is buried with Trayvon Martin. We cannot hear both sides and split the difference or reject one and embrace the other. What we do know is that a young man who was unarmed and guiltless of any crime is dead. And shouldn't there be some penalty to pay for that?

13

Black Skin Privilege
and the American Dream
(co-authored with John Perazzo)

When a Neighborhood Watch guard shot Trayvon Martin in February 2012, a chorus of civil rights activists concluded that he had been killed because of his race. Michael Skolnick, the political director for hip-hop mogul Russell Simmons, spoke for the consensus in an article he titled, "White People, You Will Never Look Suspicious."

> I will never look suspicious to you. Even if I have a black hoodie, a pair of jeans and white sneakers on ... I will never watch a taxicab pass me by to pick someone else up. I will never witness someone clutch their purse tightly against their body as they walk by me. I won't have to worry about a police car following me for two miles, so they can 'run my plates.' I will never have to pay before I eat. And I certainly will never get 'stopped and frisked.' I will never look suspicious to you, because of one thing and one thing only. The color of my skin. I am white....[1]

Skolnick spoke for those who had rushed to condemn the watch guard, George Zimmerman, calling him a racist and killer in advance of the evidence, and demanding his arrest. It was the pervasive theme of the outrage, even though Zimmerman was of

---

MISSING NOTE?
[1] "White People, You Will Never Look Suspicious Like Trayvon Martin!" Michael Skolnik, Global Grind, March 19, 2012, http://globalgrind.com/news/michael-skolnik-trayvon-martin-george-zimmerman-race-sanford-florida-photos-pictures.

Peruvian descent and not "white." To make the racial case, Zimmerman's accusers labeled him a "*white* Hispanic" and disregarded the fact that he was Latino with a great-grandfather who was black. Speaking for the many, Congressional Black Caucus member Hank Johnson claimed that Martin had been "executed for WWB in a GC—Walking While Black in a Gated Community."[2] It was the unmistakable implication of President Obama's own statement on the case: "If I had a son, he would look like Trayvon."[3] For the already convinced, Trayvon Martin was killed not because of anything he had done, but because he was a black man in a racist culture, and therefore racial prey.

The term "white skin privilege" was first popularized in the 1970s by the SDS radicals of "Weatherman," who were carrying on a terrorist war against "Amerikkka," a spelling designed to stigmatize the United States as a nation of Klansmen.[4] Led by Bill Ayers and his wife Bernardine Dohrn (later to be President Obama's friends), the Weather terrorists called on other whites to renounce their privilege and join a global race war already in progress. Although their methods and style kept the Weather radicals on the political fringe, their views on race reflected those held by the broad ranks of the political left. In the following years, the concept of "white skin privilege" continued to resonate until it became an article of faith among all progressives, a concept that accounted for everything that was racially wrong in America, beginning with its constitutional founding. As Pax Christi USA, a radical Catholic organization, explained: "Law in the U.S. protects white skin privilege because white male landowners created the

---

[2] "Mob Rule Trumps Rule of Law in Trayvon Martin Killing," *Investor's Business Daily*, March 28, 2012, http://news.investors.com/ibd-editorials/032812-605931-left-bypasses-law-on-trayvon-martin-incident.htm.

[3] "Obama: 'If I Had A Son, He Would Look Like Trayvon'," YouTube, March 23, 2012, http://www.youtube.com/watch?v=wAPtUfOs7Gs.

[4] Weatherman—http://www.discoverthenetworks.org/groupProfile.asp?grpid=6808.

laws to protect their rights, their culture and their wealth."[5] This was the central theme of *A People's History of the United States*, the most popular and most deceitful book ever written about America, now part of university curricula across the nation.

Eventually, the concept of white skin privilege was embraced even by liberals who had initially resisted it as slander against a nation that had just concluded a historically unprecedented civil rights revolution. This was because the concept of white skin privilege provided an explanation for the fact that the recently passed Civil Rights Acts had not led to an equality of results, and that racial disparities persisted even as overt racists and institutional barriers were vanishing from public life. The inconvenient triumph of American tolerance presented an existential problem for civil rights activists, whom it threatened to put out of work. "White skin privilege" offered a solution. As the unscrupulous Southern Poverty Law Center explained: "White skin privilege is not something that white people necessarily do, create or enjoy on purpose," but is rather an unavoidable consequence of the "transparent preference for whiteness that saturates our society."[6] In other words, even if white Americans were no longer racists, they were.

A parallel concept favored by progressives was "institutional racism." This was the idea that, even in the absence of actual racists, the values and standards of American institutions by their very nature discriminated against non-whites. These two sophistries made possible new battles and continued campaigns that annually lured millions of dollars into the deep pockets of "anti-racist" organizations and movements, even as racists were no longer detectable in the institutions themselves.

---

[5] "Anti-racism Training for White Activists," Beatrice Parwatikar, Pax Christi USA, June 10, 2012, http://paxchristiusa.org/programs/brothers-and-sisters-all/anti-racism-training-for-white-activists/.

[6] "On Racism and White Privilege," Jennifer R. Holladay, Southern Poverty Law Center—Teaching Tolerance, http://www.tolerance.org/article/racism-and-white-privilege.

Lynching Whites

What reality is there to the claim that white skin is privileged and black is not? Is it really the case that non-whites are the exclusive targets of racial vendettas, while whites enjoy protection from racial prejudice and collective suspicion? No sober individual could possibly think so.

In fact, for decades, white males have been the prime villains in the nation's classrooms, and the principal targets of disapprobation and presumptive guilt in the general political culture. Not that long ago, the nation witnessed a public scandal as racially charged as the Trayvon Martin case in the public lynching of three white male students at Duke University. At Duke, as at other institutions of higher learning, there are no principles more sacred than racial tolerance, diversity and inclusion. As everyone knows but few will take the risk to observe, these principles extend to every race but whites. When an anonymous individual drew a noose on the office door of an African-American faculty member at Columbia University, the entire university community concluded that it was an act of racism, and the institution was virtually shut down to express collective horror that such an event might occur. This all took place before there was any indication that its message was racial, or that its perpetrator was not the faculty member herself— which has been a not infrequent occurrence on campuses before.

But when three white members of the Duke lacrosse team were accused of rape by a black prostitute, on no evidence whatsoever, the campus not only failed to defend the presumption of their innocence but rushed with intemperate haste to punish them as though they had already been tried and convicted. The university expelled them, the lacrosse coach was fired and the lacrosse season terminated; the students' names were published and 88 members of the Duke faculty signed an open letter condemning their "racist" deed.[7] The cloud of suspicion and presumption of guilt

---

[7] "Timeline of Events in Duke Lacrosse 'Rape' Case," Fox News, April 11, 2007, http://www.foxnews.com/story/0,2933,265386,00.html.

that engulfed the students ruined their reputations and put their lives and careers on halt. This lasted for more than a year with no challenge from university officials or public authorities or the mainstream media. Yet it was entirely based on the false and malicious accusations of a local prostitute and drug addict, whose record of criminal behavior and absence of credibility were eagerly overlooked because she was black. While the faces of the innocent accused were plastered across the national media, where they were portrayed as racists and rapists, the accuser herself was protected, her name withheld throughout the case—even after her criminal libels were exposed.

The nameless accuser was a professional stripper who had been hired to entertain a fraternity party. A fellow stripper, who was also black and present at the event, denied the rape had ever taken place. One of the accused rapists proved that he was not even present when the attack was alleged to have taken place. Yet he was judged guilty all the same by the civil rights lynch mob that had decided he was guilty because he was white. White skin was enough evidence to get all three students indicted by the local district attorney, who was seeking votes in an election year among a constituency that was largely black and now racially inflamed (although the national press averted its eyes from this aspect of the case as well).

Leading the calls for punishment before trial were racial agitators Jesse Jackson and Al Sharpton. Jackson was first out, attempting to secure a conviction by decrying the long "history of white men and black women and rape and assault," as though the criminal actions of a minority implicated every person of the same gender and color.[8] Jackson also proposed to have his organization pay all tuition costs for the faceless criminal accuser should she want

---

[8] "Is The Duke Rape Story Unraveling?," Tom Bevan, *Real Clear Politics*, April 12, 2006, http://www.realclearpolitics.com/articles/2006/04/is_the_duke_rape_story_unravel.html.

to attend college.[9] The clear implication was that—unlike her rapists, whose parents (being white) could afford a Duke education—the benighted woman was denied such an opportunity by a racist society. Al Sharpton claimed: "This case parallels Abner Louima, who was raped and sodomized in a bathroom [by a New York City police officer] like this girl has alleged she was."[10] The inventor of this ludicrous connection was a man practiced in the art of racial libels, including the infamous (and almost identical) accusations made by his client Tawana Brawley, who ruined the lives of six innocent white males by making false accusations of rape against them. After six years of inflicting pain on his victims, Sharpton eventually lost a libel suit brought by one of them. But even being a convicted liar failed to disqualify Sharpton as a civil rights "leader" since *his* victims were white and therefore guilty anyway.

A professor of English named Houston Baker emerged as Duke's homegrown racial arsonist, leading a posse of Duke faculty members in condemning the accused students in an ad that appeared in the *Duke Chronicle*. Baker charged that "white male privilege" had permitted the alleged perpetrators of "this horrific, racist incident" to remain "safe under the cover of silent whiteness."[11] Whiteness had given them "license to rape, maraud, deploy hate speech and feel proud of themselves in the bargain."[12]

---

[9]"Jesse Jackson Says Organization Will Pay Alleged Rape Victim's Tuition," WRAL-TV, April 15, 2006, http://www.wral.com/news/local/story/1091599/.

[10]"Al Sharpton on the Duke Rape Arrests," Fox News, April 19, 2006, http://www.foxnews.com/story/0,2933,192277,00.html.

[11]"A Perfect Storm of Disgrace," Paul Mirengoff, Powerline, September 28, 2007, http://www.powerlineblog.com/archives/2007/09/018598.php.

[12]"Provost Responds to Faculty Letter Regarding Lacrosse," Peter Lange and Houston Baker, Duke University, April 3, 2006; http://today.duke.edu/showcase/mmedia/features/lacrosse_incident/lange_baker.html; "After Duke Prosecution Began to Collapse, Demonizing Continued," Peter Applebome, *The New York Times*, April 15, 2007, http://www.nytimes.com/2007/04/15/nyregion/15towns.html?_r=2&.

A year later, the three lacrosse players were exonerated and the district attorney sacked, when conclusive evidence showed that there had been no rape and no crime. But the mob leaders Jackson, Sharpton and Baker never had to face consequences for their malicious, racially motivated deeds; never made to apologize for their racism, or to concede that that's what it was. Call that immunity *black* skin privilege.

The Duke travesty has left the front pages and faded in memory along with the many other episodes of racial injustice to whites that were never openly acknowledged as such. Not only have we reached a national moment when innocent whites are presumed guilty on the basis of their skin color, but blacks are often presumed innocent when the evidence points to their guilt. This is true whether the crime they commit is false witness, as at Duke, or a double homicide, as in O.J. Simpson's brutal murder of his wife and a stranger. Simpson was defended by a "dream team" of the nation's best lawyers and the televised trial was closely watched by the entire nation. When a mostly black jury acquitted the murderer, the overwhelming majority of Americans who had watched the trial viewed the verdict with horror—but not black America, which cheered and celebrated this miscarriage of justice as a racial "payback." No one called *that* racism. That's another black skin privilege.

In America today, blacks generally can conduct racist assaults on whites and count on "civil rights" activists and the media not to notice. In the two months following Trayvon Martin's death, black assailants carried out at least fourteen known attacks against white victims with the idea of "avenging" the fallen youth.[13] In East Toledo, six juveniles beat a 78-year-old white man, shouting: "This is for Trayvon ... Trayvon lives, white [man]. Kill

---

[13]"'Justice for Trayvon': 15 Whites Beaten by Gangs of Black Thugs ... So Far," Bob Owens, *PJ Media*, May 2, 2012, http://pjmedia.com/blog/justice-for-trayvon-15-whites-beaten-by-gangs-of-black-thugs-so-far/?singlepage=true.

that white [man]!"[14] In Gainesville, five blacks shouting "Trayvon!" beat a 27-year-old white man, leaving his face permanently disfigured. In another Gainesville incident, a black crowd shouting "Trayvon!" assaulted and stomped on a white man who was trying to recover his female companion's purse from the hands of a black thief.[15] In Chicago, two black teenagers beat and robbed a 19-year-old white man because, as one of the attackers explained, they were angry about Trayvon Martin.[16] In Baltimore, a group of blacks beat and robbed a white man, stripping him naked, then posting a video of the assault online with the caption: "me an my boys helped get justice fore trayvon."[17] In Mobile, a white man named Matthew Owens was brutalized by twenty African-Americans armed with brass knuckles, bricks, chairs, bats and steel pipes after he had asked them to stop playing basketball

---

[14]"Man, 78, Recounts Assault by 6 Youths in E. Toledo," Taylor Dungjen, *The Blade*, April 3, 2012, http://www.toledoblade.com/Police-Fire/2012/04/03/Man-78-recounts-assault-by-6-youths-in-E-Toledo.html.

[15]"'Trayvon' Shouted as Group Attacks Good Samaritan," Chad Smith, *The Gainesville Sun*, April 12, 2012, http://www.gainesville.com/article/20120412/ARTICLES/120419865/1002/news?Title=-8216-Trayvon-shouted-as-group-attacks-Good-Samaritan.

[16]"Wave of Black Mobs Brutalizing Whites," Chelsea Schilling, *World Net Daily*, May 3, 2012, http://www.wnd.com/2012/05/wave-of-black-mobs-brutalizing-whites/;
"Suspect Claims He Attacked White Teen Because He Was Angry Over Trayvon Case, Police Say," Fox News, April 26, 2012, http://www.foxnews.com/us/2012/04/26/suspect-attacked-white-teen-because-am-angry-about-trayvon/.

[17]"Wave of Black Mobs Brutalizing Whites," op. cit. "$1 Million Bond Set for Man Charged in Videotaped Beating," Justin Fenton, *The Baltimore Sun*, April 14, 2012, http://articles.baltimoresun.com/2012-04-14/news/bs-md-ci-downtown-beating-arrest-20120413_1_victim-anthony-guglielmi-court-records-show
"Arrest Made In St. Pat's Day Mob Assault of Tourist. Update: Cameraman @CASHton_Kutcher Tweets: 'Justice for Trayvon,'" *Ironic Surrealism*, April 14, 2012, http://www.ironicsurrealism.com/2012/04/14/baltimore-aaron-parsons-charged-in-connection-to-videotaped-assault-of-tourist-held-on-at-1-million-bond/.

in the street directly in front of his home.[18] As the assailants left the scene, one of them looked back at the victim, who was bleeding profusely, and shouted, "Now that's justice for Trayvon!"[19] It is unlikely that many Americans have heard of these racial attacks, because the perpetrators are protected by a media establishment that does not want to notice that the racists are black, and their victims white.

Within weeks of the Trayvon Martin shooting, a parallel killing occurred with the skin colors reversed at a Taco Bell restaurant in Phoenix, Arizona. A 22-year-old black motorist got into an altercation with Daniel Adkins, a 29-year-old, mentally disabled "white Hispanic" who was walking by. When the argument grew heated, the motorist drew a gun and killed Adkins. When police arrived at the scene, the black shooter claimed that Adkins had swung a bat or metal pipe at him, although no such items were found at the scene. Arizona, like Florida, has a "Stand Your Ground" law that allows a person to use deadly force to protect himself when faced

[18]"White Man Beaten Near Death by Black Mob, Shouting JUSTICE FOR TRAYVON," April 24, 2012, http://www.youtube.com/watch?v=K4Oy5zEVJes;

"'That's Justice for Trayvon': Angry Mob Beats Man for Telling Them to Stop Playing Basketball ... As His Sister Claims it Was Racist Revenge Attack for Gunned Down Teen," *Mail Online*, April 24, 2012, http://www.dailymail.co.uk/news/article-2134340/Thats-justice-Trayvon-Angry-mob-beats-man-telling-stop-playing-basketball—sister-claims-racist-revenge-attack-gunned-teen.html

"'Justice for Trayvon': Alabama Man in Critical Condition After Mob Beating," *The Blaze*, April 24, 2012, http://www.theblaze.com/stories/justice-for-trayvon-alabama-man-in-critical-condition-after-mob-beating/

"Where's the Media? ... AL Man Clings to Life After Vicious Beating By 'Trayvon' Sympathetic Mob," Jim Hoft, *The Gateway Pundit*, April 23, 2012, http://www.thegatewaypundit.com/2012/04/mobile-man-clings-to-life-after-brutal-beating-by-black-mob-video/.

[19]"Mob Beats Man on His Own Front Porch 'for Trayvon' ... Press Ignores," Dave Gibson, *Examiner*, April 24, 2012, http://www.examiner.com/article/mob-beats-man-on-his-own-front-porch-for-trayvon-press-ignores.

with a life-or-death confrontation.[20] A protective media withheld the shooter's name, and there was no racial mob calling for his head. Unlike George Zimmerman, the gunman was not arrested or charged with a crime. Call that black skin privilege.

If you're black and possibly guilty but a white person is involved, the media will actively volunteer to be your advocate. This was true in the Duke case, where *The New York Times* and other papers convicted the accused in advance of any legal proceeding. In the Trayvon Martin case, the media withheld details of the crime that were damaging to Trayvon in order to protect him and indict Zimmerman. For example, that the mainly white community he had entered at night had been the target of a rash of recent break-ins and burglaries by young African-American men;[21] that the hoodie Trayvon wore was a uniform for burglars; and that Trayvon had been suspended from school after burglary tools had been discovered on his person along with unaccounted-for jewelry.[22] At the same time, the press flooded the airwaves and front pages with sentimental photos of Trayvon as an innocent adolescent, while withholding other photos of the six-foot-two, 17-year-old who beat the smaller Zimmerman to the ground, banging his head on the concrete before he fired his gun in self-defense.

---

[20]"Daniel Adkins' Killer Claims Self-defense: Unarmed Man Shot, Killed Outside Arizona Taco Bell," *Chicago News Report*, April 4, 2012, http://www.chicagonewsreport.com/2012/04/daniel-adkins-killer-claims-self.html
"Black Male Shoots Unarmed Hispanic, Remains Free, Media Mum. Taco Bell Shooting Victim was Holding Leash, Not Weapon," Fox News, April 4, 2012, http://nation.foxnews.com/daniel-adkins/2012/04/09/black-male-shoots-unarmed-hispanic-remains-free-media-mum.
[21]"George Zimmerman: Prelude to a Shooting," Chris Francescani, Reuters, April 25, 2012, http://www.reuters.com/article/2012/04/25/us-usa-florida-shooting-zimmerman-idUSBRE83O18H20120425.
[22]"Trayvon Martin Was Suspended Three Times from School," NBC News, March 26, 2012, http://usnews.nbcnews.com/_news/2012/03/26/10872124-trayvon-martin-was-suspended-three-times-from-school?lite.

Looking at the Martin case, black skin privilege means you can form a lynch mob if the target is a "white" man (the press will overlook it); you can demand a judgment in advance of the facts, and can conclude his guilt in advance of a trial. You can even take "justice" into your own hands by threatening his life as the New Black Panthers did, or twittering his home address as vigilante filmmaker Spike Lee and comedienne Roseanne Barr did in the apparent hope that someone might go after him.[23] If this isn't a rebirth of the cracker mentality of the segregated South, it is hard to know what that would be.

But it is events under the national radar that take the biggest toll. Black skin privilege means the national media will fail to report an epidemic of black race riots that have targeted whites for beatings, shootings, stabbings and rapes in major American cities, as actually happened recently. A determined reporter, Colin Flaherty, broke ranks to document these rampages in a book titled *White Girl Bleed A Lot* (after a statement made by one of the rioters).[24] As reported in Flaherty's book, there have been hundreds of black race riots in more than fifty American cities in the last few years, including more than a dozen each in Chicago, Miami, Philadelphia, New York, Las Vegas, Milwaukee, Kansas City and Denver.[25] In July 2011, to cite an illustrative example, a mob of African-Americans created what the local NBC affiliate called an "astonishing" amount of violence at downtown Philadelphia restaurants, hotels and bars.[26] Afterwards, the

---

[23]"Celebs Speak Out on Trayvon Martin Case, Use Twitter to Post Private Information of George Zimmerman and Family," Fox News, March 30, 2012; http://foxnewsinsider.com/2012/03/30/celebs-speak-out-on-trayvon-martin-case-use-twitter-to-post-private-information-of-george-zimmerman-and-family/.

[24]"Are Race Riots News?," Thomas Sowell, Creators Syndicate, July 17, 2012, http://www.creators.com/opinion/thomas-sowell/are-race-riots-news.html.

[25]Colin Flaherty, *White Girl Bleed a Lot*, CreateSpace Independent, 2012, p. 28.

[26]"Flash Mob Strikes in Philadelphia," Monique Braxton, NBC News, July 31, 2011, http://www.nbcphiladelphia.com/news/local/Flash_Mob_Strikes_in_Philadelphia_Philadelphia-126468293.html.   *(cont.)*

politically correct police chief said he feared for the safety of the *rioters*.[27] But after surveying the mayhem, the city's black mayor made an unprecedented public statement. "You have damaged your own race," he said to the culprits, and in a pointed reference to the Martin case, he added, "Take those God darn hoodies down."[28]

Crime Statistics

In the liberal culture, black skin privilege has created an optical illusion, persuading progressives that white-on-black attacks are commonplace events, rather than the other way around. In fact, there are five times as many black attacks on whites as the reverse. According to the National Crime Victimization Survey (NCVS), which relies on crime victims to identify their assailants, 320,082 whites were victims of black violence in 2010, the latest year for which statistics are available, while 62,593 blacks were victims of white violence.[29] But these raw statistics understate the pattern. In 2010, the white and black populations in the United States were 197 million and 38 million, respectively.[30] In other

---

[26]*Continued:*
   "The Return of Race Riots to America," Colin Flaherty, *World Net Daily*, October 14, 2011, http://www.wnd.com/2011/10/355449/.
[27]Ibid.
[28]"Philadelphia 'Flash Mobs': Black Mayor Takes Aim at Black Community," Patrik Jonsson, *Christian Science Monitor*, August 15, 2011, http://www.csmonitor.com/USA/Society/2011/0815/Philadelphia-flash-mobs-black-mayor-takes-aim-at-black-community
   "Philadelphia Mayor Talks Tough to Black Teenagers After 'Flash Mobs'," Dave Boyer, *The Washington Times*, August 8, 2011, http://www.washingtontimes.com/news/2011/aug/8/mayor-talks-tough-to-black-teens-after-flash-mobs/?page=all.
[29]"Criminal Victimization, 2010," Jennifer L. Truman, Department of Justice—Bureau of Justice Statistics, September 2011, Table 9, p. 11, http://www.bjs.gov/content/pub/pdf/cv10.pdf.
[30]"Overview of Race and Hispanic Origin: 2010," Karen R. Humes, Nicholas A. Jones, and Roberto R. Ramirez, United States Census Bureau—U.S. Department of Commerce, March 2011, http://www.census.gov/prod/cen2010/briefs/c2010br-02.pdf.

words, blacks committed acts of interracial violence at a per capita rate *25 times higher* than whites (849 per 100,000 versus 32 per 100,000).[31]

This pattern has been among the most consistent findings of criminal justice research for many years, and for a wide variety of crimes. Nationwide, there were an estimated 67,755 black-on-white aggravated assaults in 2010, as compared to just 1,748 white-on-black crimes of the same description. In other words, blacks committed acts of interracial aggravated assault at a rate 200 times higher than whites (181 per 100,000 population versus 0.9 per 100,000).[32]

The physical threat to African-Americans *from* whites is actually minimal compared to the epidemic of black violence *against* whites. The National Crime Victimization Survey reported approximately 13,000 black-on-white rapes in the United States in 2010, and 39,000 black-on-white robberies, both violent crimes against persons. By contrast, the numbers of white-on-black rapes and robberies reported in the same surveys were so infinitesimal that whites were estimated to have accounted for zero percent of all rapes and robberies committed against black victims in the United States.[33]

To stoke the fires of racial grievance in the face of these contrary facts, civil rights advocates pretend that the statistics lie, or that merely mentioning them is an act of racism. They tell us that black criminals aren't actually criminals; the true culprit is the white "unjust justice system" that "profiles" blacks and creates this racist illusion. "Unjust justice system" is the term favored by Los Angeles congresswoman Maxine Waters, who explains, "the color of your skin dictates whether you will be arrested or not, prosecuted harshly or less harshly, receive a stiff sentence or gain

---

[31]"Criminal Victimization, 2010," op. cit.
[32]Ibid.
[33]Ibid.

probation or entry into treatment."[34] Bill Quigley, legal director of the left-wing Center for Constitutional Rights, agrees with her conclusion: "The U.S. criminal-justice system is ... a race-based institution where African-Americans are directly targeted and punished in a much more aggressive way than white people."[35]

President Barack Obama and Secretary of State Hillary Clinton also agree. At a debate during the Democratic Party primaries in 2008, Obama ignored the facts and charged that blacks and whites "are arrested at very different rates, are convicted at very different rates, [and] receive very different sentences" for "the same crime."[36] Not to be outdone, Clinton denounced the "disgrace of a criminal-justice system that incarcerates so many more African-Americans proportionately than whites."[37] No member of the press disturbed their duet by pointing out that African-Americans commit many more crimes than whites. This is black skin privilege at work, and it illustrates how prevalent anti-white racist attitudes have become in the culture.

Through sheer repetition and lack of corrective information, the myths of white skin privilege have made a deep imprint on the culture generally and the culture of black Americans in particular. According to a recent *Washington Post*/ABC News poll, 84 percent of black Americans feel that the justice system treats them

---

[34]"My Black Crime Problem, and Ours," John J. DiIulio, Jr., *City Journal*, Spring 1996, http://www.city-journal.org/html/6_2_my_black.html "Race and Crime," *Investor's Business Daily*, February 21, 1996, http://news.investors.com/022196-326786-editorial-race-and-crime.htm.

[35]"Fourteen Examples of Systemic Racism in the US Criminal Justice System," Bill Quigley, Common Dreams, July 26, 2010, http://www.commondreams.org/view/2010/07/26-2.

[36]"Barack Obama on Crime," On the Issues, November 22, 2009, http://www.ontheissues.org/domestic/Barack_Obama_Crime.htm.

[37]"Is the Criminal-Justice System Racist?," Heather MacDonald, *City Journal*, Spring 2008, Vol. 18, No. 2, http://www.city-journal.org/2008/18_2_criminal_justice_system.html.

unfairly.[38] But while it is true that blacks are arrested in numbers greater than their percentage of the population, it is also true that they commit crimes in far greater numbers than their representation would warrant. African-Americans are 12.6 percent of the U.S. population,[39] but they account for 38.9 percent of all violent crime arrests—including 32.5 percent of all rapes, 55.5 percent of all robberies, and 33.9 percent of all aggravated assaults.[40] Is this because they are arrested for crimes they didn't commit? Are they only "guilty of being black"? In fact, the statistics are compiled by interviewing the victims of these violent crimes, which in the case of crimes committed by blacks are mostly black themselves. In 2010, black perpetrators were responsible for 80 percent of all violence against blacks (including 94 percent of homicides), while white perpetrators accounted for just 9 percent of all violence against blacks.[41]

Another inconvenient fact for the promoters of the racial "injustice system" myth is that numerous high-crime cities with majority black populations and high black arrest rates are run by African-American mayors and African-American police chiefs. Among them are Detroit, Jackson, Birmingham, Memphis, Flint, Savannah, Atlanta, and Washington, D.C. Cognizant of the methods that police use to fight crime, and the disproportionate contribution of blacks to crime rates, the former black police chief of Los Angeles, Bernard Parks, said: "It's not the fault of the police when they stop minority males or put them in jail. It's the fault of the

---

[38] "Racial Divisions Define Opinions on the Trayvon Martin Shooting," Damla Ergun, ABC News, April 10, 2012, http://abcnews.go.com/blogs/politics/2012/04/racial-divisions-define-opinions-on-the-trayvon-martin-shooting/.

[39] "Overview of Race and Hispanic Origin: 2010," op. cit.

[40] "Table 324: Arrests by Sex and Age—2009," United States Census Bureau—Statistical Abstract of the United States: 2012, http://www.census.gov/compendia/statab/2012/tables/12s0325.pdf.

[41] "Criminal Victimization, 2010," op. cit.; "Should Black People Tolerate This?," Walter Williams, Townhall, May 23, 2012, http://townhall.com/columnists/walterewilliams/2012/05/23/should_black_ people_tolerate_this/page/full/.

minority males for committing the crime. In my mind, it is not a great revelation that if officers are looking for criminal activity, they're going to look at the kind of people who are listed on crime reports."[42] But this sensible attitude has not penetrated the leadership of the Democratic Party or that of the nation's morally degraded civil rights movement.

Affirming Racism

Crime is only one of the areas where black skin privilege fogs the nation's brain on racial matters. Under the banner of "leveling the playing field," the rules of the game have been systematically rigged—against whites and in favor of blacks. Speaking for the dominant culture in our universities, and for the U.S. Supreme Court's majority, Columbia University law professor Patricia Williams, who is black, explains: "If the modern white man, innocently or not, is the inheritor of another's due, then it must be returned."[43] (Innocently or not!) Attorney General Eric Holder is of a similar mind. In February 2012, he expressed amazement over the fact that anyone could seriously think that racial preferences might be bad social policy: "The question is not when does [affirmative action] end, but when does it begin.... When do people of color truly get the benefits to which they are entitled?"[44] Or, as the late Supreme Court Justice Thurgood Marshall put it more candidly to his fellow justice William O. Douglas: "You [white] guys have been practicing discrimination for years. Now it's our

---

[42]"Profiling," Walter Williams, Townhall, March 28, 2012, http://townhall.com/columnists/walterewilliams/2012/03/28/profiling/page/full/.

[43]"Critical Race Theory: A Cult of Anti-White Resentment," John T. Bennett, *American Thinker*, March 22, 2012, http://www.americanthinker.com/2012/03/critical_race_theory_a_cult_of_anti-white_resentment.html.

[44]"Holder Talks Financial Crime, Affirmative Action at Low," Yasmin Gagne, *Columbia Spectator*, February 24, 2012, http://www.columbiaspectator.com/2012/02/24/holder-talks-financial-crime-affirmative-action-low.

turn."[45] The current Supreme Court majority is sympathetic to this view.

This collectivist view of guilt and debts that erases individuals and their accountability is now entrenched in America's institutional framework. In the 1970s, affirmative action was successfully redefined to mean racial preferences for non-whites, and a new standard was set for admissions policies at universities across the United States. Though black students' median SAT scores in any given year were at least 200 points lower than the median for white students, blacks were admitted to virtually all academically competitive schools at much higher rates.[46] The pattern of racial privilege for blacks persists to this day, not only in undergraduate colleges and universities, but also in professional training schools for aspiring doctors and lawyers. At the University of Michigan Medical School, for instance, the odds favoring the admission of black over white applicants with the same background and academic credentials have ranged between 21-to-1 and 38-to-1.[47] At the University of Nebraska College of Law in recent years, the black-over-white admission ratio was 442-to-1;[48] and at Arizona State University Law School, 1,115-to-1.[49]

---

[45]Dinesh D'Souza, *The End of Racism,* Free Press, 1995, p. 201, http://books.google.com/books?id=QNV3XwST4WIC&q=our+turn#v=snippet&q=our%20turn&f=false.

[46]"Racial Preferences: What We Now Know," Stephan Thernstrom & Abigail Thernstrom, Manhattan Institute For Policy Research, February 1999, http://www.manhattan-institute.org/html/_commentary-racial_prefs.htm.

[47]"Racial and Ethnic Admission Preferences at the University of Michigan Medical School," Althea K. Nagai, Center for Equal Opportunity, October 17, 2006, http://www.ceousa.org/attachments/article/543/UMichMedFinal.pdf.

[48]"Racial and Ethnic Preferences in Admission at the University of Nebraska College of Law," Althea K. Nagai, Center for Equal Opportunity, October 8, 2008, http://www.ceousa.org/attachments/article/544/NE_LAW.pdf.

[49]"Arizona Law Schools Discriminate," Roger Clegg, Accuracy in Academia, October 2, 2008, http://www.academia.org/arizona-law-schools-discriminate/.

Inevitably, racial bias does not stop with the admissions process. Once a university accepts black students, under-qualified for that school though they may be, it is imperative that they remain in school and eventually graduate, poor performance notwithstanding. This is because high minority dropout rates jeopardize not only a university's reputation among advocates of racial preferences but also its formal accreditation. To reduce minority attrition and "level the playing field," many professors evaluate the work of black students using a lower standard than they use for their white and Asian peers, a practice which the late sociologist David Riesman labeled "affirmative grading."[50] A blunter characterization was made by a professor at one of California's state universities, who observed: "We are just lying to these black students when we give them degrees."[51] By lowering the standards for black students—without admitting that they are doing so— universities are also lying to their graduates' future patients and clients, many of whom are likely to include large numbers of blacks themselves.

Because maintaining racially "diverse" student bodies is now a legal obligation, some schools have taken to providing monetary incentives to black students who meet normal standards, a privilege not offered to their white and Asian peers. At Penn State, beginning in the early 1990s, blacks were paid $580 if they were able to maintain a C average, while those with a B average or better were given twice that amount.[52] Monetary incentives have been implemented with younger students as well. In 2008, Harvard professor Roland Fryer spearheaded an initiative to pay underachieving black fourth-graders in New York up to $250 for

---

[50]"'Friends' of Blacks," Thomas Sowell, Townhall, September 4, 2002, http://townhall.com/columnists/thomassowell/2002/09/04/friends_of_blacks/page/full/.

[51]Ibid.

[52]Thomas DeLoughry, "At Penn State: Polarization of Campus Persists Amid Struggle to Ease Tensions," The Chronicle of Higher Education, April 26, 1989.

improving their grades, and as much as $500 for seventh-graders.[53] The ugly racial condescension that goes with these reward systems (not to mention the incentives such advantages provide to students to be content with underperforming) attracts little or no notice. There are also thousands of college scholarships and fellowships earmarked exclusively for nonwhite students.[54] These are made available by private organizations, individual schools, publicly and privately held corporations, the federal government, and state governments.

These scholarships, grants and rewards are not made to students who first demonstrate that they are actually disadvantaged by race or any other factor. Many of the recipients come from quite privileged backgrounds. The benefits are granted to these students because of their race. No one would think of providing such scholarships to white students while excluding others. That would be racist. No one pays much attention to the gross injustices done to white students, from all economic backgrounds, who are denied places because they "inherited" unspecified and undocumented advantages by virtue of their skin color.

Nor are racial privileges for blacks limited to educational institutions. Since the 1970s, most major corporations (and a host of smaller ones) have implemented wide-ranging race-specific strategies for recruiting minorities, sponsored scholarships for minority recipients, funded internship programs earmarked exclusively for

---

[53]"Should We Pay Kids to Learn," *Black Voices*, December 11, 2008, http://blogs.blackvoices.com/2008/12/11/should-we-pay-kids-to-learn/ "Paying Poor Kids for Good Grades Appears to be Working," Carmen Dixon, *Black Voices*, June 9, 2009, http://www.bvblackspin.com/2009/06/09/paying-poor-kids-for-good-grades-appears-to-be-working/.

[54]"UNCF Scholarships & Grants," Ron White, http://www.ehow.com/info_7817859_uncf-scholarships-grants.html;
"African American Scholarships," http://www.scholarships.com/financial-aid/college-scholarships/scholarships-by-type/minority-scholarships/african-american-scholarships/;
Barry Beckham, *The Black Student's Guide to Scholarships, Revised Edition: 600+ Private Money Sources for Black and Minority Students*, MADISON, 1996.

nonwhite high school and college students, paid current and former employees a "reward" merely for identifying the names of
potential "diversity candidates," and given financial bonuses to
managers for successfully recruiting and/or promoting a significant number of black employees.[55] In an effort to maintain their
diversity profiles and to keep their coveted black workers from
seeking greener career pastures, many companies have established
minority employee organizations that sponsor mentorship and
self-help programs, produce newsletters, organize fundraising
activities, and provide forums in which nonwhites in the labor
force can air their grievances.[56] And of course, all of these measures also serve to separate their workers on the basis of race.

Needless to say, since government is the real source of these
segregated arrangements, racial privileges are ubiquitous in government hiring practices. Police and fire departments nationwide
go to great lengths to recruit black applicants. Where those applicants have failed the qualifying examinations in disproportionately high numbers, departments have simply thrown out the
results, lowered the standards, or created new definitions of what
constitutes a passing grade. One of the most blatant manifesta-
tions of the obsession with diversity involved the Boston Fire
Department. A pair of white identical twins, Philip and Paul Malone, both failed the department's qualification test and consequently were dropped from the applicant pool. Two years later
they took the test again, at a time when the department was under
pressure from a court-ordered affirmative action plan to hire more
minorities. In an attempt to exploit the judicial mandate, the Mal-
ones reclassified themselves as black, claiming to have recently
discovered that their long-deceased great-grandmother was of
African ancestry. Their exam scores this time around were 57 percent and 69 percent, respectively—far below the 82 percent cutoff

---

[55]"Recruitment Hotsheet—African-Americans," http://www.nasrecruit-
ment.com/uploads/files/volume-19-african-americans-hotsheet-7.pdf.
[56]"Strategies for Retaining Diverse Employees," http://www.diversity-
council.org/retaining_diverse_staff.shtml.

point for white applicants, but more than sufficient for black applicants. The Boston Fire Department hired the "black" Malone twins.[57]

Black Racism

Like the racial injustice against blacks that preceded it, the racial injustice enforced on behalf of blacks has damaged them as well as whites. It has empowered incompetence and sown resentment, and ensured that racial tensions persist nearly half a century after the Civil Rights Acts outlawed racial barriers. A 2009 Quinnipiac University poll asked respondents, "Do you think affirmative action programs that give preferences to blacks and other minorities in hiring, promotions and college admissions should be continued or ... abolished?" Discriminated-against whites favored "abolished" by a margin of 64 percent to 27 percent, while the black beneficiaries, not surprisingly, favored "continued" by 78 percent to 14 percent.[58]

Racial bias is now such an integral part of America's political culture that in 2008 black skin privilege elected a president of the United States. Absent this privilege, is the career of our 44th president conceivable? What political novice, lacking notable legislative or professional achievements, having spent his entire career on the radical fringes of American politics, and having encumbered himself with an unrepentant terrorist and a racial bigot as his close political collaborators, could even think about winning a major party presidential nomination, let alone being elected? Absent black skin privilege, what candidate with such a checkered

---

[57]"Color Them Black," *Time*, October 31, 1988, p. 19, http://content. time.com/time/magazine/article/0,9171,968798,00.html;
Frederick Lynch, *Invisible Victims: White Males and the Crisis of Affirmative Action*, Praeger, 1989, p. 28.

[58]"U.S. Voters Disagree 3–1 With Sotomayor on Key Case, Quinnipiac University National Poll Finds; Most Say Abolish Affirmative Action," Quinnipiac University, June 3, 2009, http://www.quinnipiac.edu/ institutes-and-centers/polling-institute/national/release-detail?ReleaseID=1307.

past could go virtually un-vetted by the national press, or receive a pass from his political opponent on matters that would sink the fortunes of a candidate of any other race?

Black skin privilege guarantees not only exemptions from intellectual and political standards that others are required to meet, but from moral standards as well. What white celebrity, having shot his brother as a juvenile, dealt cocaine as an adult, and stabbed a rival business executive with a five-inch blade, could count an American president among his friends and be invited to host his political fund-raisers? But rapper Jay-Z did exactly that during Obama's 2012 re-election run, and both he and the president could remain confident that no one would suggest it was a problem.[59]

Black skin privilege is a license not only to commit no-fault crimes, but to be openly racist without adverse consequences. White celebrity bigots like Mel Gibson are routinely condemned and shunned as pariahs, as they should be. It would be hard to imagine a white counterpart boasting that he had voted on the basis of skin color, characterizing non-whites as racists, and repeatedly using the word "nigger" to salt his wisdom. When this outrage was committed by black actor Samuel L. Jackson, however, nobody gave his racism a second thought. In February 2012, Jackson told *Ebony* magazine, "I voted for Barack because he was black. 'Cuz that's why other folks vote for other people—because they look like them.... That's American politics, pure and simple. [Obama's] message didn't mean [bleep] to me. When it comes down to it, [whites] wouldn't have elected a nigger. Because, what's a nigger? A nigger is scary. Obama ain't scary at all.... I hope Obama gets scary in the next four years, 'cuz he ain't gotta

---

[59]"Jay-Z the Gunslinger," Brad Hamilton, *New York Post*, March 6, 2011, http://nypost.com/2011/03/06/jay-z-the-gunslinger/;
"Beyoncé & Jay-Z Host NY Bam Ba$h," *New York Post*, September 18, 2012, http://nypost.com/2012/09/18/beyonce-jay-z-host-ny-bam-bah/.

worry about getting re-elected."[60] This ignorant and repellent outburst (whites do vote for blacks) resulted in no consequences for Jackson; he didn't even lose his job as spokesman for Apple's popular iPhone.[61]

Racist behavior isn't even a disqualifier for civil rights leaders if they are black. Leader of a "civil rights movement" is how the media characterized Louis Farrakhan during his Million Man March, and Wikipedia still does today. What white racist could hold a march to protest black supremacy, air the grievances of white males and expect to receive respectable press coverage, let alone attract nearly a million whites to follow him? But Louis Farrakhan did just that with blacks.[62] A white racist of Farrakhan's ilk couldn't get 5,000 sympathizers to a March on Washington, let alone 500,000. That's a black skin privilege.

What white spiritual leader could support the torture-murders of South African blacks, compare Israel to Nazi Germany, and still be regarded as a moral icon? A black cleric like Bishop Desmond Tutu can.[63] What racial arsonist and convicted liar, whose incitements led directly to the incineration of seven individuals, could be regarded by the national media as a civil rights *spokesman*, and then hired as a TV anchor by NBC?[64] Only a black demagogue like Al Sharpton. Only a black racist like Sharpton could find himself

---

[60]"I Voted for Barack Obama Because He's Black," Samuel L. Jackson, http://www.tmz.com/2012/02/11/barack-obama-samuel-l-jackson/?adid=hero2#.TzgdXiNqNWM.

[61]"Samuel L. Jackson Stars In New iPhone Commercial," Timothy Stenovec, *The Huffington Post*, April 17, 2012, http://www.huffingtonpost.com/2012/04/17/samuel-l-jackson-iphone-commercial-video_n_1430054.html.

[62]Louis Farrakhan—http://www.discoverthenetworks.org/individualProfile.asp?indid=1325.

[63]Desmond Tutu—http://www.discoverthenetworks.org/individualProfile.asp?indid=2416.

[64]"8 Killed in Harlem—Arson / Gunman Among Dead," John Kifner, SF Gate, December 9, 1995, http://www.sfgate.com/news/article/PAGE-ONE-8-Killed-In-Harlem-Arson-Gunman-3018812.php.

lauded by an American president (as it happens, Barack Obama) as "a voice for the voiceless and ... dispossessed."[65]

Nor have bigoted advocacies and anti-Semitic slurs cut short the career of America's other celebrated race-hustler. On the contrary, Jesse Jackson's inflammatory rhetoric and racially motivated campaigns have endeared him to Democratic presidents and made him a millionaire many times over. Despite his success as a black man in America, he lectures Americans on how white racism is "the rot of our national character."[66] That defamatory charge is the source of his impressive income. By threatening major corporations with racial boycotts that he alone can prevent, Jackson has been able to extort lucrative ransoms, not only for the organizations he runs but for himself and his immediate family. In one celebrated case, he called off his threatened boycott of Anheuser-Busch after the company agreed to sell his sons one of its beer distributorships at a specially reduced price, making them millionaires in the bargain.[67]

Despite the baggage he carries, Jackson has been able to make two high-profile runs for the presidency and remain a national civil rights figure. During his first presidential outing, he referred to Jews as "Hymies" and New York as "Hymietown,"[68] indiscretions that would have ruined other politicians but only caused a hiccup in his campaign. He received 3.5 million votes during the

---

[65]"Obama's Leftism," Joshua Muravchik, *Commentary*, October 1, 2008, http://www.commentarymagazine.com/article/obamas-leftism/.

[66]Jesse Jackson et al., "The Continuing American Dilemma," *New Perspectives Quarterly*, Summer 1991, Vol 8. No.3, p. 10.

[67]"Jesse Jackson Exposed," Judicial Watch, June 2006, http://www.judicialwatch.org/archive/2006/jackson-report.pdf; "Jesse Shakedown Jackson Gets Beer Distributorship for Son," Sabrina L. Miller and E.A. Torriero, Solar General, April 8, 2001, http://solargeneral.com/jeffs-archive/black-civil-wrongs/jesse-shakedown-jackson-gets-beer-distributorship-for-son/; "Jackson Defends Finances," ABC News, March 8, 2001, http://abcnews.go.com/US/story?id=93897&page=1#.UKaQkWByFWM.

[68]"Jesse Jackson's 'Hymietown' Remark—1984," Larry J. Sabato, *The Washington Post*, 1998, http://www.washingtonpost.com/wp-srv/politics/special/clinton/frenzy/jackson.htm.

primaries—enough to earn him a keynote speech at the 1984 Democratic convention.[69] His anti-Semitism resurfaced in October 2008, when he predicted that an Obama presidency would provide a welcome counterbalance to the "Zionists who have controlled American policy for decades."[70]

Black skin privilege has enabled Jackson to enjoy a career that would be denied to any non-black politician, while accumulating high-level honors along the way. He has been awarded more than forty honorary doctorates by American universities.[71] He was given the Presidential Medal of Freedom by President Clinton, the highest award a civilian can receive,[72] while the U.S. Post Office put his likeness on a pictorial postal cancellation, making him only the second living person to receive such recognition.[73] He has used this undeserved respect, in conjunction with other black demagogues, to transform a civil rights movement that once stood for race-neutrality under the law, into a vigilante posse seeking one law for "people of color" and another for the rest of America.

Destroying the Diverse Union

Those who attempt to rationalize racial bigotry when it is bigotry on behalf of blacks usually claim that this injustice is designed to redress a historic one, correcting the results of previous discrimination. There is certainly a truth here. Even as black skin privilege has meant widespread injustice to others, it has also brought benefits to a historically discriminated-against group, although

---

[69]"1984 Democratic National Convention Address," Jesse Jackson, *American Rhetoric,* July 18, 1984, http://www.americanrhetoric.com/speeches/jessejackson1984dnc.htm.

[70]"The O Jesse Knows," Amir Taheri, *New York Post,* October 14, 2008, http://nypost.com/2008/10/14/the-o-jesse-knows/.

[71]"Rev. Jesse L. Jackson, Sr.—Founder and President Rainbow PUSH Coalition," http://rainbowpush.org/pages/jackson_bio; Jesse Jackson— http://www.discoverthenetworks.org/individualProfile.asp?indid=687.

[72]"Clinton Awards Freedom Medals," Anne Gearan, ABC News, August 9, 2000, http://abcnews.go.com/US/story?id=96208.

[73]"About Reverend Jesse Jackson," http://www.keephopealiveradio.com/articles/history-445549/about-reverend-jesse-jackson-9478729/.

individual blacks today would be hard put to claim that racism has been an impediment to their own achievements and successes. Many beneficiaries of racial preferences may also have put the unfair advantages they received through racial preferences to good use. But perpetuating unfairness and inflicting injustice on others because of their skin color is a dangerous proposition, whatever the benefits that may accrue to some.

Racial privilege does more than merely damage the unlucky individuals who are its victims. When enforced by government and backed by law, it tears at the very fabric of the social order, regardless of whom it benefits. The wounds that the principle of separate-and-unequal inflicts on the community are incomparably greater than the damages incurred by individuals or the benefits that accrue to them. Building racial bias into the framework of the nation compromises the neutrality of the law that governs us all. It corrupts the standards that make a diverse community possible, and creates a racial spoils system that is the antithesis of the American dream, which was Martin Luther King's dream as well. By corrupting the principle of neutrality, racial privilege breaks the common bond between America's diverse communities and undermines the trust that makes the nation whole.

"All men are created equal" is the creed that makes a diverse nation possible. But a flaw was built into the original construction, which is open to multiple interpretations, including destructive ones. The most destructive of these is the idea that government can and should "level the playing field." It is this idea that has given birth to the new racism. Obviously, all people are not created equal but are born with disparate abilities and characteristics. People are clearly unequal in beauty, intelligence, character, upbringing, and other vital aspects of personhood that lead directly to inequalities of celebrity, power, wealth and social standing. Because these inequalities are rooted in human nature, there can never be a level playing field. Moreover, the efforts to produce one must lead (and historically have led) to the loss of individual freedom. This is because the field can only be made equal—and then only superficially—by governmental force as an all-powerful state takes the earned fruits of one person's labor, intelligence and talent and distributes it to those it prefers, and does so in the name of "social justice."

America's Founders understood that there is an irreconcilable conflict between freedom and equality, between individual liberty and equal results. They understood that "social justice" in practice is just a rationale for the taking of one person's achievements and giving them to others who are favored by the party in power. What is justice to some is necessarily theft to others. It is an "injustice justice system." In order to block such levelers, the Founders created a Constitution that guaranteed property rights and instituted a system of checks and balances to frustrate their designs. History has proven the wisdom of the Founders' concern.

In a free society composed of unequal individuals, the drive to level the playing field is a totalitarian desire and a threat to freedom because it empowers government to confiscate the talents and earnings of some for the benefits of others it favors. The expansion of governmental power into every individual sphere entails a loss of freedom for all. Since the targets of the levelers are the creators of society's wealth, an inevitable result of social justice is generalized poverty and economic decline.

In a free society, composed of individuals who are unequal by nature, the highest government good is neutrality in the treatment of its citizens before the law. One standard and one justice for all. This is the only equality that is not at odds with individual freedom. It is the only equality that can make a diverse community one. A nation that respects individual rights and protects individual freedom cannot be sustained if there is one standard for black and another for white; one for rich and another for poor. It can only be sustained by a single standard—one law and one justice for all.

Index